Money, Mandates, and Local Control
in American Public Education

�֎ ✖ ✖

Jill,

You're the best sister in the world! Thanks for all your support.

Bya Obl

Money, Mandates, and Local Control in American Public Education

Bryan Shelly

The University of Michigan Press • Ann Arbor

Published in the United States of America by
The University of Michigan Press
Manufactured in the United States of America
⊗ Printed on acid-free paper

2014   2013   2012   2011   4   3   2   1

A CIP catalog record for this book is available from the British Library.

Library of Congress Cataloging-in-Publication Data

Shelly, Bryan.
    Money, mandates, and local control in American public education /
Bryan Shelly.
        p.   cm.
    Includes bibliographical references and index.
    ISBN 978-0-472-11765-9 (hardback) — ISBN 978-0-472-02673-9
(e-book)
        1. Education—United States—Finance.   2. Educational
accountability—United States.   3. Education and state—United
States.   4. Educational equalization—United States.   5. Educational
change—United States.   I. Title.

LB2825.S45   2011
379.73—dc22   2011000477

Contents

✖ ✖ ✖

Acknowledgments

❈ ❈ ❈

HAD I NOT HAD SUCH A POSITIVE EXPERIENCE in a public school district, I doubt I would have been so interested in the system as a whole. My first note of thanks must go to my teachers in the Pennridge School District for helping me grow as a person and giving me an ideal template of the type of education that I would like all students to receive. First among equals is Michael White, who served as my teacher and mentor and later morphed into a friend. The Pennsylvania Association of Student Councils has shown me public schooling at its best and has allowed me ample opportunities to help Pennsylvania's schools and students in some small way. I thank Andy Costanzo and H. James and Barrie Finnemeyer for the opportunity to serve. As an undergraduate at Tufts University, I was fortunate enough to work with Robert Devigne, James Glazer, and Vicki Sullivan, who helped develop my love of politics, big ideas, and the study of inequality.

Three institutions provided the primary support for the research and writing of this book. While a graduate student at Princeton University, I received generous support from the Department of Political Science, the Fellowship of Woodrow Wilson Scholars, and the Center for the Study of Democratic Politics. My dissertation committee showed endless patience and helped turn a cocky kid who thought he had all the answers into something resembling a professional political scientist. Jennifer Hochschild is as brilliant, kind, giving, and decent a person as her reputation suggests. Her contributions to the argument and research contained herein are immeasurable. She was also instrumental in helping me secure a position as a visiting fellow with the Department of Government at

Harvard University, whose support I also appreciate. Michael Danielson built his considerable reputation on the study of local government and calls for decentralization in American politics. I could not have asked for a chair with more profound and helpful insights and advice. Keith Whittington helped me link the politics of education to the broader study of federalism and provided valuable mentorship. David Lewis provided hours of help with statistical analyses. My fellow graduate students provided some of the most useful guidance I received and helped keep me relatively sane. In particular, I thank Jason Casellas, Amy Gershoff, and Shana Kushner for their intellectual contributions and support. Adam Berinsky, Chris Kaprowitz, Stephen Macedo, Susan McWilliams, the late Wilson Carey McWilliams, Karen Stenner, and Micah Watson provided various forms of aid that helped me survive the sometimes painful dissertation process and emerge with a project of which I am proud.

I thank Wake Forest University for its support for my research. Wake's Department of Political Science has been an ideal place for this young scholar to grow, and I thank all of my colleagues for their support and guidance. In particular, John Dinan, Katy Harriger, and Kathy Smith provided valuable insight on later stages of this project. In classroom discussions, my students pushed me and helped me refine my thinking more than they can know.

I offer a special note of thanks to Melody Herr of the University of Michigan Press. Even though this book is my first, I already know that the care, support, and attention to detail she has offered have left me with hopelessly unrealistic expectations of what an editor should be. I owe a debt of gratitude to those residents of Vermont described in chapters 4 and 6. They made me feel welcome and shaped my thinking about the topics this book discusses.

Finally, I thank those people whose love guided me through all of these periods and who made me want to write about local communities and the people who love them. I have no idea how appropriately to thank my mother, my father, and my sister, but at least I can let them see their names in print. Nancy, Willard, and Jill Shelly, I love you. Thanks also to Miriam Bruzas and the Nase family for making sure that home always felt that way. My friends occupy the space in my heart next to my family. I cannot possibly thank all of them, but some deserve special mention. Benjamin Derby, Greg Smith, Benjamin Sprows, and Luke Zimmermann made sure home was just a campfire away, and Sean Heffron always reminded me to believe in myself and in the power of skiing at the speed of light.

CHAPTER ONE

Equity and Control in School Funding

✖   ✖   ✖

WHEN ONE THINKS ABOUT PUBLIC EDUCATION, what is the first image that comes to mind? Many people will remember their own or their children's schools, particularly if one had a favorite teacher or class or caught the winning touchdown that vanquished a hated rival. Others may think fondly of the promise that public education will help all students achieve the American Dream, which may lead to thoughts about *Brown v. Board of Education* and the long struggle to provide poor and minority students with an education that will prepare them to succeed in the modern world (Hochschild and Scovronick 2003).

Others may look to the past. American mythology holds that group education began in little red schoolhouses in even the smallest towns. Until the later part of the nineteenth century, parents had a wide variety of local schools to which they could choose to send their children, and local townspeople had sole responsibility for nearly every decision concerning their schools. As the ideal goes, small towns or groups within them hired teachers to operate one-room schools that taught students of all ages a sound, basic education. The people had an intimate connection with the school and enjoyed ultimate authority and responsibility over what occurred within its walls. Parents who were unsatisfied with their children's reading levels, for example, could speak with the teachers, who were the final authority on what was taught and could dramatically change their approaches when made aware of problems. When fences fell down or roofs began to leak, local townspeople did not have to solicit competitive bids or conduct environmental impact studies. They simply got the town together and fixed the school.

Although public education in the United States underwent seismic changes in the twentieth century, the myth of the little red schoolhouse continues to hold a cherished place in the country's educational imagination. Today's public schools often serve as the glue that holds localities together. One only need attend a Friday night football game in any rural area of the country to see schools' power to unite diverse groups into a community. Urban education analysts frequently trumpet the potential of individual districts, schools, faculty, and students to close the achievement gap between minority and white students and to solve other problems that frustrate state and federal policymakers (Stone et al. 2001; Morris 2004). Conservatives and liberals alike see local control of public education as a vital mechanism to encourage parental participation in the education of their children, ensure that schools are responsive to the needs of parents and other concerned citizens, and dismantle the dehumanizing modern bureaucratic state (LaHaye 1997; Gruenewald 2003; Dillon 2004).[1] This consensus reflects the broad agreement with the National School Board Association's description of local schools as "the nation's preeminent expression of grassroots democracy" (Shannon 1994, 387). For these reasons and more, the public support for local control of public education remains high. A 2003 survey found that 61 percent of the public believes local school boards and teachers should have the most influence over American public education (Phi Delta Kappan and the Gallup Organization 2003). Today's local school officials continue to make important decisions on staffing, curriculum, budget, transportation, facilities, and a host of other issues.

Another measure of local control's popularity is the massive resistance that has developed around state and federal reform efforts inconsistent with local control. Fears that a community's schools could be "taken away" endangered the concept of the modern American public school system. In the early 1800s, Horace Mann embarked on a crusade to ensure that every student would receive free schooling, an effort that most observers recognize as the beginnings of the U.S. system of public education. Those who opposed even this first step toward public education complained that state laws requiring that all students attend school violated the local prerogative to determine attendance policies (Mondale and Patton 2001, 29–30). Fears of a loss of local control threatened to derail many of the major twentieth-century reform efforts designed to improve the education of society's most vulnerable children. In 1955, one year after its landmark decision in *Brown v. Board of Education* that public schools could no longer be segregated, the Supreme Court ruled that local school districts should be allowed to devise their own desegregation plans, effectively ceding control of desegregation to the same southern elites who had instituted and maintained the system of segregated schools. As the pace of federal desegregation efforts increased, a host of unsavory attitudes motivated some opposition, but poor whites also believed that desegregation robbed schools of their ability to serve as community centers. In 1972's landmark *Milliken v. Bradley* decision, the Court dramatically scaled back the scope of school desegregation, ruling that the federal government could not mandate interdistrict desegregation remedies in part because doing so would violate local control. Writing for the majority, Chief Justice Warren Burger said that "no single tradition in public education is more deeply rooted than local control over the operation of schools; local autonomy has long been thought essential both to the maintenance of community concern and support for public schools and to quality of the educational process" (418 U.S. 742). Critics of the 2001 No Child Left Behind Act (NCLB) have argued that its mandates of nationwide, standardized measures of academic progress and teacher qualification and a host of other provisions severely limit the discretion of local actors in areas where they previously enjoyed a relatively high level of autonomy.

Local Control and School Finance Reform

One of the areas in public education that has retained a strong local component is school funding. In the country's early years, anyone who wanted to open a schoolhouse needed to raise the funds to do so. Figure 1.1 shows the percentage contribution to the total public school funding burden across the United States by local, state, and federal governments from 1919 to 1920. For the first half of the twentieth century, local revenue sources made up more than 60 percent of the total funding for public schools. Whatever merits such a system may have, this high reliance on local funding allows areas with higher concentrations of wealthy residents to raise more money for public education than areas with less affluent residents.[2] Given that income and race are highly correlated in the

United States, this system also results in much higher average spending in school districts that serve white students. To advocates for less affluent school districts and those with large minority populations, the inequities of contemporary school funding violate the dearly held American belief that every person receive an equal chance to succeed in life regardless of background. However one defines a successful public education, U.S. students from ethnic and racial minority groups and the lowest socioeconomic brackets face barriers much higher than those confronting other groups. Advocates argue that because poor districts lack the funds necessary to educate their students adequately, the existing funding system exacerbates the already significant competitive disadvantage these children face and dooms poor children to failure. Such criticisms take on a particular urgency because they view insufficient funding of school districts with high minority populations as a betrayal of our country's commitment, starting with the *Brown* decision, to use public education as a means to overcome the lasting effects of slavery and segregation.

Since the early 1970s, these advocates have waged a war to lessen or eliminate the role of local sources in funding American public education. They have pushed state and federal governments to assume a larger percentage of total school spending so that funds may be more easily redistributed and equalized across school district lines. In 1973's *Rodriguez v. San Antonio Independent School District* decision, the Supreme Court ruled that the federal government had no constitutional basis to consider state education funding. *Rodriguez* effectively eliminated the federal government as a potential venue for finance reform and forced reformers to pursue their objectives at the state level. Most state government constitutions contain provisions requiring a quality education for all students. For example, the New Jersey Constitution requires the state to provide a "thorough and efficient education" to all its children, while the Vermont Constitution requires that schools be "competent." Since 1970, reformers have filed suit in state courts against governments in forty-five states, claiming that the reliance on local taxes to fund education creates disparities that prevent less affluent children from receiving a quality education and therefore violates the state's constitution (Access 2005b). In twenty-eight states, plaintiffs representing poor districts have won at least one court victory (Access 2005a).[3] Despite such victories, in every state except Hawaii, local sources still make up a significant portion of total education funding. Table 1.1 shows that

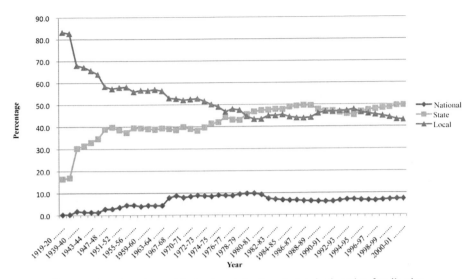

Fig. 1.1. Local, state, and federal contributions to total education funding by percentage, 1919–20 to 2000–2001

for the 2000–2001 school year, local sources of funding provided an average of 40.5 percent of all U.S. public school funding.

Even slight changes in a state's school funding formula can result in a redistribution of hundreds of millions of dollars, so the tremendous controversy that has accompanied reform movements is no surprise. Reform proposals have ignited some of the most contentious and bitter debates found in state politics, and officials who have sought to reduce the heavy reliance on local funding often have felt voters' wrath on Election Day. In the early 1990s, public backlash over efforts to meet the New Jersey Supreme Court's demand for more equitable school funding was one of the primary causes contributing to both the defeat of Democratic governor Jim Florio and the election of Republican majorities in both houses of the state legislature for the first time in almost twenty years.[4] In 1998, reaction against Act 60 allowed Republicans to seize a majority in Vermont's House of Representatives for the first time in sixteen years (Associated Press 1998).

One of the most frequent arguments against finance reform proposals is that they would compromise local educational control.[5] School finance reform battles are fought in state rather than federal courts in part because of the U.S. Supreme Court's respect for local control. In *Rodriguez*, the Court ruled that the federal government had no obligation to remedy inequities in school funding in part because the justices were unwilling to disturb the system of local control.

The persistence of attachment to government at the lowest level where education is concerned reflects the depth of commitment of its supporters. In part, local control means . . . the freedom to devote more money to the education of one's children. Equally important, however, is the opportunity it offers for participation in the decision-making process that determines how those local tax dollars will be spent. Each locality is free to tailor local programs to local needs. Pluralism also affords some opportunity for experimentation, innovation, and a healthy competition for educational excellence. . . . Justice [Louis] Brandeis identified as one of the peculiar strengths of our form of gov-

TABLE 1.1. Local Contribution to School Finance Burden by State, 2002–3

State	Locally Funded (%)	State	Locally Funded (%)
Nevada	59.1	Wisconsin	38.2
Illinois	56.4	Oregon	37.2
Connecticut	55.8	Arizona	37.1
Pennsylvania	53.7	Louisiana	36.6
Missouri	52.3	Montana	35.1
Maryland	52.0	Utah	32.3
Virginia	51.8	Kansas	31.2
Nebraska	51.7	California	30.3
Massachusetts	51.6	Indiana	30.1
Rhode Island	50.2	Idaho	29.5
New Jersey	50.1	Arkansas	28.8
South Dakota	47.5	Kentucky	28.5
Texas	47.0	Mississippi	27.8
New York	46.6	Oklahoma	27.6
Colorado	46.4	West Virginia	26.9
Maine	46.3	Delaware	26.8
Ohio	45.3	Michigan	26.6
New Hampshire	43.6	Washington	26.0
North Dakota	42.8	Alabama	25.7
Georgia	42.0	North Carolina	24.2
Florida	41.9	Vermont	23.7
Iowa	40.9	Alaska	23.3
Tennessee	39.6	Minnesota	17.1
Wyoming	38.9	New Mexico	11.1
South Carolina	38.4	Hawaii	0.8

Source: National Center for Education Statistics, *Digest of Education Statistics 2005*, Table 153.
Note: U.S. average: 40.5 percent.

ernment each State's freedom to "serve as a laboratory; and try novel social and economic experiments." No area of social concern stands to profit more from a multiplicity of viewpoints and from a diversity of approaches than does public education. (411 U.S. 50)

Acting as defendants in state court cases, many state governments have argued that greater state funding is incompatible with strong local control. In California's *Serrano v. Priest* (1971), the first state court case to challenge local funding, the state argued that a ruling requiring equalized spending across all districts would compromise local autonomy not just in education but in all policy areas where local government had power (Malen 2000). State courts often have found such arguments compelling. By 1992, nearly a dozen state supreme courts had used local control to justify rulings against finance reform. Even courts that ruled in favor of finance reform have taken care to craft and approve remedies that respect local control (Briffault 1992). Elected officials voice similar concerns. In 1995, Governor Jim Guy Tucker of Arkansas urged his legislature to find some way to increase spending in poor school districts without raising state taxes because he felt that increased state taxes would threaten local control of schools (*Memphis Commercial Appeal* 1995). Available evidence suggests that nothing erodes popular support for court decisions that mandate more equitable school funding schemes more than the fear that localities will lose control over their school districts (Reed 2001). School funding opponents often describe the link between the level of government that funds a program and the level that controls its other aspects through the proverb, "He who pays the piper, calls the tune." I thus refer to the relationship as the Piper Link.

Does Funding Equal Control?

Left unsaid in many cases is how the Piper Link should function: what exactly "local control" means and how its defenders worry it will be compromised. Centralization of finance at the state level obviously endangers the ability of some individual communities to set their tax rates at preferred levels, but defenders usually extend their argument, explicitly or implicitly, to convince the general public that centralization of finance will lead to a vast increase in the number of decisions made at the state level. In the case of school finance, those who believe that control follows money argue that finance centralization at the state level, or the movement of the state share of the finance burden toward 100 percent of the money spent, will lead state governments to become more active in regulating areas traditionally left to the discretion of local school boards—curriculum, student evaluation, and teacher qualification, among others. Finance centralization may also decrease local school and school district ability to implement strong policies independent of state influence. Through both of these processes, financial centralization will erode the autonomy of local actors and institutions. Writing for the majority in the *Rodriguez* decision, Justice Lewis Powell argued,

> The people of Texas may be justified in believing that other systems of school financing, which place more of the financial responsibility in the hands of the State, will result in a comparable lessening of desired local autonomy. That is, they may believe that along with increased control of the purse strings at the state level will go increased control over local policies. (411 U.S. 53)

Piper Link advocates might also expand their analysis and worry that increased federal spending leads to more decisions being made at the federal level at the expense of local and even state governments. Any attempt to describe the relationship between funding and control in contemporary education policy must consider the role of the federal government, which has become a major actor in both the funding and regulation of education. As figure 1.1 shows, the federal government contributes a small but significant and growing portion of all education funding—8.5 percent ($37.5 billion) for the 2000–2001 school year (National Center for Educational Statistics 2007). As the federal government has increased its financial contribution, it has increased its education regulations and its demands on state and local school governments. The additional funding of the 1960s came from new laws, including the Elementary and Secondary Education Act (ESEA), which denied schools access to the new funding until they offered plans for full desegregation. Southerners bitterly complained that the federal government had overstepped its place and severely compromised their local control. The federal government has subsequently expanded its regulation of public schools, a trend that NCLB exacerbated. Many observers now worry that the $90.9 billion that the American Recovery and Reinvestment Act of 2009 (commonly referred to as the stimulus package) committed to schools, combined with the decreasing state and local revenues resulting from the recession, will leave schools heavily dependent on the federal government and will marginalize communities in the decision-making process. President Barack Obama's plans to toughen federal teacher quality and academic requirements only heighten these fears (Dillon 2009).

On first consideration, the Piper Link seems intuitively true and to explain the trend toward escalating state and federal regulation of education during the twentieth century. Today, local funding makes up a smaller percentage of the total school finance burden than at any other time in U.S. history. Those who accept the Piper Link argue that the centralization of finance has given centralized levels the leverage to lean on schools and school districts to implement any regulation the centralized levels choose to pass. If proponents of this view are correct, these dynamics may suggest that further school finance centralization to achieve equity goals will diminish what local control remains. As more decisions are made farther and farther from local schools and school districts, those who seek to preserve strong, independent local decision making may wonder if reducing the dependence on federal funds is the key to halting or reversing the trend toward centralization.

An Alternative Explanation: Unfunded Mandates

While some observers worry that increased state and federal funding leads those levels to become more active in regulating education, others are concerned about a very different possible relationship between funding and control. While state and federal regulation and funding have increased since the mid–twentieth century, they have not increased at the same pace. Beginning with the original ESEA, the federal government adopted a series of programs for selected groups of students that state and local governments had to implement. The ESEA charged state and local governments with integrating public schools, and subsequent reauthorizations have retained a strong focus on boosting racial and ethnic minorities' performance. In the 1970s, federal special education legislation required schools to develop plans to educate students with learning disabilities. In part as a consequence of federal funding that allowed state governments dramatically to increase the sizes of their departments of education, states began to take a much more active role in regulating education, especially after the release of *A Nation at Risk*, the 1983 Reagan administration report that sparked the first great wave of state learning standards and testing (U.S. Department of Education 1983).

State and local officials have complained vehemently that many of these regulations are unfunded mandates. Strictly speaking, that label is not accurate. Most federal and state programs are voluntary and provide some money for implementation. Given the inherent resource constraints on decentralized levels, however, state and local officials seldom feel that they can refuse any money, regardless of the conditions attached, so, however reluctantly, they accept the funding. These officials therefore are complaining about what one might call underfunded mandates. Despite the federal government's expanding role in public education over the past thirty years, total federal funding for K–12 education has never accounted for even 10 percent of total spending, and the money at risk for noncompliance with specific programs is often much less.[6] If this relationship process represents the biggest challenge that intergovernmental financing poses to state and local actors, the problem with funding from more centralized levels is not too much but too little. Specifically, if state and federal governments mandate that local school governments adopt certain programs without providing enough funding for implementation, local officials must expend their funds and effort to serve goals not of their design.

Scholars who focus not on education policy but the broader studies of federalism and intergovernmental relations argue that local governments often welcome funding from the state and federal levels and not just because such funding offsets the costs of state and federal regulations. Because people and businesses can change their locations at relatively low cost, local governments cannot levy high taxes without driving companies and/or people out of the area. To provide the level of service constituents expect, local governments must rely on state and federal grants for most funding. For more centralized levels, mobility offers a less viable option to escape taxation. At those levels, therefore, taxes can be levied and funding can be raised to amounts far higher than what local governments can do on their own. Thus, most local officials believe that increases in centralized-level funding allow localities to offer more services and increase rather than decrease autonomy (Berman 2003). In poor areas that have greater difficulty raising adequate funding, these dynamics are even more pronounced, and centralized-level funding is even more essential. Indeed, the plaintiffs in *Rodriguez* argued that poor school districts could not raise funding sufficient to ensure even a basic level of local policy activity.

The Broader Context: Funding and Control in Intergovernmental Relations

Thus, depending on the observer's perspective, two dynamics could explain the relationship between federal and state funding and local autonomy in public education. On one hand, opponents of school finance reform argue that increased regulation will accompany all increased federal and state funding, so that funding increases will always compromise local autonomy. On the other, education practitioners complain that state and federal officials have been all too willing to regulate without providing the necessary funding and that the key to reviving strong local control of public education is having centralized levels adequately fund their mandates. In short, one side sees increased federal and state funding as a problem, while the other sees it as a solution.

Very little empirical work has been conducted on the funding/control relationship in public education.[7] Most scholars and commentators spend only a sentence or two describing the relationship, meaning that the same person may often seem to argue that both dynamics are true.[8] The failure to understand how the Piper Link works and what kind of financial policy most compromises locally controlled education makes the construction of rational education policy far more difficult than it need be. When deciding issues associated with school finance reform, NCLB, and countless other state and federal public education reform proposals, policymakers consider the distribution of billions of dollars and the welfare of the nation's children. Too often, debates marginalize or ignore the effects of all of these proposals on local control of public education, an ideal Americans profess to adore. This book seeks primarily to bring evidence to the funding/control problem so that officials can understand the effects of state and federal funding on local autonomy and accurately weigh these concerns when creating policy.

This book also presents evidence that the relationship between federal funding and state autonomy functions similarly to the relationship between federal and state funding and local autonomy. NCLB marked a new era of much greater federal involvement in public education, and President Obama has indicated that he intends to maintain many of the new requirements implemented by the Bush administration and NCLB. A book about the contemporary relationship between funding and control cannot ignore the federal government's effect on state governments.

Moreover, examining whether and how the federal government ensures compliance with its mandates even though its relative share of the school finance burden is the smallest of the three levels reveals a critical piece of the puzzle for understanding the Piper Link relationship more generally.

This book also seeks to provoke scholarly interest in how centralized-level funding affects the autonomy of all units of local government in policies outside of education. The debates this work considers are critical to understanding not just public education but how the three levels of government in the United States interact. While scholars have always scrutinized the dynamics of intergovernmental funding, it came to the forefront of political consciousness during the 2009 debate over the Obama economic stimulus package. Numerous Republican governors expressed the same fear as opponents of school finance reform: more money from the federal government would come with strict conditions that would compromise state and local autonomy. At least six Republican governors raised the possibility of refusing federal funding, potentially hampering their states' economic recovery but reducing dependence on Washington (Madden and Winant 2009). As Mississippi governor Haley Barbour put it, "It's not a possibility of strings being attached, it's a certainty . . . and until we get a look at what finally passes and all of the implications, it is my belief that there may be some things that we'd be better off not to take" (West 2009, A1). While the publicity surrounding state resistance to the stimulus was relatively new, since 1990 state and local officials have been increasingly willing to threaten to refuse federal funding that came with burdensome conditions (Shelly 2008). One of the most high-profile instances of such behavior was the debates that raged in most state capitols about whether to opt out of NCLB and endanger the state's share of the $44.8 billion the federal government annually provides to public K–12 education (National Center for Education Statistics 2007, table 163). The lessons of NCLB help show scholars of federal, state, and local governments how funding from the centralized levels influences control and autonomy at the decentralized recipient levels.

While the strings attached to federal aid have been a notable concern of state and local officials in the new millennium, debates over intergovernmental relations during the 1990s largely centered on the explosion in unfunded federal mandates. Federal regulation of state policy activity has increased dramatically since 1970, but the financing to implement such regulations has lagged far behind. State and local officials have complained vehemently about this trend through lobbying and seeking waivers to individual requirements, to little avail (Posner 1997; Cho and Wright 2001). When the Republicans took over Congress in 1994, they promised that sufficient funding would accompany all federal regulations, but the much-heralded Unfunded Mandates Reform Act of 1995 does not apply to a whole host of mandates, conditions on grants-in-aid, or instances where some observers have argued that states have little real choice about whether to accept a mandate and therefore are in effect subject to an unfunded mandate. Recent attempts at passing constitutional amendments limiting federal power have failed almost as soon as they have begun (Dinan 1997).

Given the obvious ramifications of the debate, it seems right to ask which phenomenon—regulations without funding or funding with regulation—most compromises the autonomy of the recipient level of government. Federal politicians constantly promise to embrace decentralized governments as equal partners, usually right before they enact some policy that encroaches on state and local prerogatives. This book shows how federal and state governments can treat local governments better and in the process respect one of the great traditions of American democracy.

The Stakes: The American Tradition of Local Government

Americans have always valued their local governments. One of the most cherished ideals of American political life is the New England town meeting, an institution so American it seems to have jumped right out of a Rockwell painting.[9] Alexis de Tocqueville observed how small-scale, participatory government could instill democratic virtue in the populace:

> The New Englander is attached to his township because it is strong and independent; he has an interest in it because he shares in its management; he loves it because he has no reason to complain of his lot; he invests his ambition and his future in it; in the restricted sphere within his scope, he learns to rule society; he gets to know those formalities without which freedom can advance only through revolutions, develops a taste for order, understands the harmony of powers, and in the end accumulates clear, practical ideas about the nature of his duties and the extent of his rights. (Tocqueville 1969, 70)

Other democratic theorists have praised local governments' ability to inspire citizen participation in their own affairs, to ensure that government responses to problems are tailored to diverse local conditions, and to serve as "laboratories for democracy," with each government sharing its successful innovations with the others (Zimmerman 1995; Derthick 2001; Oliver 2001). At the end of the nineteenth century, James Bryce observed that "the towns . . . are to this day the true units of political life in New England, the solid foundation of that well-compacted structure of self-government which European philosophers have admired" (1910, 597).

Even as the federal government grew and became the dominant partner in U.S. intergovernmental relations, localism and decentralization remained powerful ideas in American political culture. Polls show that people believe that local government is more efficient in its use of money and performs the best in numerous policy areas, including education (*Spectrum* 1997; Cole, Kincaid, and Parkin 2002).[10] Appeals to the merits of local government and decentralization also help politicians get elected. Since the Eisenhower administration, the Republican Party has made decentralization a key part of its political philosophy (Kincaid 1998). President Richard Nixon said that the

> idea that a bureaucratic elite in Washington knows what is best for people everywhere and you cannot trust local government [is] completely foreign to the American experience. [Local government is] the government closest to the people, it is more responsive to the individual person; it is the people's government in a far more intimate way than the Government in Washington can ever be. (Danielson 1976, 214)

Few politicians embraced the ideals of decentralization more than President Ronald Reagan, who promised in his speech accepting the 1980 Republican presidential nomination that "everything that can be run more efficiently by state and local governments we shall turn over to state and local governments, along with the funding sources to pay for it" (Williamson 1989, 5). Reagan spawned a generation of leaders who rode promises to devolve responsibility for a host of social welfare programs to control of Congress in the Republican Revolution of 1994 (Williamson 1989). Seeing Republicans' success, many "new" Democrats embraced the rhetoric of decentralization during the 1990s, with President Bill Clinton famously declaring that "the era of big government is over." Today, politicians of every stripe want to be known as proponents of returning power to local and state governments because "federalism became good politics" (Bowman 2002, 8). President Obama has signaled a willingness to accept "progressive federalism," where state and local officials lead the way on environmental and consumer protection policy (Schwartz 2009).

Despite local governments' alleged popularity, they have been losing power almost since the ink on the Constitution dried, a trend that reached lightning speed in the twentieth century (Bryce 1910). Whatever good they achieved, political developments including the Progressives' campaign against local political machines, the New Deal, and President Lyndon Johnson's desegregation efforts and War on Poverty granted more power to state and federal governments at the expense of the states (Derthick 2001, 10). Today, "localities have often been restricted from making meaningful decisions or undertaking important service activities. In some states, the legislatures have whittled down the value of county and municipal home rule and made it difficult for local governments to function effectively" (Berman 2003, 88). Observers of intergovernmental finance have speculated that the Piper Link might be largely responsible for the loss of local autonomy and even appropriated a proverb of their own to describe the relationship: "He who controls the purse strings controls the sword."[11] In 2004–5, about 46 percent of all local government revenue came from state and federal funding (U.S. Census Bureau 2007). If the Piper Link functions, the decline of local governments' self-reliance in funding can help explain why their powers have ebbed.

Those who hope to preserve what powers local governments retain or return responsibilities to them have good reason to care about the relationship between state and federal funding and local autonomy. Even as state and federal officials have infringed on other traditionally local policy areas, public education has retained a strong local component and thus provides a useful test case with lessons from other policy areas. The loss of power other forms of local government have suffered has led supporters of local education control to cherish it even more. Many observers believe

> that the local school district is the last stronghold of direct democracy in American public affairs. This view tends to rest on the belief that the local school district "belongs" to its citizens. . . . It gains in political importance as other levels of governmental decision making become further and further removed from the voter. (Iannaccone and Lutz 1970, 15)

If the commitment to local funding has helped local schools and school districts retain a level of autonomy above what other types of local government enjoy, the politics of education may provide advocates a method by which to preserve or revitalize the autonomy of other units of local government. Generalizing the findings presented in this book will require further research on the relationship between finance and control across a wider variety of policy areas, but these results can certainly provide hypotheses for those who wish to pursue such studies.

CHAPTER TWO

Mechanical Advantage?

How the Piper Link May Work

A PROVERB IS AN ATTEMPT TO EXPRESS the essence of a complex truth in a few words, but the relationship between funding from centralized levels of an intergovernmental system and the autonomy of decentralized levels is anything but simple. Even those who believe in a strong relationship between the two would agree that the failure more clearly to hypothesize the Piper Link has made the critical empirical research needed to confirm its existence difficult. This chapter presents four main theoretical questions that guide the subsequent empirical analysis of the Piper Link: the definition of local autonomy; the relationship of federal, state, and local governments to each other; the effect of increases in centralized-level finance share at different parts of the 0–100 percentage continuum of possible contributions; and the lag between finance centralization and the hypothesized loss of local autonomy. Scholars of intergovernmental relations and federalism literature may find these factors worthy of inclusion in a framework that describes the conditions under which centralization promotes regulation and decreases local autonomy across all policy areas.

What We Already Know

Some major works in the study of state politics have posited a strong relationship between state financing and state regulation of local affairs.

Joseph Zimmerman writes, "In view of the fact that the exercise of local discretionary authority is dependent to a great extent upon the adequacy of local financial resources, [local financial autonomy] may be viewed as an approximate measure of the degree to which political power is centralized in each state" (1995, 68; see also Berman 2003, 10). Other scholars who have directly addressed Piper Link–type concerns have argued that money and control can be separated (see, for example, Hovey 1989). For the most part, these observations are offered more as suggestions than as empirical truths, and holding any of these authors to a few sentences in book-length works would be a mistake. The Piper Link simply has not received much attention from the contemporary fields of intergovernmental relations and federalism. Some older studies find that finance centralization may lead to an increase in state regulation of local fiscal policy, but other studies find that a host of mitigating factors lessen or erase this connection.[1]

Perhaps because of the importance of local control in public education, the study of education policy has produced a few studies on the Piper Link. A 1972 report by the President's Commission on School Finance and the Urban Institute examined the relationship between state share of finance and state control in eleven other educational policy areas (including curriculum, budget, tax policy, and personnel) in ten states. The commission found "little direct relationship between the percentage of state aid provided and the degree of state restrictions on the operation of local school boards" (249). The commission's findings are based on correlations between state finance share and variables measuring other state education regulations. Correlations between two variables do not control for the effect of other factors that may influence state education policy, meaning that the commission's results do not describe school finance's independent causal effect on state regulation.

Frederick Wirt (1982) uses ordinary least squares regression analysis on a 1972 data set to attempt to identify whether finance centralization has an independent effect on an index that measures the strength of thirty-six state education regulations: he finds that state finance share has no impact on his index. By using multivariate statistical techniques, Wirt extends the findings of the President's Commission. For contemporary policy debates, his study still has some drawbacks. It focuses only on state laws that may curtail local autonomy and cannot measure their effects on school and school board behavior. His results speak to the effect of state funding on regulation without describing whether finance centralization changes how school boards approach writing a budget, how extensive they view their discretion in curriculum and teacher hiring, and so on. Wirt acknowledges that his results cannot describe how finance centralization affects what local school districts do and argues persuasively that laws still matter. Nevertheless, a full examination of Piper Link dynamics must consider both state regulations and their effects on local actors.

The primary drawback of both the Wirt and Presidential Commission studies is their age. Several seismic shifts in state and federal involvement in public education have occurred since the data for these studies were gathered. State policy activity has exploded. Movements in favor of standardized testing, charter schools, and a host of other reform proposals either did not exist or were in their infancy in 1972. With the passage of No Child Left Behind (NCLB) and the increased complexity of federal regulations such as the Individuals with Disabilities Act, the federal government has expanded its regulation of education to unprecedented levels. With these changes, one can reasonably posit that the relative importance of factors that influence centralized-level education regulation has changed and that the centralized levels' share of the school finance burden has become more important as they have become more active in regulating education.

A second advantage in a reexamination of the Piper Link is methodological. More advanced statistical modeling techniques now allow us to estimate the effects of multiple factors on dependent variables much more accurately than was possible when these studies were done. Recent studies have used such methods and tested whether state finance share and other independent variables lead to an increase in specific forms of education regulation. Michael Mintrom and Sandra Vergari (1998) find that the ratio of state to local finance share does not predict whether states will consider or approve school choice plans. Martin Carnoy and Susanna Loeb (2002) find that state finance share has no effect on the strength of a state's pre-NCLB accountability system. These studies examine finance share's effects on only a few regulations and do not attempt to describe how regulation changes the behavior of local school actors, but their methodology provides a starting point for the statistical analyses in chapter 3.

A more recent study by economist Carolyn Hoxby (1997) compares state share of the school finance burden with student graduation rates, average student future earnings, and state unemployment rate. She concludes that "local school funding is not separable from well-functioning local control" (2). She bases her conclusions on comparisons of raw data from states that increased their share of school finance from 1980 to 1990 with those that did not. Such a technique cannot isolate the independent causal effect of school finance centralization on her measures of local autonomy (or even the level of correlation between the two concepts). Also, as important as graduation rates, average student future earnings, and state unemployment rate are, they are not good measures of local schools' autonomy.[2]

Theoretical Issues at Play

Negative and Positive Local Autonomy

One of the problems with an examination of the Piper Link is that "local control" has meant different things to different people. Thus, the first theoretical task an empirical examination of the Piper Link must undertake is to define and measure local control. Describing something as complex and nuanced as "control" as a single concept is reductive. Saying that a local school district has control of its own affairs or that a certain state respects the traditional prerogatives of local school districts to control education could mean that districts determine everything from K–12 mathematics curricula to lunch menus. The problem with such a broad concept is that identifying the uncountable number of small decisions that local school actors could make, let alone hypothesizing and examining which ones finance centralization will affect, is impossible. A state might give local school districts considerable leeway in one policy area, such as setting tax rates, while heavily regulating another area, such as curriculum.

This study does not presume that control can be reduced to a single measure or that its limitless manifestations can be measured. It does assume that it is possible to measure the amount of control local school districts can wield over the most important decisions involved in governing public schools. It also assumes a relationship between finance centralization and local-level control functions similarly across the different parts of a policy area. That is, if the Piper Link is true, one expects finance centralization to exert pressure toward centralization on most or all other aspects of educational governance. The empirical work presented in subsequent chapters recognizes potential variance in finance share's effects on different parts of a policy area, but the remaining text often discusses finance share as a single concept to help simplify the presentation of the theoretical framework and findings.

This study uses the definition of local autonomy provided by David Berman, a prominent scholar of state and local government. Local autonomy is

> the general right of local governments to initiate policies that they deem appropriate and to be protected from outside interference in a sphere of activity reserved solely to them. . . . Some, too, equate local autonomy with local power, by which is meant the ability of local officials to make meaningful decisions. (2003, 1)

This definition identifies two equally important parts of local autonomy. The first is a lack of constraints and commands from centralized levels. States decide the boundaries of local school districts, so local governments and school boards are constitutionally subservient to the state and have autonomy only to the extent that the state recognizes that autonomy. By passing regulations that require local governments to undertake or avoid certain actions, state and federal governments compromise local governments' ability to chart their own courses and therefore inhibit local autonomy. I refer to this aspect of local autonomy as *negative autonomy*. If the Piper Link functions strongly, one would expect finance centralization to lead state and federal governments to become more active in regulating other aspects of education policy, thereby decreasing the negative autonomy of local school districts. In education governance, the Piper Link suggests that increased finance centralization will lead states to become more active in regulating areas traditionally left to the discretion of local school boards, among them curriculum, student evaluation, and teacher qualifications.

Many plausible reasons exist to think finance centralization will compromise negative local autonomy. Centralized-level finance bills present the opportunity to attach riders with nonfiscal requirements.[3] Having donated a larger share of money, centralized levels may demand a greater role in defining positive or negative outcomes and greater accountability of local actors. Centralized levels also may feel a greater sense of obligation to make sure children receive a good education and are more likely to enact programs designed to define and ensure such an education, such as stronger accountability and teacher certification systems. Finance centralization may cause a growth in centralized-level bureaucracy and its ability and willingness to review local actions, which may lead to increases in regulations and reporting to policymakers at the state and federal levels on the problems the bureaucrats believe require centralized-level intervention.

Most local government scholars maintain that autonomy is more than a lack of centralized-level regulation. Local governments must also have the power to act—that is, to initiate policy and make independent decisions. In practice, local governments have a great deal more power than whatever legal independence state governments bequeath to them (Mansfield 1967). Thus, any study of local autonomy must examine not only what the state and federal levels allow but what and how much local governments do given their constraints. I refer to this aspect of local autonomy as *positive autonomy*.[4] Most existing studies, including those referenced earlier in this chapter, do not measure the relationship between state and federal action and this aspect of local autonomy, a shortcoming this book remedies (Wirt 1985).

Finance centralization may threaten local positive autonomy in several ways. Increasing the dependence of local school districts on revenue outside of their direct control may decrease their confidence in the resources available to them, which may in turn lead local officials to undertake fewer or less ambitious independent programs. Finance centralization may erode the perception that local school institutions can address problems in which citizens are most interested, thereby decreasing citizen participation in local affairs and consequently making these institutions less efficacious. Scholars have argued that people will become less involved in local school affairs as boards lose the ability to decide important issues (Wirt and Kirst 1997; Stone et al. 2001, 95). Budgetary issues may generate the most citizen interest in local affairs, so losing control of financial matters may be particularly damaging to citizen participation (Hoxby 1997; McDermott 1999).

Then again, one should not assume that centralized-level funding and regulation will necessarily hurt decentralized-level autonomy. Wirt (1985) argues that the balance of power between state and local governments need not be zero-sum and that state regulation has the potential to expand the policy options available to localities. Citing the fact that state and national governments award grants that allow decentralized levels of government to do things they otherwise could not, some theorists make compelling arguments that decentralized levels can only be vital when they receive funding from centralized levels (Grodzins 1966; Anton 1989; Berman 2003). At the state level, the federal government funded a massive expansion of state departments of education during the 1960s so that states could monitor schools' progress toward desegregation. Larger departments of education enabled states to be more ambitious with their reforms, leading to the explosion of state government activity in public education over the past forty years (Manna 2006). Empirical evidence is needed to ascertain whether finance centralization and all state regulation has a beneficial, harmful, or negligible effect on local control.

School Finance and General Intergovernmental Funding

This project is concerned with multiple types of financial centralization. The primary focus of chapters 3 and 4 is the relationship between state educational funding and local control of public education. School finance reform efforts have excited most of the debate about the Piper Link, and the stakes are high in terms of money involved and children at risk. This book also aids those studying the relationship between all funding by centralized levels of the intergovernmental system and the autonomy of decentralized levels. This book explains the effect of U.S. federal and state contributions on local autonomy and federal contributions on state autonomy. Figure 2.1 depicts these relationships visually.[5] The focus on education means that these results can speak definitively only to the politics of education, but in the process, the research generates a series of hypotheses that can guide further explorations in other policy areas.

Expanding the scope of analysis to all intergovernmental funding also allows this study to consider U.S. education funding in its totality. Were the project to consider only state funding of education, it would have to limit its claims to how increases in state funding from 30 percent to 90 percent compromise local autonomy. For the 2002–3 school year, state government contributions to the total funding spent on K–12 public education varied from 30.2 percent in Nevada to 90.1 percent in Hawaii (National Center for Education Statistics 2007). Expanding the study to encompass federal education funding, which makes up less than 10 percent of the total education spending nationally, and its effects on local and state autonomy allows this study to consider almost the entire range of the possible movements from 0 percent to 100 percent centralized-level funding. As discussed later in this chapter, there are good reasons to believe that movements from 0 percent centralized-level funding to some small part of the total funding have the greatest effect on decentralized-level autonomy and that movements in the 30–90 range will result in no

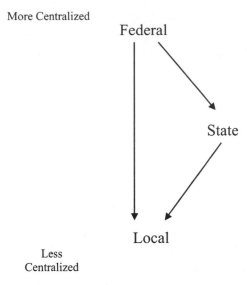

Fig. 2.1. Describing the links between levels (arrows denote direction of funding)

or negligible loss in autonomy. Understanding whether movements at different parts of the 0–100 interval have different effects on local control may better help education policymakers choose a level of funding that allows them to preserve or enhance the desired level of local autonomy. If this hypothesis is correct, a study that considers movements only in the state share of the school finance burden would miss the most significant way in which funding affects local educational control. Also, the inclusion of federal funding allows for an examination of how it affects state educational autonomy, a topic that state and federal policymakers will need to consider every five years when the ESEA comes up for reauthorization. Authorities at all levels of the intergovernmental system have said that they do not want NCLB and its successors to challenge states' traditional role as the primary decision makers in public education, but nearly everyone agrees that NCLB has severely curtailed state discretion.[6] The results presented here should help the federal government craft an improved NCLB during reauthorization that sets federal funding at a level that preserves the preferred amount of state authority.

The inclusion of the federal government assumes that the relationships between federal education funding and local autonomy, federal funding and state autonomy, and state funding and local autonomy function similarly, an assumption some readers may question. These relationships differ in several meaningful ways, not the least of which is the legal status of state and local governments. The Tenth Amendment states that "the powers not delegated to the United States by the Constitution, nor prohibited by it to the states, are reserved to the states respectively, or to the people." The amendment has been taken to protect states' primacy in many policy areas, including education. By contrast, local governments legally have only those powers conferred by state governments (Zimmerman 1995). Concerns about the equivalency of the two relationships are valid, but judgments about whether state/local and federal/state and local fiscal dynamics are similar should be made only after evaluating the evidence presented in the remainder of this book. This evidence suggests that many of the legal protections to state autonomy have eroded over the past thirty years, leaving state governments in an increasingly subservient position that resembles the position in which local officials have always found themselves. Whatever theoretical arguments may support the idea of differences in the two relationships, in practice they appear quite similar.

Are All Funding Increases Equal?

One of the most critical issues in an examination of the Piper Link is whether an increase in the centralized-level funding share from X percentage to X + Y percentage functions the same at any point on the 0–100 percent continuum or whether the same shift has different effects depending on where it falls on the continuum. In plain terms, this consideration means one must ask whether an increase from, say, 5 to 6 percent state funding has the same effect on local autonomy as does a move from 49 to 50 percent. Given the steady trend toward school finance centralization in the second half of the twentieth century, this study assumes that no state will contribute less than a 20 percent share of the total finance burden in the future.[7] Because local and federal sources of funding are unlikely to disappear completely, this study assumes that no state will contribute much more than 90 percent of the total finance burden. Based on these ideas, this study assumes that the entire range of possible state contributions to the total burden of K–12 public schooling falls between 20 percent and 90 percent. One can expect the point of contention in most school finance reform movements to be where to locate the state share of the school finance burden within the 20–90 range. Therefore, for

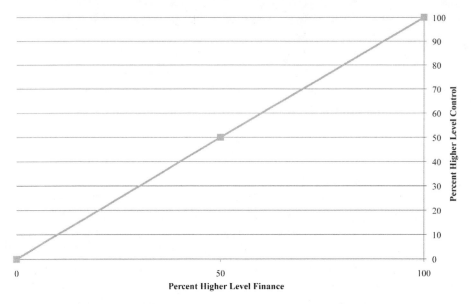

Fig. 2.2. A linear relationship between finance and control (hypothesized)

centralization stemming from school finance reform movements to have a detrimental effect on local autonomy, movements within the 20–90 range must cause a significant loss of local autonomy.

Figure 2.2 represents a hypothetical relationship in which finance centralization in the 20–90 range affects local autonomy. This relationship posits a proportional loss of local autonomy for every increase in funding centralization. That is, when states finance 0 percent of a given policy area, this version of the Piper Link expects the state to control very few or no aspects of that policy area. Any increase in state funding will result in a corresponding proportional increase in state control of other aspects, so that at 50 percent state funding, the state controls approximately 50 percent of a program's other aspects; at 75 percent funding, it can control 75 percent; and so on. If this version of the Piper Link is true, one can expect school finance reform movements that centralize finance at the state level within the 20–90 range to have a detrimental effect on local educational control.

Most scholars of intergovernmental relations and federalism would doubt the hypotheses that figure 2.2 represents. One of the most relevant threads of the federalism literature argues that centralized levels currently exercise control over decentralized levels using less money than in the past. From the 1970s onward, the federal government has sought to influence state and local policy not only by imposing conditions on grants-in-aid but also via direct and often unfunded mandates, even though the latter strategy can put significant strain on decentralized levels. Decentralized-level officials face a daunting array of factors that promote compliance, including an erosion of constitutional safeguards against regulation and popular support for many of the ideas regulations attempt to enforce. In addition, if the regulations come with even a little additional funding, local officials may feel they cannot say no. Local governments face significant constraints on their fund-raising ability and consequently rely heavily on state and federal funding. To provide even a minimum level of acceptable service, local governments may need to accept any and all centralized-level funding, regardless of what strings are attached (Kincaid 1990). The federal government is depending on this dynamic to ensure NCLB compliance. Chapter 6 describes how U.S. state and local governments risk no more than 5 percent, on average, of their total school spending. If the threat of loss of such a small part of the total funding drives states and local governments to comply with NCLB, centralized levels can achieve a great deal of compliance by providing relatively small contributions to the total funding burden.

If centralized levels of an intergovernmental system can exercise large amounts of control with relatively small financial contributions, the hypothetical proportionality between funding and control specified in figure 2.2 is not accurate, and an alternative specification of the Piper Link is needed, perhaps looking like figure 2.3. Figure 2.3's design accounts for the idea that centralized levels can exert a significant amount of control through regulations even while providing no funding. It also holds that because decentralized-level governments can become dependent on even limited funds from centralized levels, centralized levels of the federal government can gain a disproportionate level of control over a policy with a very small total percentage of funding. Thus, as the centralized-level financial contribution increases from 0 percent of the total funding burden for a policy or program, the amount of control gained rises very quickly. This model predicts that because state and local governments cannot afford to give up even the relatively small share of funding NCLB noncompliance risks, they will comply despite any objections.

A second notable feature of the figure 2.3 logic is how little control

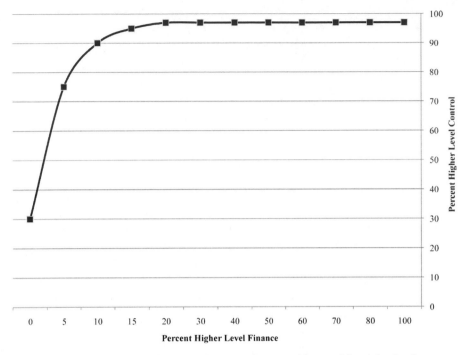

Fig. 2.3.   A curved relationship between finance and control (hypothesized)

centralized levels gain with funding contributions above a certain percentage. Because they gain so much control with so little funding, funding increases above a certain percentage yield very small or no gains in control. This model predicts that not all funding increases are created alike. For example, an increase from 5 to 6 percent of total program funding results in a far greater centralization of control than a movement from 30 to 31 percent or even from 20 percent to 90 percent. This model predicts almost no movement in the 20–90 percent range and therefore implies that very little local control is at stake in contemporary school finance debates. Whether a state government contributes 20 percent, 90 percent, or some amount in between of the total school funding, it retains basically the same amount of leverage to force local school governments to adopt most of its policies.[8] If this relationship is true, it makes very little sense to oppose school finance centralization for equity's sake because of the negative effects on local autonomy: little local autonomy is lost by the level of centralization at play in finance reform.

When? Time Is on Your Side

An examination of the Piper Link must also address how long finance centralization will take to undermine local autonomy. School finance reform opponents' greatest fear is that the choice to centralize finance will lead to an inevitable, unavoidable increase in regulation, regardless of whether state elected officials plan to increase regulation at the time of finance centralization. Opponents fear that finance centralization will have a lagged effect on centralization of other aspects, for finance centralization at time T to lead to other centralization at time $T + U$.

This project does not consider instances in which state funding centralization and increased state regulation occur simultaneously. No reason exists to think that finance centralization will lead to immediate increases in regulations unless policymakers want such to be the case. Lawmakers certainly can package together funding and regulation increases. For example, in the 1990s, both Kentucky and New Jersey enacted extensive curricular changes with school finance reform packages. These examples appear to represent conscious choices. A simultaneous centralization of school finance and other aspects of educational governance must be considered a political decision and an example of one set of political values trumping another, not the result of the inevitable deterioration of local control that the Piper Link posits.

Plan of the Book

These theoretical concerns guide the analysis presented in chapters 3–7. Chapters 3 and 4 ask whether finance centralization at the state level affects both negative and positive autonomy. Chapter 3 presents a statistical analysis of how the percentage of total school finance burden each state government provides affects the likelihood of that state adopting a series of regulations that can compromise negative autonomy. Chapter 4 analyzes the effects of Vermont's Act 60 school finance reform on both types of autonomy, with a specific focus on positive local autonomy. To show that Vermont's politics are not exceptional, chapter 4 also describes the politics surrounding Michigan's school reform efforts in the 1990s. The two chapters report that little evidence exists to support the claim that finance centralization in the 20–90 percent range has any effect on local autonomy, suggesting that the linear model of the Piper Link presented in figure 2.2 is not accurate. Chapter 5 asks why the Piper Link still matters so much in school finance reform debates when little to no control is in play and looks for an answer in the public opinion dynamics surrounding finance reform in five states. Chapter 5 resolves the matter of local control in the school finance reform debate, but further evidence is needed to understand whether higher-level funding (or the lack thereof) has any impact on local autonomy. Chapter 6 returns to Vermont to describe how un- and underfunded mandates are much more harmful to decentralized-level autonomy than is finance centralization. Chapter 7 examines the politics surrounding NCLB's implementation, finding that the federal government has exerted a tremendous amount of control over the decentralized levels and ensured overwhelming compliance with NCLB using leverage created through a relatively tiny contribution to the total finance burden. This evidence suggests that movements in the 20–90 range do not affect local autonomy because centralized levels gain a great deal of control from small financial contributions. In other words, the curved model in figure 2.3 best represents the relationship between money and control in education.

CHAPTER THREE

The More Money We Come Upon

Finance Centralization and
Negative Local Autonomy

✖ ✖ ✖

ALTHOUGH LOCAL CONTROL IS MADE UP OF hundreds of possible decisions, some decisions are more central to the core mission of public education and therefore more important than others. All else being equal, a school district that can independently choose its curriculum has more local control than one that can choose only its lunch menu. Fortunately, for many of the biggest decisions that determine the course of contemporary public education, aggregate statistical data exist describing how extensively each state has pursued some of the most popular contemporary education reform strategies such as standardized testing. As states pursue such regulations, they decrease local actors' negative autonomy, or their ability to act without compulsion or constraints from centralized levels of the intergovernmental system.

This chapter presents estimates of multivariate statistical models employing as dependent variables measures of state standardized testing, high-stakes testing, teacher certification requirements, school safety legislation, and state takeovers of failing school districts. The key independent variable in all models is the state share of the school finance burden. The statistical techniques employed allow for the control of numerous other factors that political science scholars have found to influence state government regulation and isolate the independent effect of finance centralization on the level of each regulation. The ability to examine all fifty states in a systematic fashion and identify, as far as is possible, finance centralization's role in promoting state regulation provides powerful evidence regarding the existence of the linear Piper Link. If finance centralization in the 20–90 range leads to a loss of negative autonomy, one would expect state governments that contribute a higher share of total school spending to regulate other aspects of education more extensively.

Other Factors That May Influence State Education Policy

The level of state funding is not the only factor that may cause states to adopt a centralized level of education regulation. This chapter's statistical analyses include variables that control for the effects of several factors that can influence state education policy and state policy-making in general. These controls allow one to see the independent effect of finance centralization on education regulation.

One possibility is that the level of government that contributes the greatest share of the total funding may be less important than the total funding itself. More affluent states may be more able than poor states to afford to regulate public education. To be fully implemented, these regulations require adequate funding. Systems of statewide standardized testing that use results to diagnose problems and craft solutions require personnel and equipment to grade the tests and a bureaucracy capable of monitoring both the results and compliance with any mandated changes.[1] At the local level, school districts must have the resources to comply with reporting requirements and to implement mandated changes. States with high centralized levels of educational funding may feel they have the resources to attempt ambitious and costly statewide reform efforts. Poorer states may feel that extensive regulation costs more than they can afford, forcing them to adopt a much lower level of regulation.

The racial and ethnic composition of a state's populace may have a powerful effect on the course of state education policy. Scholars have shown that the size and diversity of a state's racial and ethnic populations significantly affect a host of social policies, including education (Morgan and Wilson 1990; Hero and Tolbert 1996). In most measures of academic achievement, African American and Hispanic students lag behind students from other racial and ethnic groups, suggesting that states with larger shares of these students may be more likely to adopt programs designed to eliminate this gap, such as extensive systems of standards and tests and state takeovers of academically failing districts. Mainstream American society has painted areas in which African Americans and Hispanics live as dangerous, which may lead (primarily white) state legislators to regard schools in those areas as unsafe and to pass more school safety legislation. Others may point out that many of the most highly publicized school shootings occurred in suburban and rural districts and hypothesize that race and ethnicity variables will have a negligible or negative effect on school safety regulations.

Partisanship may also affect a state's willingness to regulate public education, with high levels of support for Democrats leading to centralized levels of regulation. Recent scholarship has established the strong role of public opinion and partisan control of the elected branches on state policy process (Barrilleaux 1997; Burstein 2003). Despite President George W. Bush's advocacy of No Child Left Behind (NCLB), the Democratic Party still advocates a higher level of involvement for state and federal government in public education. As a consequence of their traditional affinity for limited government, state-level Republicans are more likely to oppose expansion of public education policy (Mintrom and Vergari 1998).

Scholars have shown that the composition and relative strength of a state's interest group population influence its policy output (Jacoby and Schneider 2001; Hunter, Brunk, and Wilson 2002; Gray et al. 2004). Any study of state education policy must consider the role of teachers' unions. Thanks to their extensive resources and broad membership, they are among the most powerful special interest groups in state politics. Teachers' unions have a reputation—deserved or not—of being hostile to most education reforms, perhaps because they seek to insulate their members from changes that would increase their workloads or because unions recognize the challenges of implementing politically negotiated reforms in actual classrooms. States with stronger teachers' unions would be expected to adopt fewer education regulations.

Methodology

To analyze the effect of finance centralization on state regulation, I assembled a data set containing variables with observations from all fifty states. The data set contains standard variables political science scholars use to measure various factors, including each state's Hispanic and

African American population and percentage of the 2000 vote Bush received. To measure the availability of resources, I include Census Bureau data on each state's median income. To gauge of the strength of unions in each state, I used data from the U.S. Department of Education's 1999–2000 Schools and Staffing Survey (2005) on the percentage of each state's teaching force that belongs to unions.[2] The critical independent variable in all models is percentage of total school revenue that comes from state sources, data that the Department of Education collects annually for each state. Because of the lag time expected in the Piper Link's effect, two variables measure state finance share from three and six years prior to the observations used for the dependent variables.[3] Of extreme importance is the range of the three finance share variables the models include. For the 1995–96 school year, state government finance share varied from a high of 89.8 percent to a low of 7 percent; during the 1999–2000 school year, the high was 88.8 percent and the low was 29.1 percent; for 2002–3, the high was 90.1 percent and the low was 30.2 percent. This range means that these results cannot provide evidence on the relationship between finance centralization and state regulation for the full 0–100 percent spectrum. As discussed in chapter 2, for the foreseeable future, state finance share is unlikely to fall below 20 percent, so these results will speak to the effect of school finance centralization only in the 20–90 percent state funding range.

The dependent variables measure five state policies that increase state government involvement in various parts of public education governance. These state policies were selected for both the availability of data that enable rigorous quantitative testing and the clear threats these policies represent to negative local autonomy. These policies clearly and dramatically limit local school districts' choices and therefore compromise local control. Each policy, its effect on centralizing education decision making at the state level, the scaling of the dependent variable that measures it, and the method of model estimation used are presented in separate sections on each policy. Table 3.1 presents the sources and summary statistics for all variables.

For each regulation, the corresponding table first presents estimations of models containing every independent variable except the finance share variable.[4] The number of cases each model considers is fifty (one for each state). In statistical models with so few observations, fewer independent variables are preferable, so a second model estimation presented in the table contains only the independent variables that meet a minimal

TABLE 3.1. Description of Variables

Dependent Variables

Variable (year of measurement)	Source	Min. Value	Max. Value	Mean (std. var.)
Standardized testing (2002)	*Education Week* 2002	0	5	2.74 (1.7935)
Teacher certification (2001)	*Education Week* 2002	0	3	1.9 (1.1473)
High-stakes testing (2001)	*Education Week* 2002	0	1	0.36 (.4849)
Safety (2006)	*Education Week* 2007	0	3	1.98 (.8449)
State takeover (2002)	Education Commission of the States 1998	0	4	0.96 (1.4702)

Independent Variables

Finance 03	National Center for Educational Statistics 2007	30.2	90.1	50.446 (11.9981)
Finance 00		29.1	88.8	51.68 (12.0469)
Finance 98				
Finance 97		7	89.8	49.396 (14.5033)
Finance 95				
Black	U.S. Census Bureau 2000	0.3	36.3	9.902 (9.5801)
Bush vote 00	infoplease 2007	32	68	50.48 (8.7113)
Hispanic	U.S. Census Bureau 2000	0.7	42.1	7.786 (8.9147)
Income/1,000	U.S. Census Bureau 2002	30.1	55.6	43.094 (6.5675)
Union share	NCES 2005	0	100	71.1474 (37.06784)

Controls

Standardized testing (1998)	*Education Week* 1999	0	5	2.08 (1.7361)
Teacher certification (1998)	*Education Week* 1999	0	4	1.9 (1.1645)
High-stakes testing (1997)	*Education Week* 1998	0	1	0.32 (.4712)
State takeover (1996)	Education Commission of the States 1998	0	4	0.56 (1.0333)
Safety (2002)	*Education Week* 2003	0	3	1.76 (.9806)

$N = 50$

standard of statistical significance in the first model. In the third and fourth models, estimates including the covariates from the second model and a variable measuring state finance share (the key independent variable) three and six years before the measurement of the dependent variable are presented, allowing readers to gauge the relative importance of finance share's effect in terms of both size and impact on the overall fit of the model. Evidence that state governments that contribute a higher percentage of the total school finance burden enact higher levels of regulation, even when other factors are controlled, strongly suggests that finance centralization leads to increased regulation generally and to a corresponding loss of local control.

Results: The Effect of Finance Centralization on State Regulation

Standardized Testing

The first state policy considered is the extent of each state's pre-NCLB standardized testing.[5] In the 1980s, standardized testing became a very popular program among state governments to address the perception of unsatisfactory levels of student achievement. By 2000, prior to NCLB's passage, every state had implemented some form of testing to measure student achievement. Standardized testing represents a departure from the traditional prerogative of local schools and school boards to be the sole judges of whether a student has learned required material. Both school board members and administrators believe standards greatly curtail their autonomy (Feuerstein and Dietrich 2003). Researchers have shown that standards have a significant effect on teachers' classroom practices and the content of a school's curriculum (Malen and Muncey 2000; Swanson and Stevenson 2002). Some state governments use results from these tests to decide how much control to exercise over an individual school or school district, with the ultimate recourse being to take over a district deemed failing.[6]

The *standardized testing* dependent variable measures how much states hold schools accountable for performance on standardized tests. *Education Week* recorded whether states issued report cards on individual school test scores, rated individual schools on their performance, and offered rewards, assistance, and/or sanctions for performance levels for the 2002–3 school year. Such requirements require local actors to implement programs they would be unlikely to undertake without compulsion. Possible scores for the dependent variables range from 0 if a state had adopted none of these regulations to 5 if they had adopted all of them. The data also allow for the construction of a control variable measuring the same five state testing policies for the 1997–98 school year to ensure that the model estimations reflect the change in state testing policies caused by the other independent variables.

Table 3.2 presents estimates of ordered logit models using the standardized testing variable as the dependent variable.[7] In Models 1 and 2, the only statistically significant predictor of the dependent variable in addition to the measure of previous testing levels is the percentage of a state's vote Bush received in 2000, with a larger Bush vote share associated with lower levels of the dependent variable.[8] Democrats are more likely to support state tests monitoring student achievement than are Republicans, who may find it hard to reconcile testing with their traditional affinity for local educational control and small government.[9] No other independent variable employed in Models 1 or 2 has an effect that approaches statistical significance, meaning that we cannot accept their effects as real. In Model 1, the union share and black variables come closest, so they are retained for subsequent models.

Models 3 and 4 present estimates of ordered logit models very similar to those described earlier. The only difference is that Model 3 includes a variable measuring state finance share for the 1999–2000 school year and

TABLE 3.2. Standardized Testing

	Model 1	Model 2	Model 3	Model 4
Finance 00			.0016 (.0209)	
Finance 97				.0038 (.0195)
Black	.0372 (.0438)	.0399 (.0412)	.0407 (.0428)	.0409 (.0415)
Bush vote 00	−.0817 (.0384)*	−.0841 (.0379)*	−.0841 (.0379)*	−.0846 (.0381)*
Hispanic	.0063 (.0349)			
Income/1,000	.0200 (.0559)			
Union share	−.0156 (.0121)	−.0136 (.0103)	−.0135 (.0105)	−.0132 (.0105)
Testing 98	1.0202 (.2321)**	1.0209 (.2210)**	1.0183 (.2237)**	1.0216 (.2212)**
Model Summary Statistics				
N	50	50	50	50
McKelvey and Zavoina's R^2	.604	.603	.603	.604

Note: Estimates of ordered logit models with dependent variable measuring extent of state standardized testing in 2002–3 school year as described in table 3.1 and methods section.
*$z < .05$ **$z < .01$

Model 4 includes a variable measuring state finance share for 1996–97. Measuring finance share three and six years prior to the dependent variable should catch any possible effects of finance share centralization on state regulation, but no effect is present. In neither Model 3 nor Model 4 does the effect of the finance centralization variable approach statistical significance. The evidence presented here suggests that centralization of school finance at the state level does not have an independent effect on the likelihood that states will adopt more extensive combinations of standardized testing and the reporting, rewards, and sanctions that can accompany it.

High-Stakes Testing

The full potential of standardized testing's force as an agent of centralization can be seen in the rise of high-stakes testing. Some states have decided that testing students merely to identify areas for schools to target for improvement is insufficient. To ensure that students have mastered content deemed appropriate for their grade level, these states require that students pass standardized tests to advance to the next grade and/or to graduate from high school. In removing promotion and graduation decisions from local schools, high-stakes testing increases state control of education even more than conventional standardized testing does. Researchers have shown that high-stakes testing leads to changes in instruction (Firestone, Mayrowetz, and Fairman 1998; Roderick, Jacob, and Bryk 2002). The *high-stakes testing* dependent variable is a dichotomous variable that measures whether states required students to pass a test to advance to the next grade or graduate for the 2002–3 school year. A control measuring whether states employed such tests for 1996–97 is employed as an independent variable.

Table 3.3 presents estimates of logit models using the high-stakes testing variable as a dependent variable.[10] Model 1 shows that the effect of every independent variable achieves or approaches statistical significance except the income variable. These effects are robust across the different models presented in table 3.3, suggesting that their effects are real. Both the black and Hispanic variables achieve statistical significance, with larger percentages of these residents associated with higher scores of the dependent variable. These results conform to expectations. In almost every measure of educational achievement, most African American and Hispanic students lag behind their counterparts in other racial and ethnic groups. Many observers hope that high-stakes testing will ensure that these students must master basic skills to advance and graduate. Higher levels of Bush voters are associated with increases in the dependent variable.[11] This result bucks the hypothesis that Democrats will favor more state activism than will Republicans, perhaps because of the desire, commonly associated with conservatives, to have students master the basics and to hold students to rigorous performance standards. Relative to some of the other reforms this book discusses, including school finance reform, high-stakes testing can be relatively inexpensive, thereby potentially increasing its appeal to fiscal conservatives who want to help poor children without increasing government spending

Models 3 and 4 present estimations of logit models identical to Model 2 except for the inclusion of the 1999–2000 finance share variable in Model 3 and the 1996–97 finance share variable in Model 4. Neither of these variables is a statistically significant predictor of changes in the dependent variable. This evidence suggests that state finance share does not increase the likelihood that states will adopt high-stakes testing. Combined with the results from the standardized testing models, these results provide no evidence for the proposition that finance centralization at the state level leads to increases in the extent or severity of state accountability systems.

TABLE 3.3. High-Stakes Testing

	Model 1	Model 2	Model 3	Model 4
Finance 00			.0212 (.0396)	
Finance 97				.0242 (.0370)
Black	.3818 (.1274)**	.3746 (.1236)**	.3835 (.1284)**	.3867 (.1299)**
Bush vote 00	.1401 (.0956)	.1407 (.0923)	.1372 (.0930)	.1357 (.0935)
Hispanic	.1313 (.0570)*	.1300 (.0567)*	.1299 (.0565)*	.1312 (.0568)*
Income/1,000	−.0415 (.0932)			
Union share	.0450 (.0956)	.0411 (.0215)	.0413 (.0213)	.0415 (.0213)
High stakes 97	1.6554 (1.1291)	1.6499 (1.1030)	1.5543 (1.1051)	1.4948 (1.1059)
Model Summary Statistics				
N	50	50	50	50
Pseudo R^2	.5478	.5447	.5491	.5514

Note: Estimates of logit models with dependent variable measuring use of state required high-stakes tests in 2000–2001 school year as described in table 3.1 and methods section.
*$z < .05$ **$z < .01$

Teacher Certification

In the days of the little red schoolhouse, deciding whether a teacher had adequate credentials was the job of either the community or the local school government, but those days are long gone. By 2002, forty-one states required that beginning teachers pass at least one test to receive their teaching licenses, and many states require more tests. Regulations determining who can begin teaching may discourage motivated individuals from becoming teachers or discourage districts from hiring noncertified individuals for fear of public backlash. Thus, the teaching pool and options for local actors are reduced.[12] The *teacher certification* dependent variable measures the testing states require beginning teachers to pass before they can become certified for the 2000–2001 school year. *Education Week* recorded whether states required beginning teachers to pass tests in basic teaching skills, specific subjects, and subject-specific pedagogy skills before receiving beginning teacher licenses. The result is a categorical, ordered variable with possible values ranging from 0, where a state did not require beginning teachers to pass any of these tests before entering the classroom, to 3, where a state required teachers to pass all three of these tests. The models include a control measuring states' beginning teacher certification policies for the 1997–98 school year.[13]

Table 3.4 presents estimates of ordered logit models using teacher certification as the dependent variable. In Models 1 and 2, two variables

TABLE 3.4. Teacher Certification

	Model 1	Model 2	Model 3	Model 4
Finance 98			.0042 (.0213)	
Finance 95				−.0085 (.0199)
Black	.0704 (.0483)	.0784 (.0465)	.0790 (.0468)	.0781 (.0460)
Bush vote 00	−.1034 (.0515)*	−.1063 (.0495)*	−.1050 (.0498)*	−.1073 (.0495)*
Hispanic	−.0120 (.0327)			
Income/1,000	.0328 (.0576)			
Union share	−.0196 (.0132)	−.0156 (.0117)	−.0152 (.0119)	−.0164 (.0119)
High stakes 97	1.2243 (.3473)	1.1652 (.3306)	1.1742 (.3338)	1.1683 (.3301)
Model Summary Statistics				
N	50	50	50	50
McKelvey and Zavoina's R^2	.631	.626	.626	.630

Note: Estimates of ordered logit models with dependent variable measuring beginning teacher certification requirements for the 2000–2001 school year as described in table 3.1 and methods section.
*z < .05   **z < .01

have notable effects on the dependent variable. Once again, the Bush vote variable has a statistically significant impact on the dependent variable, with a higher percentage of the Bush vote associated with lower levels of the dependent variable. This result fits with the perceptions that Republicans are more suspicious of an activist centralized government in education policy-making than are Democrats, who rely on teachers' unions as part of their electoral coalition and are likely to increase the professionalism requirements for entry into teaching.[14] The effect of the African American variable approaches significance.[15] A higher black population is associated with increased levels of the dependent variable. African Americans, whose schools are staffed with a disproportionate number of uncertified teachers, may see increased certification requirements as key to improving the quality of instruction students receive.

Models 3 and 4 are identical to Model 2 except that they include finance share variables for the 1997–98 and 1994–95 school years. Neither of their effects approaches significance. This evidence suggests that finance centralization does not make states more active in regulating minimum teacher requirements.

School Safety

One of the more recent state education regulations to become popular is legislation designed to ensure that students are safe when they attend school. Propelled by public reaction to such horrible acts of school violence as the Columbine massacre, by the 2005–6 school year, forty-seven states had enacted some form of school safety legislation. The aims of such legislation are beyond reproach but represent a significant expansion of state regulation of public education that creates a new set of procedures local districts must follow. The *school safety* dependent variable measures whether states required schools to put safety data on report cards, funded programs to reduce bullying and harassment, and forced schools to adopt specific bullying and school violence policies for the 2005–6 school year. The resulting variable is ordered and categorical with possible values ranging from 0, where a state has adopted none of the four safety policies, to 4, where they have adopted all four. The data allows for the construction of a control to be inserted as an independent variable, with its observations taken from beginning teacher certification policies for the 2001–2 school year.

Table 3.5 presents estimations of ordered logit models using school safety as the dependent variable and the independent variables specified earlier.[16] In Models 1 and 2, the black variable has a statistically significant effect on the dependent variable, with increases in the African American variable associated with increases in the dependent variable. While most of the high-profile school shootings of recent years have occurred in school districts with large majorities of white students, violence is often perceived as a particular problem for African American communities, a phenomenon that may make state legislators, most of whom are white, more apt to support legislation designed to combat violence. A lower per capita income is associated with increases in the dependent variable at a statistically significant level. If one accepts that the threat of violence seems more real in less affluent environments, this result makes sense.[17]

Models 3 and 4 incorporate finance share variables from the 1999–2000 and 2002–3 school years into Model 2.[18] In neither model does the finance share variable's effect approach statistical significance. Thus, these models provide no evidence that state finance centralization leads states to adopt more school safety regulations.

State Takeovers

The most dramatic instance of state control over education involves state takeovers of school districts deemed to be failing. For reasons including

TABLE 3.5. Safety Legislation

	Model 1	Model 2	Model 3	Model 4
Finance 03			.0273 (.0250)	
Finance 00				.0296 (.0253)
Black	.1055 (.0423)*	.1078 (.0400)**	.1166 (.0413)**	.1170 (.0412)**
Bush vote 00	−.0102 (.0395)			
Hispanic	.0095 (.0417)			
Income/1,000	−.0784 (.0558)	−.0760 (.0556)	−.0804 (.0564)	−.0759 (.0561)
Union share	.0112 (.0128)	.0127 (.0116)	.0144 (.0117)	.0146 (.0117)
Safety 02	1.5423 (.4105)**	1.5920 (.3853)**	1.5575 (.3888)**	1.5456 (.3892)**
Model Summary Statistics				
N	50	50	50	50
McKelvey and Zavoina's R^2	.509	.510	.521	.523

Note: Estimates of ordered logit models with dependent variable measuring school safety legislation enacted for the 2005–6 school year as described in table 3.1 and methods section.

*$z < .05$ **$z < .01$

academic underachievement, crumbling infrastructure, fiscal misman-
agement, and corrupt administration, eighteen states have taken over the
operations of at least one school district. In such cases, the state charges
its department of education with the management of all school district
activities (Education Commission of the States 1998). It is hard to imagine
a more invasive state regulation, in that takeovers institute literal state
control over public education in a school district. The *state takeover* variable measures the number of school districts of which each state government had assumed control by the end of the 2002–3 school year. Values
range from 0, the value attributed to the thirty-two states that had not
taken over any district, to 4, for the six states that had taken over four districts. The data allow for the construction of a control to be inserted as an
independent variable, with its observations taken from beginning
teacher certification policies for the 1996–97 school year.

Table 3.6 presents estimates of Poisson maximum likelihood models
employing state takeovers as a dependent variable.[19] In Models 1 and 2,
in addition to the control, three independent variables have effects that
achieve or approach statistical significance. The Bush vote variable has a
statistically significant effect at the $z \leq .01$ level, with increases in the Bush
vote associated with decreases in the dependent variable. This effect may
stem from the pressure Democrats receive from urban residents, who
make up a key part of the party's electoral coalition, to do something to
help ailing school districts. This rationale also helps interpret the effect of

TABLE 3.6. State Takeovers

	Model 1	Model 2	Model 3	Model 4
Finance 00			–.0193 (.0165)	
Finance 97				–.0135 (.0158)
Black	.0316 (.0193)	.0334 (.0176)	.0299 (.0180)	.0313 (.0178)
Bush vote 00	–.0830 (.0306)**	–.0781 (.0256)**	–.0734 (.0360)**	–.0727 (.0259)**
Hispanic	.0048 (.0156)			
Income/1,000	–.0529 (.0389)	–.0584 (.0330)	–.0734 (.0360)*	–.0695 (.0362)
Union share	–.0029 (.0084)			
Takeover 96	.8171 (.1202)**	.8322 (.1152)**	.8711 (.1251)**	.8642 (.1254)**
Model Summary Statistics				
N	50	50	50	50
Pseudo R^2	.4444	.4431	.4522	.4479

Note: Estimates of Poisson maximum likelihood models with dependent variable measuring number of state school districts deemed failing before and including 2002–3 school year as described in
table 3.1 and methods section.
*$z < .05$ **$z < .01$

the black variable, which approaches statistical significance.[20] Because African American children disproportionately attend the nation's lowest-performing school districts, their parents may be most likely to pressure their elected officials (most of whom are Democrats) to assume control of these districts. The income variable has an effect one can be reasonably sure is real, with a higher per capita income associated with fewer takeovers.[21] Less affluent states generally have poorer schools, potentially increasing demand for state action.

Models 3 and 4 present estimates similar to Model 2 except for their inclusion of the finance share 1997 and 2000 variables. Neither variable has an effect on the dependent variable that approaches statistical significance. Thus, there is again no evidence that finance centralization at the state level leads to an increase in state takeovers of failing school districts.

The Results as a Whole

While these results provide critical insight into the dynamics of the Piper Link, they also offer evidence about which other factors influence state education policy. For four of five regulations, the partisanship variable has an effect that achieves or approaches conventional definitions of statistical significance. The two parties seem to have very different plans for state governments' role in education, with Democrats favoring a more active role in determining curriculum and day-to-day operations for local school districts. Republicans seem to support allowing local school actors more leeway, a stance consistent with traditional conservative respect for local control. With such support for local control comes a demand that districts prove they are providing a quality education through a more extensive system of standardized testing. In the post-NCLB era, it will be important to measure whether this distinction between the parties continues or whether bipartisan support for NCLB has led to a convergence of the parties' philosophies regarding education reform. During the 2007 debate over the law's reauthorization, congressional Republicans indicated a desire to scale back the federal role in public education, and many of the states that have resisted NCLB the most are quite conservative (Dillon 2007). These developments may represent the post-Bush Republican Party's desire to return to its traditional championing of local control. All five of the regulations this chapter considers undeniably increase state control over public education. Even though Republicans are less likely to support many of the reforms presented here, they do support high-stakes testing, which takes evaluation and promotion decisions out of the hands of teachers, principals, and other local officials. Even the party that more frequently appeals to local control supports some policies that undermine it.

For four of five regulations, a relatively large African American population is associated with higher levels of regulation at statistically significant or near-significant levels. Given that public education is seen as the great engine of upward mobility in American society, even legislators from the most conservative districts may face constituent pressure to do something to address the achievement gap, but not at the expense of radically changing the existing system. The public is generally satisfied with the state of American public education. Parents, who are understandably among the most vocal groups when decisions on public education are to be made, have favorable impressions of the schools, with 67 percent grading the school their children attend as an A or B (Phi Delta Kappan and the Gallup Organization 2007). Thus the public is not likely to approve of school finance reform, voucher systems, desegregation, and other measures that challenge or eliminate the existing system. Thus, legislators seeking to help African American students must embrace approaches such as standardized testing that seek to improve black achievement rates without disturbing the majority of school districts. Also, the support of the African American community would seem an almost necessary condition for a state takeover to have a chance of reversing the developments that caused the takeover. No matter how poorly performing a school may be, the specter of a disproportionately white state government assuming control of an urban school district, where the leadership may be overwhelmingly black, raises legitimate fears about racial paternalism. If the general African American population supports the takeover, such fears may be mitigated.

This chapter's most important finding is a series of nonresults. The models show absolutely no evidence that centralization of finance leads to increases in state education regulation. States with more centralized systems of school finance are no more or less likely to adopt strong student accountability systems, pass extensive teacher certification or school safety regulations, or take over failing school districts than those states that rely more heavily on locally generated revenue to fund public education. The evidence shows no sign that the Piper Link functions—that school finance centralization leads to a decrease in local negative autonomy. These results suggest that states can centralize their systems of school finance without fearing an inevitable increase in state regulation in the future. A state's location in the 20–90 percentage range of possible finance share simply does not affect local negative autonomy.

Skeptics may argue that states' decisions to adopt standardized testing, curricular standards, and the other reforms discussed here can be attributed to a wide variety of factors and that states are not trying to curtail local autonomy by passing such measures. For example, conservative proponents of curricular standards and testing would dispute the idea that their proposals are designed to erode local government's power. Whether or not this argument holds true, it does not change the fundamental point that the reform proposals described in this chapter pursue other goals while disregarding concerns about the proper balance between state and local authority in a way that educational experts from two generations ago would find inconceivable. Whatever else standardized tests do, they undeniably "impose external measurements to determine how well students are performing" that dramatically limit schools' and school boards' ability to devise independent evaluation systems (Hochschild and Scovronick 2003, 98). State governments may take over failing school districts for noble reasons, but this action still strips local school boards of their traditional authority. These trends clearly represent a centralization of educational authority and a significant threat to local educational control, but finance centralization does not influence the passage of such measures. At least for the 20–90 percent range of the school finance share independent variable in these models, this is strong evidence against the dynamics hypothesized by the Piper Link.

CHAPTER FOUR

Sharks and Wolverines

The Effect of School Finance Centralization in Vermont and Michigan

"A small town is like a big family."
Wall hanging at Blanche and Bill's Pancake House, Bridgewater Corners, Vermont

THE RESULTS OF CHAPTER 3 may indicate that a state's finance share has no effect on its level of regulation but cannot speak to whether state finance share undercuts local governments' ability to undertake independent actions—that is, on their level of positive local autonomy. A strong local government is not just free from restriction. Its leaders must also feel empowered to act, to diagnose and fix problems in their community. Fully understanding whether finance centralization harms local control in the 20–90 range requires examining whether local actors seem less able to act independent of state government in a system of relatively higher financing.

This chapter presents results of case studies of finance reform movements in Vermont and Michigan. During the 1990s, both states embarked on remarkable and extensive school finance centralizations, albeit under radically different conditions. These two very different states had very different school finance reform movements, yet finance centralization had similar effects on local control. The aggregate data necessary to understand all of what local school boards do are not available, requiring us to venture into the messy, idiosyncratic, and utterly wonderful world of local school politics.

School Finance in Vermont

"In Vermont, local control is as much a part of life as maple syrup and country stores."

Joetta L. Sack

Prior to the 1990s, public schools in Vermont were as dependent on local sources of funding as almost any state in the Union. During the second half of the twentieth century, the state share of the school finance burden hovered between 20 and 30 percent of total education spending, with the vast majority of the remainder coming from local sources. This method created large disparities in per-pupil spending between rich and poor towns, with the richest district in the state spending almost three times as much as the poorest district (Mathis 2000). The heavy reliance on local funding also meant that because property in poor areas was valued much lower, local governments in these areas needed to maintain much higher property tax rates to raise money for their schools. Because rich areas' property values were much higher, their governments could raise the same amount of money with a much lower tax rate. State representative Jack Andersen estimates that the town of Stratton, located in a wealthy ski community, could raise per-pupil spending one thousand dollars by increasing its property tax rate by one cent, while the poorer town of Richford needed to raise its tax rate fifteen cents to generate an additional one hundred dollars per pupil. The bottom line was that a property in a less affluent area could be and was taxed at 10 times the rate of a similarly valued property in an affluent area without generating the same amount of resources for schools (Kilborn 1999).

In 1995, plaintiffs on behalf of the state's poor districts filed *Amanda Brigham et al. v. State of Vermont*, alleging that the state had failed to live up to its constitutional obligation to provide equitable education and taxation.[1] On February 5, 1997, the state supreme court agreed, ordering the legislature to provide an equitable distribution of education resources. The state's response to the *Brigham* decision was quick, sweeping, and, to those with knowledge of finance reform movements in other states, almost unbelievable. In most instances of school finance litigation where plaintiffs have received a favorable verdict, the elected branches of state government have complied reluctantly and tried to design a remedy that disturbed the existing finance system as little as possible. On June 26, 1997, Vermont governor Howard Dean signed Act 60, a law that would have made school funding in Vermont as equitable as any system in the country if fully implemented.[2] It instituted a statewide property tax and promised every school a block grant of five thousand dollars per pupil. Local towns could vote to spend any amount over the block grant, but if they spent more, they also had to contribute money to a sharing pool designed to ensure that poorer towns would be funded at the same level.

Act 60 had dramatic results, helping the state make significant progress toward equity in per-pupil spending (Baker 2001; Jimerson 2002). At least 82 percent of the state's residents and 168 of Vermont's 251 towns saw their property tax rates reduced from pre–Act 60 levels, and 198 towns received more money back from the state for their local schools than they paid in property taxes (Goodman 1999; Kilborn 1999; Mathis 2000). Before Act 60, the affluent town of Stowe spent more than nine thousand dollars per pupil with a relatively low tax rate of seventy cents per one hundred dollars of assessed property value. Act 60 required Stowe to send seventy cents of every dollar it raised above the block grant amount to the state sharing pool for redistribution. By 1999, Stowe residents paid 50 percent higher taxes while receiving back only 58 percent of their pre–Act 60 per-pupil spending (fifty-one hundred dollars) from the state (Goodman 1999).

For the purposes of this book, the most significant feature of Act 60 was that it rapidly increased the state's share of the school finance burden. The level and speed of Vermont's school finance centralization is unmatched in U.S. history. In the 1996–97 school year, before Act 60 was signed, the state government contributed 28.6 percent of the total funding for public education in the state, with local revenue sources contributing 64.9 percent (National Center for Education Statistics 1999). By 1998–99, the first year Act 60's funding scheme was in effect, the state share had jumped to 74.4 percent (National Center for Education Statistics 2001). Vermont's rapid and dramatic program is one of the qualities that make the state an ideal place to test finance centralization's effects on positive local autonomy. This centralization encompasses a significant amount of the 20–90 variation in contemporary state government finance shares, which suggests the effects of finance centralization on Vermont before and after Act 60 may provide as good a test for Piper Link dynamics as the statistical models presented in chapter 3. If the linear model of the Piper Link represents the true relationship between money and control, a rapid and substantial centralization of school funding such as the one Vermont undertook in the late 1990s should cause a dramatic decrease in local school board decision-making authority. Even if finance centralization's effect on local school boards has some kind of lag, by the time this research was conducted in 2004, a centralization the magnitude of Vermont's should show at least some effect on the number and scope of decisions Vermont's school boards make.

Local Control in Vermont

A second reason Vermont is a good place to study the Piper Link is because the state is as attached to the principle of local government as any place in the nation. The New England town meeting that Tocqueville romanticized and the rest of the country has largely abandoned still occurs in Vermont. Citizens come together once a year to decide matters of local concern through direct democracy. Proud Vermonters proclaim that they have "a little democracy at every crossroads" (Mathis 2000). Frank Bryan of the University of Vermont, by all accounts a quintessential Vermonter, named his recent opus on Vermont's town meetings *Real Democracy* and clearly holds a special place for them in his heart:

> Above all else, town meeting is public talk—common people *standing* for something. . . . It is in the speaking, the direct face-to-face link between talk and power, that real democracy transcends nearly every other definition of democracy issued since the Greeks. This is what enfolds our imagination, sparks our sense of democratic adventure, and conjures up ancient and hopeful possibilities. (2004, 140)[3]

Vermont's love of local control has always extended to education. "There is no truer symbol of self-government than our local school boards. A school board member who sees her or his responsibility as primarily local serves democracy in the finest way" (Sandberg 1997). Throughout the state's history, Vermonters have jealously guarded the prerogatives of local school boards against any attempt by the state to take a more active role in what schools taught, whom they hired as teachers, or the condition of their facilities (Lane 2002). Unlike most other states, Vermont has resisted consolidating its tiny schoolhouses into large regional school districts with one school board supervising many schools: each of Vermont's 252 towns has its own school board. Most of them continue to operate at least an elementary school even though many are extremely small and economies of scale suggest consolidation.[4] Towns continue to operate their own schools because they value the sense of community that schools instill in both their children and the town as a whole and because, as one former Rutland Northeast school board member says, "They hate taking things away from towns and giving them to the state." According to former Leicester Central School principal Ruth Anne Barker,

> I don't think that these small schools are particularly cost-efficient, but I'm not sure that it would be a good idea to close them. Many of these smaller towns wouldn't have any focus or any heart and soul if they didn't have their school. In many cases, the school provides identity and a common ground for people to meet, especially in these rural areas that don't have a real town.

The state's passion for locally controlled educational governance makes the opposition to Act 60's school finance reform unsurprising, and the relationship between higher funding and local autonomy was a prominent part of the debate. The state supreme court acknowledged the state's tradition of local control in the *Brigham* decision but argued that "regardless of how the state finances public education, it may still leave the basic decision-making power with local districts" (*Amanda Brigham* 1997, 20). Act 60's opponents disagreed with the court and cited a "growing body of research" that claimed that local control depended on local funding and predicted that as the state assumed a greater share of the finance burden, it would become more active in areas such as curriculum and collective bargaining (Act60.org 1997). School boards would lose the ability to make policy and be reduced to running schools "in accordance with an increasingly complex and demanding array of state goals, mandates, plans, standards, and penalties" (McClaughry 1997). Today, Representative Jack Andersen of Woodstock and others worry about how much control boards have retained in the post–Act 60 era: "Local control as we knew it is gone. That old definition of local control was that everything was intradistrict—our tax base, our tax rate, our school, our superintendent, our principal, our school, our kids. Now, with the statewide system, local decisions are only made within this larger context."

Vermont's love of local government and the centrality of local control concerns to the Act 60 debate make Vermont the perfect case for the linear version of the Piper Link to demonstrate its effects, if it functions. The commonsense assumption about the Piper Link is that of course money should influence control. However, chapter 3 provided compelling evidence that the Piper Link does not function within the 20–90 range. Given the disconnect, the Piper Link deserves the chance to demonstrate its effects in an area where local governments may have retained significant power and people are hypersensitive to its effects and, if anything, will overstate the loss of local autonomy. The passion local government excites makes Vermont such a place. For the Piper Link to erode local control, some version of relatively strong local control must exist. As chapter 1 describes, most scholars believe local governments across the nation lost significant power during the twentieth century. Vermont's commitment to the ideal of the New England town meeting may have allowed it to buck trends and retain a system of strong, active local school boards. If so, it retains a level of strong local autonomy on which the Piper Link could exert its influence. The commitment to the local ideal should also make residents aware of any encroachments, which is an advantage for a study that is looking for evidence that the linear Piper Link functions. Opponents of Act 60 live in a political culture where local government is a prominent part of the vocabulary and receives nothing but praise. Their hatred of Act 60 and their love of local government should combine to make them notice even the smallest decision that local governments could make independently prior to but not after Act 60's implementation. If Vermonters do not perceive a link between finance centralization and local autonomy, little reason exists to expect that residents of other states will perceive such a link.

Methods

Case Selection

I chose six town schools and school boards for this analysis: Woodstock and Sherburne Elementary Schools and Woodstock Union High School from the Windsor Central Supervisory Union and Neshobe Elementary School, Leicester Central School, and Otter Valley Union High School from the Rutland Northeast Supervisory Union. A supervisory union is a loose amalgamation of independent schools that performs most of the same functions as school districts do in other states. Although less than forty-five miles apart, the greater Woodstock and Rutland areas could hardly be more different and represent the Act 60 experiences of a much broader sample of Vermont towns and schools.[5]

The towns of Woodstock and Killington (where Sherburne Elementary is located) are relatively affluent areas. From Sherburne's entrance, several of the peaks of Killington Ski Resort are visible, and in Vermont, money follows skiing. Located less than twenty miles from Killington, Woodstock is a picturesque New England small town that attracts the ski crowd, antique shoppers, and other out-of-state tourists. Because of their advantageous locations, both Killington and Woodstock had high property values before Act 60 and were able to raise a relatively large amount of money for their schools while keeping their property tax rates relatively low. Act 60 could not have been more unpopular in either of these "gold towns." Residents of Woodstock, Killington, and other such towns led the resistance to Act 60, dubbed its sharing pool the "shark pool," and claimed that the law punished their children.[6] To reinforce the use of these three schools to represent the experiences of affluent schools in the state, I refer to Sherburne Elementary as RS1 (Rich School 1), Woodstock Elementary as RS2, and Woodstock Union as RS3. RT1 (Rich Town 1) refers to the town of Killington, and RT2 refers to the town of Woodstock.

The Rutland Northeast schools represent the schools and towns that benefited financially from Act 60's changes to the funding formula. Leicester and Brandon (home to Neshobe and Otter Valley) rank in the bottom half of the state's towns in median household income and have a higher percentage of children receiving free and reduced lunches than the state average of 26.4 percent.[7] Prior to Act 60, such areas imposed relatively high property tax rates yet generated relatively little school funding. Such schools and towns were the intended beneficiaries of Act 60, with the goal of providing higher per-pupil spending at lower tax rates. The remainder of this work refers to Neshobe as PS1 (Poor School 1), Leicester as PS2, and Otter Valley as PS3. PT1 (Poor Town 1) refers to the town of Brandon, and PT2 refers to the town of Leicester.

Data

The bulk of this chapter's data comes from in-depth interviews conducted in 2004 with school board members, superintendents, principals, officials, and other elites associated with these towns. Table 4.1 lists their names and positions. All of them served in some relevant capacity both before and after the implementation of Act 60, so they were able to speak to how the law had changed their responsibilities.[8] These people took seriously their roles as civil servants and stewards of the school and community and offered thoughtful responses. The information they provided tells a story about local educational politics in a depth that quantitative data simply cannot match. What they can tell the scholarly community about the effects of centralized finance on local government performance is significant.

Each interview lasted roughly an hour. I sought to discover how school board members viewed their roles, responsibilities, and interaction with other key actors; the school's autonomy from state interference; and citizen participation in school affairs. I asked questions designed to test several hypotheses regarding how finance centralization might change local educational governance. Finance centralization may in-

TABLE 4.1. Interviewees and Positions

Jack Andersen, State Representative, Woodstock

Ruth Anne Barker, Former Principal, Leicester Central School and Current Principal, Clarendon Elementary

Rachael Benoit, Board Member and Chairwoman, Woodstock Union High School

Tom Bourne, Former Board Member and Chairman, Woodstock Union High School

Sonia Burnham, Business Manager, Windsor Central Supervisory Union

Greg Camp, Former Member, Woodstock Elementary School Board

Tom Carmady, Woodstock Town Clerk

Connie Carroll, Board Member and Chairwoman, Otter Valley Union High School

Phoebe Chestna, Former Board Member, Neshobe Elementary School

Pat Eugair, Board Member, Otter Valley Union High School

Steve Finneron, Board Member and Chairman, Sherburne Elementary School

Brenda Flemming, Director of Business and Finance, Rutland Northeast Supervisory Union

Mary Ellen Gallagher, Superintendent, Windsor Central Supervisory Union

Allen Hitchcock, Board Member and Former Chairman, Otter Valley Union High School

Ron Jaynes, Former Director, Woodstock Education Fund

Steve Jeffrey, Executive Director, Vermont League of Cities and Towns

Dave Lewis, Town Manager, Killington

William Mathis, Superintendent, Rutland Northeast Supervisory Union

Peter Mello, Former Principal, Neshobe Elementary and Current Director of Castleton College Center for Schools

Diane Mott, Board Member, Otter Valley Union High School

Mitchell Pearl, Former Board Member and Chairman, Neshobe Elementary School

Charles Peterson, Former Board Member and Chairman, Woodstock Elementary School

Donna Pidgeon, Town Clerk, Leicester

Jan Sherman, Former Board Member, Leicester

Marion Withum, Principal, Sherburne Elementary School

crease the state's willingness to pass laws regulating other aspects of educational governance, including curriculum and teacher certification, and thus curtail local officials' negative autonomy. Any increase in regulation associated with finance reform may also have an indirect effect on positive local autonomy. Citizen school boards may not know what the state government requires, forbids, and permits them to do and may surrender decision-making authority to educational professionals who have the time and the expertise to make sense of government regulations.[9] A greater reliance on state funding may lead to greater insecurity about the reliability and constancy of state funding, which in turn may lead local actors to undertake fewer or less ambitious initiatives. If finance centralization causes these or other changes, it may disrupt the way local actors relate to others or change their decision-making process, which may make it more difficult to undertake ambitious independent policy.

Several forms of data complement the interview analysis. I analyzed school board minutes from the three Rutland Northeast schools and RS1 from 1995–96 through 1999–2000, from RS2 from 1996–97 through 2000–2001, and from RS3 from 1998–99 through 2000–2001.[10] The first and most basic information this analysis provides is the number of motions passed. If the Piper Link exists, one would expect school boards to pass fewer motions because finance centralization would decrease their ability to make meaningful decisions. Second, seeing if the types of decisions these six Vermont boards made changed over time should help determine whether Act 60's finance centralization affected the scope or content of school board decision making. If finance centralization restricts the range of areas in which boards can make policy, they would be expected to make fewer policies in a narrower set of these six categories after the measure's 1998 implementation. A marked decrease in the number of motions in the most important areas in which boards can make policy, such as curriculum, would show that finance centralization decreases local control in areas where many citizens would most like to retain it. This analysis employs a system Kathryn A. McDermott (1999) developed to classify issues school boards address.[11]

Advocates of local government cite the values participatory democracies instill in the populace as a key argument for keeping decision making local, so one of the most harmful ways finance centralization could undermine local control is to cause a decrease in public participation in school affairs. School board minutes recorded the number of non-board-members present at each meeting, and town records contain voter turnout information for school elections in the study's four towns from 1991 to 2003. If Act 60 had a negative effect on local participation, fewer people would be expected to attend meetings and to vote in school elections.[12] Because so much local education governance occurs informally and outside of general meetings, general meeting minutes cannot tell the whole story of citizenship participation. Local elites' recollections of general patterns probably better reflect true levels of participation, so I asked my interview subjects whether they thought participation had changed in the wake of Act 60.

The Big Picture

Taxes and Spending

The first question is whether Act 60 accomplished its lofty goals of changing the relative distribution of public education resources in Vermont, and the answer is an unqualified yes. The available records show that Act 60 dramatically changed taxation and spending patterns in all four towns. Figure 4.1 shows the property tax rate for PT1 and RT1 for the 1991–92 through 2002–3 school years. Figure 4.2 shows the school tax rate for PT2 and RT2 for the same years. When Act 60 was implemented, affluent towns such as Killington and Woodstock saw their taxes increase dramatically, because their previous tax rates were well below the new state property tax rate and the state funding formula demanded that more affluent areas send money to the state for every dollar in per-pupil spending above the five-thousand-dollar baseline. Figures 4.1 and 4.2 also show that Act 60 provided substantial initial tax relief for Brandon and especially Leicester.[13] Perhaps for the first time ever and as a result of funding from the state sharing pool, poor towns could cut their tax rates without dramatically decreasing school funding. Instead, under the new finance scheme, both Brandon and Leicester were clear financial winners. Figures 4.3 and 4.4 show the total approved school budgets for the four towns from the 1991–92 through 2003–4 school years: Act 60 increased the funding available in poor towns. Though spending went up in Killington and stayed the same in Woodstock, per-pupil spending decreased in both towns.[14]

The Windsor Central schools were clear financial losers under Act 60. Because schools and school boards in these towns relied so heavily on local taxes before Act 60, they should most dramatically demonstrate any

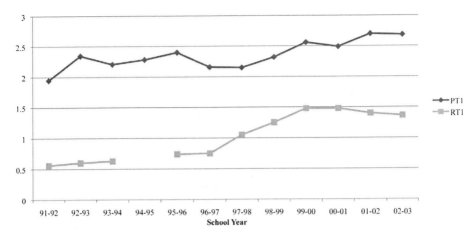

Fig. 4.1.   Total property tax rate for PT1 and RT1, 1991–92 through 2002–3 (RT data missing for 1994–95 school year)

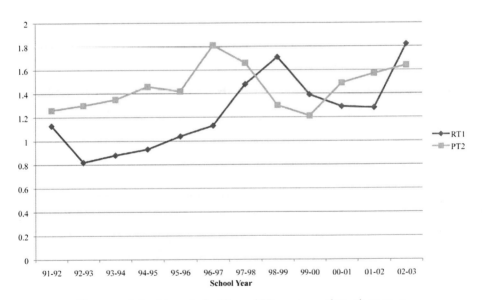

Fig. 4.2.   School tax rate for PT2 and RT2, 1991–92 through 2003–4

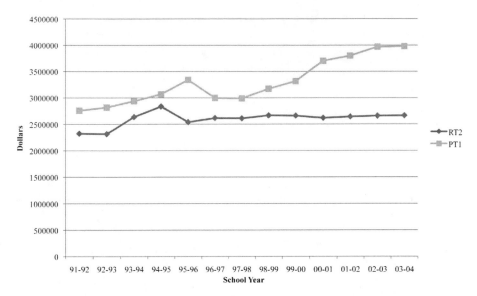

Fig. 4.3. Total approved school budgets for PT1 and RT2, 1991–92 through 2003–4

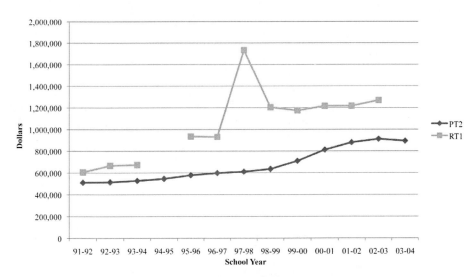

Fig. 4.4. Total approved school budgets for RT1 and PT2, 1991–92 through 2003–4 (RT data missing for 1994–95 school year)

loss of autonomy the Piper Link predicts from funding centralization. In addition, the strong resistance from residents of such areas should make them more likely to perceive and point out the law's negative consequences. Act 60's effect on poor areas is harder to predict. An increase in available funding might enable local school boards in such areas to broaden their policy-making scope. If the Piper Link functions as its proponents say it does, the Rutland Northeast school boards would enjoy less autonomy from the state even as their financial status improved.

Local Control

While Act 60 changed education in Vermont, it did not change local educational control. Almost all of the evidence from interviews and numerical data suggests that Act 60 had no negative effect on local autonomy. None of the twenty-five interview subjects, including those who raised the concerns about local control discussed later in this chapter, thought that Act 60 had a significant effect on how their schools were governed, how decisions were made, how many or what type of decisions they made, or what responsibilities the interviewees performed. These observations were consistent across all positions, including school board members, principals, supervisory union officials, and town officials. Both board members and supervisory union administrators reported that Act 60 did not increase board reliance on central administration in any way, including how members of the two groups worked together to create a budget. It did not change how schools made decisions about curriculum, hiring or firing, or any other area that goes into running schools. The subjects reported that their schools still undertook a wide variety of locally initiated projects, from block scheduling to teacher salary reform to a horticulture program at RS3 that organized field trips to places such as the Galapagos Islands. None of the interviewees felt that the scope of local decisions had decreased or that Act 60 had made the school or any of its officials more dependent on the state. Subjects from both the rich and poor schools shared these impressions. Local officials spoke with a unified voice, saying that local autonomy remained about the same. As one former board president said, "I can't think of a single case in which we made a decision based on the ramifications of Act 60." As Rutland Northeast superintendent William Mathis put it, "Act 60 is not a world in which [board members] live. They're worried about their local issues—a complaint about a teacher, bus stops, making sure we have instructional supplies."

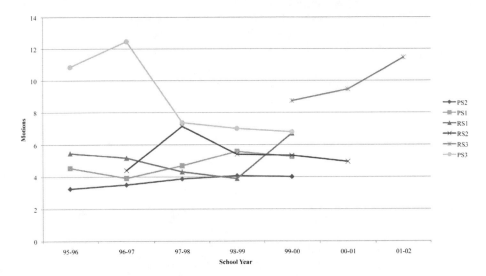

Fig. 4.5.   Average motions per school board meeting, 1995–96 through
1999–2000

The numerical data also suggest that what and how much school
boards do did not change because of Act 60. Figure 4.5 shows the average
number of motions each school board passed in varying years around the
1998–99 implementation. The number of motions per meeting that PS1,
PS2, and RS1 passed remained almost entirely constant for the three
years before Act 60 and the first two post-implementation years. Relative
to the 1996–97 and 1997–98 school years, RS2 did not pass appreciably
more motions per meeting in the 1998–99 and 1999–2000 school years. Although the board minutes for RS3 were not available for the years prior
to Act 60's implementation, the trend for the available years hardly suggests a school board that is losing decision-making authority, with averages rising from 8.73 in 1998–99 to 11.36 by 2000–2001.

Nor do the minutes from RS1, RS2, PS1, and PS2 suggest that the
types of decisions these boards are making changed because of Act 60.
Figures 4.6–4.10 show the motions from the five school boards for which
data were available sorted by year and type of motion. The number of decisions school boards made in each category remained relatively constant, as no board saw a sustained rise or fall in the number of motions in
a given category after Act 60's implementation in 1998. Especially noteworthy is the stability of the number of curriculum-related motions

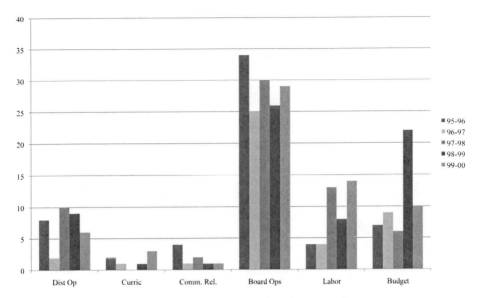

Fig. 4.6.   PS1 school board motions by type and year

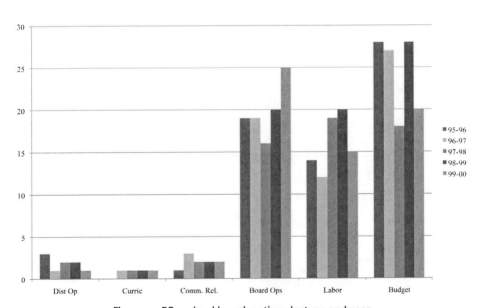

Fig. 4.7.   PS2 school board motions by type and year

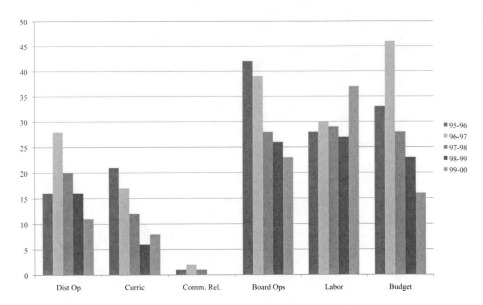

Fig. 4.8.   PS3 school board motions by type and year

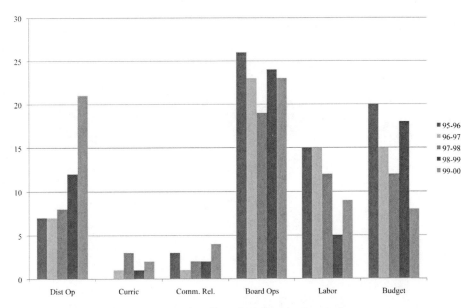

Fig. 4.9.   RS1 school board motions by type and year

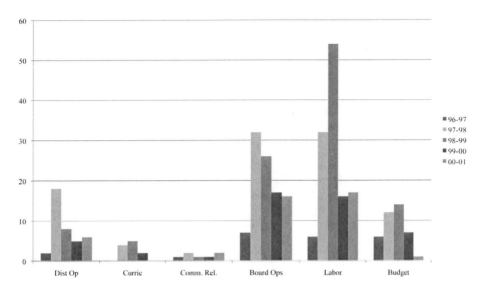

Fig. 4.10.   RS2 school board motions by type and year

across the four school boards. Act 60's finance centralization had no effect on the number of decisions school boards made about what is taught in the classroom, a finding that should alleviate the fears of those concerned with retaining some local control over what children learn.[15] A few of the trends in RS1's motions (figure 4.9) are noteworthy. Specifically, the number of labor motions in 1998–99 and 1999–2000 is lower than in the three previous years, and the number of district operations motions for the same two years increased. Without further examination, it is difficult to determine whether these trends are likely to continue. The interview subjects, the school board minutes, and the rest of the data in this section strongly suggest that these findings are short-term anomalies.

The most compelling evidence in support of the hypothesis that Act 60's finance centralization decreased local school board discretionary authority comes from an analysis of the PS3 board minutes. As figure 4.5 shows, PS3's board passed 12.46 motions per meeting during the 1996–97 school year but fewer than 8 per meeting for the three years thereafter. Figure 4.8 shows that PS3's motions decreased from their 1996–97 highs in several categories, including district operations, curriculum, board operations, and budgets. Supporters of the Piper Link could argue that this evidence suggests that PS3's board changed its behavior in response to

Act 60's passage because state funding and the accompanying requirements restricted the board's policy-making authority. Furthermore, the
losses in budgetary and curricular authority may suggest that Act 60 led
to a narrowing of the range of policy options available to local boards.

Further examination suggests that changes in PS3's personnel and procedures are a more likely explanation for the decreases in motions in specific categories. In the first three years, one December or January meeting
contained numerous motions changing specific items in the budget the
board proposed to the voters. Such meetings appear to not have occurred
in 1998–99 or 1999–2000, perhaps suggesting that more of the budgeting
process happened through the informal channels that characterize most
school board decision making (Iannaccone and Lutz 1970; Wirt and Kirst
1997). The vast majority of the curricular motions in the first two years involved granting formal approval to school group field trips. No reason exists to imagine that such approvals represent a particularly meaningful
manifestation of local control or are linked to the level of state funding PS3
received. The decrease in motions across all categories also coincides with
a change in the board's recording secretary in April 1997, suggesting that
differences in recording styles may account for some of the drop.[16]

Other evidence suggests the Piper Link is not at work at PS3. The consensus among PS3 and Rutland Northeast Supervisory Union officials
was that financial centralization has not changed their roles or power in
any way. Board member Connie Carroll indicated that she still believed
that local control remained strong and unchanged after Act 60: "It makes
me proud to be part of the system. If we see something isn't working, we
have the power to change it." More specifically, none of the six interviewees connected with RS3 saw a loss of curricular or budgetary authority. Because so much school and school board policy is decided outside the structure of formal board meetings, the impressions of RS3
officials are much more trustworthy than the average motion statistic. Finally, the findings from the other five schools considered here suggest
that something other than the Piper Link is responsible for the decrease
in motions at PS3 meetings. If five schools show no evidence of the Piper
Link, it is likely that a different phenomenon explains the change in motions in the sixth. Very few reasons exist to think that the Piper Link
would affect one of three relatively poor schools but not rich schools,
which experienced a loss of funding and hence much greater change.

In summary, local school governance in Vermont shows every indication of chugging along in almost exactly the same manner as it did before Act 60. The only major difference appears to be that some schools now do so with more money and some with less.

The Details, Part 1: Local Nonbudgetary Control

Act 60's Nonfinancial Components

This is not to say that Act 60 did not do anything in Vermont other than redistribute the tax burden and the funds it generated. It extended the state government's reach into almost every conceivable aspect of public education. Its most notable nonfinancial component was the standardized testing designed to test students' mastery of *Vermont's Framework of Standards and Learning Opportunities*, which contain detailed curricula in English, history and social science, science, math, and technology.[17] The state required that each school's instruction and assessment systems "include the state level assessments, be aligned with the Framework or comparable standards, and be consistent with the Vermont Comprehensive Assessment System" (Vermont Department of Education 1999, 5). Act 60 forced schools to report standardized test scores to their communities, specified maximum class sizes, mandated numerous course offerings and graduation requirements, and contained provisions on early reading failure, professional development, special education, transportation, construction, and countless other areas of educational governance. Combined with its reform of school finance, the new testing made Act 60 the most ambitious and encompassing legislation on public education in Vermont's history. Many schools had to change or abandon numerous programs to comply with the measure.

> Previously, a fierce tradition of local autonomy in Vermont would have allowed developers to go back to their local schools and do whatever they believed is right. Because the Brigham decision declared equity a state responsibility, however, aligning the system to test results has gained ascendancy over local programs designed to meet individual needs. (Clarke 2001, 3)

The nonfinancial parts of Act 60 represent a threat to local autonomy, but Act 60's financial centralization does not appear to have caused that threat. The nonfinancial components of Act 60 are an extension of the policy goals the state had been pursuing throughout the 1990s. The contemporary effort to increase state government's role in shaping curriculum dates back at least seven years before Act 60 was passed. In 1990, Vermont's Department of Education published *A Green Mountain Challenge: Very High Skills for Every Student: No Exceptions, No Excuses.* The report called for the development of state learning standards to which every student would be held accountable. In 1992, the department published the first *Vermont's Core Curriculum,* and by 1996 the department had developed *Vermont's Framework of Standards and Learning Opportunities,* a comprehensive set of learning standards and criteria for evaluating student performance. Act 60 gave the state an opportunity to implement curricular standards it had already designed.[18]

State policymakers' curriculum reform took into account concerns about compromising local control, establishing and following new procedures designed to preserve or strengthen it. Vermont's efforts to design curricular standards began with eleven communities (including PT1) holding independent "focus forums" of parents, teachers, students, and community members to define local learning goals and resource priorities. To aid the design of the 1992 *Vermont's Core Curriculum,* the state used these focus forums as a model and conducted similar gatherings in other towns (Clarke 2001). Former PS2 principal Peter Mello indicated that the state relied on the suggestions generated by these forums in designing its learning standards. To strengthen local control, Act 60 created the "action planning process," which required board members, teachers, administrators, and parents to diagnose areas in their schools that needed improvement and design detailed plans to achieve their goals.[19]

Interview respondents generally had favorable impressions of Act 60's testing/accountability and action plans. These stakeholders valued action planning as a way to stimulate critical and innovative thinking among the entire school community and felt that the state gave them an admirable amount of leeway to use this process as they saw fit. As one RS3 board member said, "Nobody dictated what your action plans had to be. You picked your own soft spots, and I think we did some good things." Interviewees believed that the state learning standards were helpful tools that focused the school on common goals and helped lend cohesion to learning goals across grades. According to Barker, before the Act 60 standards, "we were being asked to put together our own curriculum from the grassroots up—can you imagine?" Interviewees thought that Act 60's testing was used to guide instruction and diagnose areas for improvement rather than to punish schools.[20] They report changing programs in several curricular areas as a result of test scores and being happier with the new programs.

Mello summarized the general sentiment of this study's local elites on Act 60's nonfinancial components:

> The sledgehammer of "every school must subscribe to these other components" drove the agenda and upped the ante a little. It made teachers say, "We'd better fix the test scores. We can't let some of you do science, some of you do math. We *all* have to pay attention to what are we going to do as a school to improve our kids' reading analysis and interpretation skills." We really took a hard look at our curriculum. We took a hard look at our practice. We took a hard look at the time we allotted for reading and math. We added more time for math instruction. For reading for younger students, we added a literacy block in the primary grades. . . . *That* was Act 60, that was its heart. I have a road map now. I have a guide. I can access resources according to this guide based on our needs.

What caused the state government to become more involved in curricular matters during the past twenty years? Subjects suggested that Vermont is following the broader national trend toward greater state and federal government involvement in education policy. They were remarkably sophisticated in identifying several broader features of modern life that have contributed to marginalization of local government authority over such decisions. One former PS3 board member invoked the need to prepare students for a global economy: "You can say, 'Okay, we're not going to do any of this this year. We won't buy any more computers,' but there's a lack of control there. If you're going to educate your kids to go into society, they need to have some of these things." Vermont League of Cities and Towns executive director Steve Jeffrey blamed mass media and political incentive structures for state and federal elected officials. One respondent even cited Robert Putnam's *Bowling Alone* (2000) and its emphasis on the loss of social cohesion. A full explanation of the causes behind the rise of the standards movement is outside the scope of this work, but this evidence strongly suggests that causes other than the centralization of school finance are driving the general trend toward greater state regulation and lessened local autonomy.

Centralization and Public Involvement

Three of the Windsor Central interview subjects worried that Act 60 had driven down support for public education. Former RS2 board member Greg Camp said that support for school spending dropped as Act 60 moved financial decision making away from the town level. He argued that people perceived their increased taxes as going not to children in impoverished areas but to the state government in Montpelier and that they are most willing to spend money on their local schools: "Their kids, of their concern, are living in this town." RT1 town manager Dave Lewis also believed that people are now more likely to challenge school budgets: "Because taxes are going up, they're taking an adversarial role toward education. Because they don't understand the whole Act 60/Act 68 mechanism, they take a much more simplistic view of, 'We've got to cut education because that cuts taxes.'" Windsor Central superintendent Meg Gallagher worried that Act 60 eroded public faith in numerous state institutions, including public schools.

Does the available evidence support the claim that centralization of finance erodes public support for education? No poll has ever measured support for education among Vermont residents, but the 2002 Vermonter Poll, conducted by the Center for Rural Studies at the University of Vermont, found that residents see education as one of their most pressing problems, even after the implementation of Act 60. Vermonters ranked education as the second-most-serious issue facing the state in the coming decade, a figure that does not suggest massive public revolt against public education in the wake of Act 60 (Center for Rural Studies 2002).[21]

Participation in school affairs is a useful if imperfect measure of public support. If support for public education decreases, one might expect to see a corresponding decrease in participation. Because the idea of self-government is such a critical virtue of local control, changes in patterns of participation are an important phenomenon. In none of the four towns did Act 60 affect public participation in educational governance. Figure 4.11 presents information on average attendance at board meetings by people other than board members and administrators.[22] This evidence suggests that people were no more or less likely to come to board meetings after Act 60, even at RS1, RS3, and other schools that suffered financially as a consequence of the law. At RS3, the average audience size jumped from 4.67 people in 1998–99 to 17.45 people in 2000–2001. Average attendance at RS1 board meetings dropped from 2.15 people in

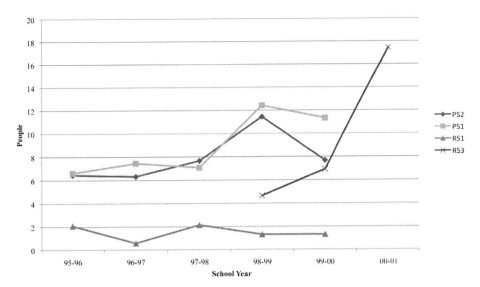

Fig. 4.11. Average attendance (excluding board members and administrators) at school board meetings, 1995–96 through 2000–2001

1997–98 to about 1.3 people for the two years thereafter, but that drop probably has less to do with a decrease in total participation and more to do with an increase in the number of budget meetings designed to respond to Act 60 and possibly the change in the board's recording secretary. At the board meetings from the two poor schools, both of which were winners under the new finance formula, attendance increased— from 7.08 in 1997–98 to 12.42 in 1998–99 at PS1, and from 7.67 in 1997–98 to 11.44 in 1998–99 at PS2. Perhaps the greater resources these schools enjoyed under Act 60 allowed boards to undertake more ambitious projects, which in turn excited more citizen participation in board meetings. More likely, the differences are coincidence, and finance centralization had no effect.

Nor is there much evidence to suggest that citizen voting behavior changed as a consequence of Act 60, especially in the places where the strongest theoretical arguments suggest that such changes would occur. Figure 4.12 shows that turnout out at RT1's annual school meetings for the five years after the law's implementation (an average of 67 people) was comparable to what it was for the three years prior to implementation (an average of 70 people).[23] Figure 4.13 shows that average voter

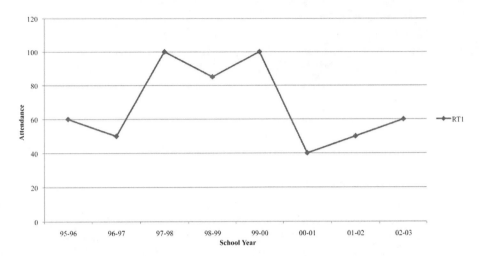

Fig. 4.12.   Attendance at RT1 annual school meeting, 1995–96 through 2002–3

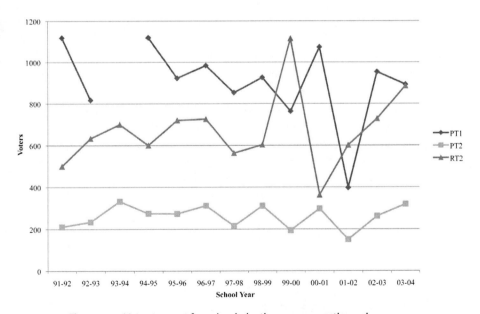

Fig. 4.13.   Voter turnout for school elections, 1991–92 through 2003–4

turnout in RT2 was higher in the six elections after Act 60 (716) than in the seven elections before it (634). In PT2, an average of 264 people voted in the seven elections before implementation, whereas an average of 255.5 people voted in the six elections after implementation. The disparity is more striking in PT1: the averages dropped from 969 between 1991 and 1997 to 834 between 1998 and 2003. A large part of this surprising result came from the 2001 election, when a major snowstorm depressed turnout throughout western Vermont. Without those results skewing the averages, voter turnout in PT2 was higher on average (276.6) after Act 60.[24] In PT1, average turnout after Act 60 jumped to 921.4 (discounting the 2001–2 election), still lower than the pre–Act 60 average of 969. Thus, the best evidence that Act 60 depressed citizen participation in local school affairs is a drop of 38 people in the average voter turnout in a town of almost 4,000 people. Given the bulk of the evidence, however, other factors were probably at work in PT1.

Every interviewee, including the three who worried about diminished public support for local education, stated that citizen participation in school affairs remained unchanged after Act 60. They described volunteerism for parent-teacher organizations and coaching positions as very good and saw no differences in such behavior after Act 60. Participation in school board decision making is a different story. The respondents debunked any potential notion of a Vermont in which a love of small-scale democracy so possesses residents that they constantly, universally, and intensely follow local government affairs. Interview respondents reported attendance at board meetings during normal times to be extremely low, with board members and administrators sometimes outnumbering the audience. When asked what voters wanted from a school board, one former RS1 board member answered, "Number 1, they want to be left alone." Said Mathis,

> I would like to give you a more civic answer than that. I would like to say that people come out every week in order to be edified about the workings of their community. But they don't. The fact of the matter is that school board meetings are, for the most part, incredibly dull. I'm sorry. They are.

Some respondents thought that participation had declined over time, in part because many towns now decided important issues at traditional voting booths rather than at annual town meetings. "People just figure, 'I'm going to get to vote, so why should I go to a meeting?'" said a former

PS3 board member. Citizen involvement is periodic and centers on controversial issues such as cuts to popular extracurricular activities, changes in bus routes, parent access to school facilities, and other logistical matters. One of the most contentious issues leaders at PS2 could remember was when school leaders decided the school would no longer serve the jelly doughnuts a local bakery donated to the students.

Some subjects reported that Act 60 increased citizen participation in some ways. The most obvious example was the private fund-raising foundations that sprung up in RT1 and RT2. According to former Woodstock Education Fund chair Ron Jaynes, these foundations sought to circumvent the Act 60 funding mechanism by soliciting donations from residents of more affluent towns and donating them directly to the local schools. This strategy allowed towns directly to finance their children's education and kept their tax rates down because they did not have to send matching money to the state. The money raised could be quite significant, with private donations to RS1 in the three years after Act 60 totaling more than $1.8 million. Jaynes said he treated his role as a full-time job and estimated that approximately thirty people were part of the group. He said that approximately 66 percent of RT1's property owners contributed in the fund's first year, but participation rates slowly declined over the next two years, leading to the fund's discontinuation after three years. Camp also reported that RS2 established partnerships with local groups and citizens in an attempt to provide services that the school could no longer afford.

It would be a mistake to make too much out of the new forms of participation that Act 60 generated. Even people most intimately connected with schools that benefited from private giving expressed regret at the need for it. A former RS2 board member described the Woodstock Education Fund as a noble and helpful endeavor that nonetheless represented "effort and time for fund-raising that, in an ideal world, could have gone elsewhere." Such foundations also show every sign of being temporary. Act 68 outlawed private foundation giving to public schools. Jaynes also indicated that the Woodstock Fund did not seek to influence any of the boards' affairs or schools' governance. The limits Jaynes describes will certainly disappoint proponents of democratic participation, who want citizens more involved in decision making. Likewise, it is difficult to construct a convincing theoretical argument that school finance reform increased voter turnout in RT2 and PT2 or participation at board meetings at RS3, PS1, and PS2. But the evidence in this section also does not offer much support for the contention that Act 60 depressed citizen support for public education. It simply seems not to have made much of a difference.

Centralization and Municipal Government

Several municipal officials worried that Act 60 had made their jobs more difficult. Town officials in RT1, RT2, and PT2 thought that the state's assumption of control over the property tax had created more work for their offices and decreased the available flexibility and discretion. According to RT1 town manager Dave Lewis, the state now charges municipalities with collecting and sending to the state the level of tax revenue the state says they should raise. Municipalities must send this exact amount, even if it means borrowing money to make up for delinquent taxes. Lewis and others believe that the state seems to take credit for whatever good comes out of education finance reform without doing any of the dirty work.

> The state doesn't have any responsibilities, nor do they have any culpability. . . . Interestingly enough, refunds are sent individually to the taxpayers with nice state letterhead saying, "The State of Vermont is sending you this money." They get the credit. The town, of course, gets the blame for all the taxes.

Since Act 60, the share of total property tax revenue available to noneducation municipal governments has decreased. Jeffrey estimates that their share has decreased from one-third to one-quarter of the total and that towns are under pressure not to request ambitious budgets: "People feel they can't say no to schools, but they can say no to municipal governments." According to PT2 town clerk Donna Pidgeon, accompanying this reduced share is frustration that she must now wait for the state budget estimations for PS1 before setting the town's tax rate. In 2002, the state provided these figures in September. PT2 collects its taxes on November 1, and she and other town employees were forced to work overtime to meet that deadline. Baicker and Gordon (2004) find that this trend characterizes all states that reformed their systems of school finance in the 1980s and 1990s for equity's sake. In such states, school districts, particularly less affluent ones, have received funding increases, but nonschool local government agencies have reduced their level of taxation and thus have less funding available than was the case prior to reform.

Jeffrey, Lewis, and Pidgeon did not think that the types of municipal government actions or their ability to perform their roles had changed since or as a result of Act 60. As they have for years, Vermont town governments still maintain roads and bridges, provide fire and police departments, handle sewer and water services, and so forth. Town officials generally do not believe that Act 60 inhibits local control. Nonetheless, they have clearly pointed to a way in which Act 60 has made their roles more difficult and their resources more scarce and less predictable. As Pidgeon indicates, these difficulties exist in at least one of the towns that benefited from Act 60's financial provisions. Their observations about the unintended consequences of the law suggest that finance centralization affected local control, albeit in a small way.

The Details, Part 2: Act 60 and the Loss of Budgetary Authority

The evidence thus far does not suggest that Act 60's financial centralization harmed local control of public education in Vermont, but residents of more affluent districts argue that Act 60's dramatic funding equalization has robbed their districts of the ability to provide an education that exceeds the state's bare-bones standard. Wealthier communities feel that they are becoming less able to provide the things that once made education in their towns special. Residents voiced these concerns through their views on the threat of school consolidation and the loss of student electives.

Centralization and Consolidation

The increase in taxes that Act 60 has spurred in Windsor Central has some residents considering what was once unthinkable: towns voting to close their schools and send their students to larger regional schools. Relative to larger schools that serve multiple towns, small schools are not cost-efficient and suffer from economy-of-scale pricing disadvantages. Heating bills, building maintenance, and the like are relatively fixed costs regardless of school size, and smaller schools with access to less total (as opposed to per-pupil) funding must use a greater share of their budgets on such items. Higher taxes have made this burden harder to ignore. RS1 officials were particularly concerned with a question a resident asked at the 2004 town meeting about whether "tuitioning" students to other schools would be more cost-effective than continuing to keep RS1 open. When towns pay tuition so that students can attend schools outside town boundaries, local citizens lack the ability to vote in board or budget elections at the receiving schools. Their only method of protesting decisions is to move their students elsewhere. The transportation challenges in such a mountainous, rural state may severely limit or eliminate choices in tuition schools, leaving residents who close their local schools without a voice in the design of their children's education. As RS1 principal Marion Withum points out, "You talk about loss of control—you can't control whether your school is going to close anymore." Gallagher believes that some of Windsor Central's smaller schools inevitably will have to close as a result of Act 60.

Under Act 68, which now governs Vermont's school funding, tax rates for most affluent towns, including RT1 and RT2, have remained much higher than their pre–Act 60 levels. At some point, schools that might have been able to stay open under the old funding formula might decide to close their doors, but this process has not yet begun. John Nelson (2004), the executive director of the Vermont School Board Association, reports that only two towns have closed their schools since Act 60 was passed in 1997. The centralization of finance and resulting higher tax rates in more affluent towns may have been responsible for one closing, in the resort town of Winhall. It is much harder to argue that Act 60 was responsible for the closing in Athens, a poorer town, since the new funding formula was designed to increase the money available to such towns. Thus, the fear that funding centralization will cause school closing has not been realized, and finance centralization appears to have a negligible effect on whether towns can afford to keep their schools open.

Even if Act 60 eventually makes it harder for some schools in more affluent areas to continue operating, it also may make it easier for more schools to stay open and allow all schools to confront rising costs with relatively equal resources. Mathis suggests that Whiting Village School, with a total K–6 enrollment of twenty-three students, has remained open only because of the reduced tax rates and increased spending that Act 60 provided. Vermont's smaller towns have long had to pay a premium to keep local schools open and have done so for a variety of reasons, including the state's relatively low population density, the logistical nightmare of transporting students across a mountainous state with relatively few good roads, and a philosophical commitment to small, local schools. But necessities such as electricity and heating grow ever more costly, and the definition of an education that will allow students to succeed in the modern world expands. Without some unspecified fundamental change, costs will rise, and every Vermont town will have to ask how much having a school in the community is worth. Act 60's financial reform simply means that schools will confront these decisions on relatively equal financial footing.

Centralization and Electives

Interview subjects from Windsor Central maintained that the character of their school changed because the new funding formula made them cut student programs. Camp noted how each Windsor Central school had a set of elective offerings that distinguished it from the other schools in the supervisory union: Pomfret Elementary had a good theater program, Woodstock Elementary was strong in music and language, and so on. Such programs did not directly affect students' ability to meet state learning standards and were among the first items to be scaled back or eliminated when the spending cuts Act 60 forced took effect. Interview subjects from all three affluent schools reported having to cut funding to programs they thought were essential to their children's education. Camp reports that Act 60 forced the board to scale back some of RS2's elective teaching positions from full time to three or four days a week. One RS1 board member portrayed the cuts as far more drastic: "We're pretty much down to state requirements. We're not allowed by the state to have a nurse in here at least one day a week. We're not allowed to offer a foreign language. We're not allowed to offer music and art and these programs."

It would be naive to think that Act 60 has not had a negative effect on some towns and the children who attend school in them. It is not possible to listen to a committed educator such as RS1's Withum discuss Act 60 and not admire her commitment to her students. She has presided over cuts to elective programs she feels are essential for the development of her children. Consolidation, an idea never seriously considered prior to Act 60, is now on the minds of at least some of her town's residents. These developments disturb her greatly: "Everybody wants to help all children in America get the brass ring, but once they get it, it's almost like, 'Now we're going to punish you. Now you don't deserve to be applauded. We're going to get you.'" The students of schools located in more affluent areas such as Windsor Central have lost some part of the liberal arts education ideal, something that the taxpayers who fund their schools provided in the past and would almost certainly still provide had Act 60 not changed everything. Local governments losing the ability to do what they once did is the definition of a loss of local control.

Of course, the rich towns of Vermont represent only one disproportionately small side of the Act 60 story. A total of 79 percent of the state's schools now have greater financial resources. With this increase in funding has come a corresponding increase in what poorer areas can offer their children. The interview subjects from poor schools indicated that Act 60's new funding allowed them to offer services that affluent districts have long taken for granted. Mello said that PS2 was able to start a prekindergarten program with Act 60 funding, and Rutland Northeast director of business and finance Brenda Flemming reports that Whiting Village School, a school from one of the supervisory union's poorest towns, began offering part-time music and art programs. In another part of the state, Goodman (1999) finds that poor schools used their increased funding to move out of cramped, outdated schoolhouses with rotting floors and hire new teachers to relieve overcrowding. However, the affluent Stowe High School was forced to cut a librarian, a nurse, and a custodian. Likewise, the schools of Windsor Central scaled back programs but still maintain a level of service above that offered by schools with similar enrollment numbers in Rutland Northeast. As Barker put it, affluent

> schools said "Oh my God, what are we going to do? We can't have five days of music now. We can't afford it. We have to have four." Look at some of these poor towns that barely have it at all—certainly no instrumental or choral program. It was just really ironic to hear all these wealthy schools complaining and complaining.

These counterarguments are not meant to minimize the cuts Act 60 has caused at rich schools. The cuts are both real and painful, they have compromised the quality of education these schools offer, and they clearly represent a loss of local control. These losses must be weighed against the gains in local control in the vast majority of the state's schools. Even if poorer schools are still providing a level of electives below that of more affluent schools, they are now clearly able to do more of what they want. When it comes to the loss or gain of extras such as electives, Act 60 may have hurt local control in a few districts, but it also may have helped it in far more.

Another Perspective: Michigan's School
Finance Reform in the 1990s

The evidence from Vermont strongly suggests that finance centralization in the 20–90 range does not compromise local autonomy, but is Vermont's school finance reform representative of similar movements in other states? Vermont is exceptional for reasons that go beyond its historic commitment to local control.[25] It is small in both total area and population and lacks large urban centers. Courts in states with more homogeneous populations have been more likely to demand that those states implement more equitable funding schemes, so the size of a state's racial and ethnic minority populations is critical to the shape of school finance debates (Swenson 2000). Vermont's population is 96.8 percent white, which is hardly representative of the entire U.S. population (U.S. Census Bureau 2000). As a mountainous state, the transportation difficulties in moving toward a system of larger, regional school districts might make Vermont's school leaders more reluctant to consolidate than their counterparts in other states. Nevertheless, the dynamics in chapter 3 function across all fifty states, and the entire country does not share the demographic characteristics of the two coasts. Thirty states lack cities of more than half a million people, and eleven states have populations that are at least 90 percent white (U.S. Census Bureau 2000). Nonetheless, an examination of another state's experience with rapid school finance centralization shows that the Vermont experience holds lessons for predicting how the Piper Link will function elsewhere.

Michigan and Proposal A

Michigan is very different from Vermont. With just over ten million people, Michigan is the eighth-largest state. Michigan resembles many other large states, with one major urban center (Detroit, the nation's tenth-largest city) with surrounding suburbs, and the rest of the state made up of rural areas and smaller metropolitan areas (such as Flint and East Lansing). Although Michigan has a relatively small Latino population, African Americans make up 14.8 percent of the population, compared to 13.4 percent of the total U.S. population (U.S. Census Bureau 2000). While local control is part of the rhetoric of public education in Michigan, it does not occupy the same sacrosanct position as in Vermont.

Both Michigan and Vermont dramatically reformed their educational systems in the 1990s. Prior to reform, Michigan was as reliant on local sources of revenue as was Vermont.[26] In the 1990–91 school year, 65.2 percent of the total revenue for Michigan schools came from local sources, a higher percentage than all but two other states (Courant, Gramlich, and Loeb 1995). Most local funds came from property taxes, which had become deeply unpopular within the state. In 1993, Governor John Engler campaigned for a second term on a promise to reduce property taxes by 20 percent; fulfilling that promise required some form of school finance reform. Thus, backers of school finance reform had allies in a popular governor and his supporters who were also very eager to change the system, albeit for different reasons (Courant and Loeb 1997). On July 23, 1993, as the State Senate debated Engler's most recent reform proposal, Democratic senator Debbie Stabenow, a potential challenger to Engler in the 1994 election, proposed the complete elimination of local property taxes as a method of school funding. Most observers believe Stabenow intended the proposal to be symbolic, but within two days, both the Michigan House and the Senate had approved the proposal. Engler signed it into law soon thereafter, meaning the state had eliminated $6.5 billion for the 1994–95 school year (Courant and Loeb 1997).

No one had any intention of allowing schools to go without more than 60 percent of their previous operating budgets. Engler and the legislature presented a plan to the public, and on March 15, 1994, the voters of Michigan passed Proposal A into law by a two-to-one margin. Proposal A instituted a radically new system for raising and distributing school funding that relied on a mix of state sales, income, and property taxes as well as revenue from liquor sales, industrial and commercial fees, and the state lottery. The new system compensated for a $2.9 billion reduction in property tax revenue with increases in other taxes and federal funds. Property tax reformers were satisfied. Total revenues increased by more than fifteen hundred dollars per pupil, so the education establishment had no reason to block the reform (Cullen and Loeb 2004).

Under Proposal A, Michigan made great gains in the equity of its school spending. In the 1993–94 school year, under the old system, thirty-two states had more equitable distributions of per-pupil revenues across all school districts. One year later, under Proposal A, only seventeen states had more equitable distributions, and the distribution of school funds in Michigan has subsequently become more equitable (Arsen and Plank 2003). The state achieved greater equity mainly through bringing up the spending of the 365 of the state's 527 school districts that had spent less than five thousand dollars per pupil in 1993–94 (Courant, Gramlich, and Loeb 1995). Revenues for Detroit's schools increased by 35.2 percent, Flint's by 41.2 percent, and Lansing's by 35.3 percent. Poor rural districts fared even better (Cullen and Loeb 2004). More affluent districts faced restrictions on their ability to raise money outside of the state system and a cap that forced their spending to increase at a set pace below the scheduled increases for less affluent districts, which meant that the spending increases in poor districts brought their per-pupil spending closer to that of rich districts. However, the state guaranteed rich districts funding increases based on their previous levels of spending, thereby en-suring that the state moved closer to but would never achieve perfect eq-uity, and children in wealthier districts would continue to have more spent on their education than children in middle- and low-income dis-tricts (Courant and Loeb 1997; Cullen and Loeb 2004).[27] As chapter 5 shows, such compromises are often necessary to ensure that the affluent do not scuttle finance reform.

The state thus became the dominant actor in school finance. In the 1995–96 school year, state revenue sources accounted for 66.8 percent of total K–12 education spending in the state, and the state government funding share has remained above 60 percent every year since (National Center for Education Statistics 2007). Because the state now controls the local property tax levy, the state's role in determining the level of funding for schools is even greater than its portion of the total spending indicates (Courant, Gramlich, and Loeb 1995). Michigan therefore saw a shift from local to state revenue sources of a magnitude on par with Vermont in a similarly short period of time. If the Piper Link functions in the 20–90 range, Michigan should have shown decreases in some form of local au-tonomy in the time since Proposal A's implementation. If school finance centralization does not affect local autonomy in either state, it is unlikely to have such an effect in most states.

Proposal A and Local Financial Autonomy

While Proposal A's complete restructuring of Michigan's school finance system enjoyed broad support, it did excite concern about several issues, including fears about a loss of local control. "The great advantage" of such measures "is that they equalize spending across districts. The great disadvantage is that they eliminate all local control" (Courant and Loeb 1997, 124). The most obvious concern about a loss of local control under the Proposal A system is that with the increased reliance on state funding and new state regulations on the levels and use of local taxes, the state government had assumed the leading role in school finance, a role local school governments previously occupied. As in Vermont, many Michigan observers worried that finance reform would rob more affluent school districts of the ability to fund the programs that made them unique. Prior to Proposal A, some middle-income communities spent less on education than some less affluent districts (Arsen and Plank 2003). One of the virtues of strong local autonomy is that different localities can provide different bundles of services from which consumers can choose through their choice of where to live, a process referred to as "voting with their feet" (Tiebout 1956; Peterson 1995). Seen through this lens, the residents of these affluent communities chose lower taxes over education spending, while the residents of poorer areas made the opposite choice, but both groups found a bundle of services and expenses that matched their tastes. A system of centralized funding with equalized per-pupil spending threatened to deprive residents of such choices (Courant and Loeb 1997). Writing soon after the implementation of Proposal A, Ronald C. Fisher and Robert W. Wassmer (1995) wondered whether the public would long tolerate the elimination of almost all local choice in setting spending levels.

Under Proposal A, however, the state did not assume control of school construction and other infrastructure improvement. Local districts retain the bulk of that responsibility, which they usually fund through bond issues. More affluent school districts have been more likely to issue bonds after Proposal A's implementation and may be using bond issues as a way to raise funding for items that are not related to capital projects (Zimmer and Jones 2005). The state also permits intermediate school districts, which contain one or more school districts, to levy an additional three mill property tax, further increasing the ways in which a cluster of local districts can raise additional revenue and maintain some fiscal autonomy (Arsen and Plank 2003). It would be foolish to argue that the Proposal A system did not take away some choice in spending levels in more affluent districts, but the state clearly permitted these districts some avenues for raising more money to meet local needs. Another measure that shows that more affluent school districts have not felt their positive autonomy constrained is the lack of sustained popular opposition to the reforms (discussed in chapter 5).

Another concern was that the caps that limit total district spending and taxation would prevent local districts with unique, hard-to-educate populations from raising extra money to address those needs. Rural districts face higher transportation costs than do suburban districts and may need funds above a general state-set per-pupil amount. Many urban Michigan districts face declining enrollment but the same fixed costs for heating, maintenance, and so forth that do not decrease when students leave a district. Under the current system, these districts cannot supplement their state funding, which is based on the number of pupils in a district and thus decreases with declining enrollment, with tax rates above the state rate, leading to concerns that schools faced with these situations would suffer (Arsen and Plank 2003).

The state has shown itself willing to adjust funding to accommodate each district's unique situation. For example, it has allocated extra money to small, rural districts to offset declining enrollments and added travel costs. More fundamentally, even observers who raised this concern argued that the solution for districts with unique needs is usually more state money, not less. The districts that face the greatest concentration of costly-to-address challenges have benefited the most from Michigan's school finance centralization. Under Proposal A, poor rural and urban districts have received more money to confront their unique challenges than they could raise on their own under the old system. Leaders of poor school districts certainly felt that Proposal A afforded them the ability to provide programs they previously could not provide. Speaking during the Proposal A debate, Detroit Board of Education member Penny Bailer said, "We get about $5,300 per child. . . . I want every child in Detroit to have 22 children per classroom. I want every child in Detroit to have performing arts, athletic teams, and physics and chemistry, and higher mathematics and pre-calculus. We can't do that" (*Crain's* 1994, A1). As in Vermont, the vast majority of Michigan districts have seen an increase in per-pupil spending, meaning that most districts in the state can better afford smaller class sizes, more athletic teams, or whatever else their local leaders deem necessary to educate their children in the way they choose.

Proposal A changed the way school districts must secure funding to meet local needs. Today, rather than passing a tax millage as in the past, local districts must persuade state officials that the district's policy priorities deserve funding. The benefit to such a system is that local leaders in most of Michigan's districts now have a much better chance of receiving the funding necessary to meet their specific local problems.

Charter Schools

Like Vermont, Michigan did not enact school finance reform in isolation from other education reforms. All parties involved acknowledge that Governor Engler controlled the state's education reform agenda efforts in the 1990s. Engler is a staunch proponent of school choice and initially spoke of implementing a broad school voucher program. His support was the key factor in driving the enactment of Michigan's Public Act 362 of 1993, commonly called the Public School Academies Act, which made Michigan one of the nation's strongest supporters of charter schools. Table 4.2 describes the number of charter schools in Michigan in each school year, the number of pupils enrolled, and the charter schools' percentage of Michigan's total school and pupil population. Within five years of the Academies Act's implementation, various chartering agencies had opened 174 charter schools, 10 percent of the nation's total (Bettinger 2005).

Scholars debate the extent to which various school choice proposals promote and/or hurt the virtues traditionally associated with democratic local control.[28] It is not necessary to take a position on school choice's impact on local control in the abstract to analyze the Academies Act's effect on local educational control in Michigan, simply because charter schools have not reached a critical mass sufficient to demonstrate any hypotheti-

TABLE 4.2. Number of Michigan Charter Schools and Charter School Students, 1994–95 to 2003–4

School Year	Number of Charter Schools	Percentage of Total Schools in State	Number of Pupils in Charter Schools	Percentage of Total Pupils in State
1994–95	14	2.2	1,151	0.1
1995–96	44	6.7	5,546	0.3
1996–97	78	11.3	12,685	0.8
1997–98	108	15.0	20,651	1.2
1998–99	137	18.4	32,801	1.9
1999–2000	174	21.9	49,673	2.9
2000–2001	184	23.1	56,651	3.3
2001–2	189	23.6	64,510	3.7
2002–3	189	23.7	67,276	3.8
2003–4	199	24.6	72,152	4.1

Source: Addonizio 2005; Michigan Department of Education 2009.

cal effect on Michigan's educational system.[29] Table 4.2 shows that by the 2003–4 school year, Michigan's 199 charter schools made up an impressive 24.6 percent of the total schools but served only 4.1 percent of the state's students. Even charter school supporters concede that such a limited student population makes it hard for competition dynamics to spark the innovation, widespread excellence, and other changes that school choice promises. Some scholars suggest that part of the reason charter schools have not expanded more rapidly is Michigan's loyalty to neighborhood schools, interscholastic athletics, and other manifestations of traditional local control (Plank and Sykes 1999).

Despite these caveats, charter school legislation represents a level of state involvement in maybe the most basic decision that government can make: what a public school can look like. While the effect of such legislation on local control is unclear, it represents an expansion of state regulation of education much in the same way as the accountability system Vermont passed as part of Act 60, leading to the question of whether Proposal A's finance centralization caused the passage of the Academies Act. Without extensive qualitative fieldwork, it is not possible to rule out the possibility that finance centralization helped to cause Michigan's embrace of charter legislation, but that possibility seems very remote. If anything, causation seems to run in the opposite direction, with some evidence suggesting that the charter school movement might have played a slight role in pushing forward Michigan's finance reform.[30] Engler's advocacy of school choice formed the center of his early education platform, and he came to see switching to a state-dominated funding system as a way to move toward a system where schools were funded on a per-pupil basis rather than based on available local revenue. When the state knew how much it was spending on a child's education, it also had the ability to move that amount of funding from a traditional school to a charter (Arsen, Plank, and Sykes 1999). No other state has paired finance reform with major school choice measures. Engler built a political coalition that united the two movements, but, as the Vermont example shows, other coalitions are certainly possible. No reason exists to think that finance centralization should force state governments to adopt school choice.

Consolidation

Early discussions of possible effects of Proposal A contained a striking number of references to consolidation, which echoed the fears of some

Vermont respondents that the loss of funding affluent districts may endure in equity-minded finance reform schemes would bring them one step closer to closing their schools or districts. Several supporters of school finance reform in the early 1990s spoke favorably of consolidation. In speaking about ways that the state might undertake finance reform and still provide adequate funding for all districts, Bailer spoke words that might chill the heart of advocates for small rural districts and schools: "An issue that was not addressed as I had hoped was consolidation of school districts. The fact that we have over 500 [districts, each] with a superintendent, school board and administrative structure seems ludicrous" (*Crain's* 1994, A1). Analysts offered consolidation as a strategy for offsetting lost revenue. "Despite the tradition of local control in Michigan's public school system, there is growing recognition that cooperative ventures involving multiple schools and school districts can enhance efficiency and service quality. It no longer makes sense for all Michigan school districts to provide a full array of services . . . 'in house.' One possibility is consolidation, in which two or more local school districts agree to merge into a single, larger district" (Arsen and Plank 2003, 2). Who knows how many Michigan residents encountered such sentiments and concluded that Proposal A was the work of some evil liberal coalition of inner-city minorities and snooty academics who cared nothing for the survival of the state's smaller schools and school districts?

The fears about Proposal A's effect on consolidation have not come to pass. Table 4.3 shows the number of local education agencies (Michigan's term for school districts) and public elementary and secondary schools from the 1989–90 to 1999–2000 and 2004–5 school years, with the 1994–95 school year highlighted as the first school year the funding scheme was implemented. During the first six school years of the new scheme, the number of school districts remained the same; ten years later, Michigan had only three fewer districts. Given the other factors that are pushing small school districts to consolidate, it is safe to assume that school finance centralization had an extremely small or no effect on the number of school districts. After Proposal A's passage, the number of schools increased dramatically, which is contrary to the expectations of the Piper Link in a situation of rapid finance centralization. The increases in the number of charter and total public schools are correlated at the .9999 level, meaning that they tracked together almost perfectly and strongly suggesting that the growth in the number of schools resulted almost entirely from the increase in the number of charters and not because of any stimulation finance reform caused. For the first ten years of the Proposal A era, the number of traditional public elementary and secondary schools remained constant, and finance centralization almost certainly placed no pressure on smaller school districts or schools to consolidate.

Instead, the new funding scheme may have helped some smaller districts to stay open, as the case of the Kalkaska School District shows. Kalkaska was a small, rural, low-spending district that had to close its doors as a consequence of lack of funding. But Kalkaska closed during the 1992–93 school year, under the old Michigan funding system, with its high reliance on local revenues, because the district's voters would not approve a property tax millage sufficient to provide what the school board and educators thought to be a minimally adequate education. The Kalkaska case received national attention and increased Michigan lawmakers' sense of urgency regarding reform of the state's school finance system (Courant and Loeb 1997). Thus, as lawmakers designed the Proposal A system, they were certainly conscious of the challenges of keeping small, rural districts alive. Rural districts benefited most from the new system, and more money gave rural districts a better chance of staying independent (Cullen and Loeb 2004). As in Vermont, centralization of finance had no negative effect on a school or district's ability to stay open and may have helped less affluent districts continue operating.[31]

TABLE 4.3. Number of Local Education Agencies, Public Schools, and Charter Schools, 1989–90 to 1999–2000 and 2004–5

School Year	Local Education Agencies	Public Elementary and Secondary Schools	Number of Charter Schools
1989–90	562	619	0
1990–91	561	618	0
1991–92	559	616	0
1992–93	557	616	0
1993–94	557	615	1
1994–95	555	628	14
1995–96	555	656	44
1996–97	555	690	78
1997–98	555	720	108
1998–99	555	750	137
1999–2000	555	783	174
2004–5	552	825	216

Source: Michigan Department of Education 2009.

Conclusion and Discussion

Chapters 3 and 4 present evidence from statistical modeling of data from all fifty states and more in-depth qualitative evidence from two states. Almost all of this evidence suggests that the linear version of the Piper Link does not function as hypothesized, that finance centralization in the 20–90 range need not lead to an increase in state regulation of education or a decrease in local school and school board autonomy. In Vermont, interviews with local school officials and an analysis of their meetings show that boards make about the same number and types of decisions now as they did before finance centralization. Finance centralization did not depress citizen participation in school board affairs or school elections. In neither Vermont nor Michigan has any measurable consolidation of small schools and school districts occurred, and the availability of greater resources may have helped poorer areas keep small schools open. Two pieces of evidence provided limited support for the Piper Link. First, noneducational municipal governments saw their resources squeezed and new state-imposed chores added to their plates. Second, affluent schools in Vermont have had to curtail the electives offered; however, most schools offer more electives as a consequence of the increased funds provided.

In both Michigan and Vermont, other education reforms accompanied school finance reform, but these other reforms were enacted as a consequence of political choices rather than of any inevitable process by which state money demanded state control. Act 60 increased Vermont state government involvement in nonfinancial aspects of educational governance, but this increase is a deliberate continuation of trends in state policy that predate Act 60 and should not be blamed on finance centralization. At the same time Michigan centralized school finance, it adopted an ambitious charter school law, but the charter school legislation is more likely to have had some causal influence on the passage of finance reform than vice versa. In terms of negative autonomy, these findings confirm chapter 3's conclusion that finance centralization need not lead state legislatures to enact more regulations on public education that inhibit local school officials' actions. States certainly can choose to enact curricular standards, school choice legislation, and other regulations simultaneously with finance reform, but state officials also have the option not to do so. Blaming school finance reform for the rise of regulations ignores this choice, as well as the fact that regulation of numerous other parts of educational governance has proceeded in most states regardless of the level of funding the state government provides. In many cases, state regulation has grown much more quickly and completely than attempts to centralize finance.

In terms of positive autonomy, the Vermont results show that school boards appear to retain the same authority over the same types of issues and enjoy (or endure) the same level of citizen participation before and after centralization. These findings should encourage those who might support equity-minded school finance reform but worry that it will undermine local autonomy and the ideal of small-scale, participatory government. The evidence suggests that local officials in all school districts make the same number and kinds of decisions both before and after finance reform. The sole difference is that after finance reform, some make these decisions with more money, and some do so with less. States can pursue interdistrict equity while leaving local governments with the ability to make meaningful decisions, thereby allowing local government to provide the benefits democratic theorists attribute to it. That the reality of local school governance does not fulfill these dreams results from forces other than the level of government that funds education, as later chapters describe.

The only substantial threat financial centralization poses to local autonomy is when it is done in such a way that more affluent school districts see spending on their children decline and thus erode their ability to continue to provide numerous electives. Isaiah Berlin defines positive liberty as "the wish on the part of the individual to be his own master. I wish my life and decisions to depend on myself, not on external forces of whatever kind" (1969, 133). External forces are preventing the residents of RT1 and RT2 from making their own decisions, as they had in the past. Residents of wealthy districts in any state that undertakes such extensive finance centralization can expect to have their positive local autonomy compromised in similar ways, yet even this loss may disguise wider gains in positive autonomy. Provided that finance reform comes without conditions that dictate what local actors must do in nonfinancial matters, it appears to increase the positive autonomy of school districts whose total resources increase. It is critical that 80 percent of Vermont's schools benefited financially from Act 60, expanding their ability to undertake new policies. Michigan's strategy narrowed the gap in spending but preserved the relative advantage of and ensured continued spending increases for more affluent districts, a system that may have saved local leaders from making painful cuts. By acting as these two states did and ensuring that a majority of districts benefit, state governments can undertake school finance reform and increase aggregate local control.

The advantage of reforming a finance system as Vermont and Michigan did is that either strategy may win public support from many middle-income districts that history has shown tend to oppose finance reform movements. In their examination of New Jersey's finance reform movement of the early 1990s, two high-ranking members of Governor Jim Florio's education reform team claim that funding reform's ultimate failure stemmed from the state supreme court's ruling that reform focus exclusively on poor districts, which denied the legislature and the governor the tools they needed to get public approval and ensured middle-class opposition. The study concludes that for a reform package to garner the political support necessary for implementation, the middle class must be able to see benefits (Scovronick and Corcoran 1998). The trick is to achieve the right balance between including enough districts as recipients to increase aggregate local control and public support and still generate enough revenue to help the poorest districts narrow the spending gap. No one should pretend that such a balancing act is easy, but the examples of the two states considered here suggest that it can be done.

The increases in positive autonomy enjoyed by most of Vermont's schools show that the relationship between state action and local control need not be zero-sum. If state action is designed in a way that it helps local actors diagnose problems and gives them the time, resources, and independence to fix those problems, local actors can do their jobs better. Most respondents felt that when Vermont's system of standards and testing finally gave schools realistic learning targets, local officials took meaningful steps that helped ensure that their children learned, in part because the state provided a structure in the action planning process. In Michigan, poorer districts maintained that more state funding would allow them more vigorously to attack their problems. In short, two states that undertook school finance centralization still found ways to strengthen local educational governance.

CHAPTER FIVE

Taxes and Tocqueville

*Local Control and Public Opinion in
School Finance Reform*

❊ ❊ ❊

BOTH THE AGGREGATE STATISTICAL ANALYSIS from all fifty states and the case studies of Vermont and Michigan show that for the 20–90 range of possible state shares of total school funding, local autonomy is not compromised in any measurable way. Why, then, has the Piper Link been such an issue in so many school finance reform movements? The answer may lie in the dynamics of public opinion. Reform movements almost always generate tremendous opposition, which Douglas S. Reed (2001) attributes to the public's support for local control. He analyzes public opinion data from five states where courts have been active in school finance debates and finds that nothing erodes popular support for school finance reform more than people's fear that they may lose control over their school districts. Support for local control has a larger and more consistent effect than even those factors that public opinion scholars find influence attitudes about social welfare policies in general, such as ideology, partisanship, class, and age.

An explanation for opposition to finance reform based on local control makes a certain amount of sense. While the Piper Link seems not to function in the 20–90 range, "He who pays the piper calls the tune" sounds like it should be true, and it is understandable that people would assume that a state government taking more control of revenue will increase its leverage to force local schools and school districts to do its bidding. This result might trouble a broad segment of the public, which generally claims to support local control. Table 5.1 shows that across multiple polls, a majority of the public thinks local school boards and teachers should have more influence over American public education than state and federal governments have. While localism has a distinctly strong place in American public education, it is also popular more generally. Polls show that people believe that local government is more trustworthy, gets the most out of the money it receives, and performs the best across numerous policy areas, including education (Conlan 1993; *Government Finance Review* 1999; Cole, Kincaid, and Parkin 2002).[1]

As plausible as this logic sounds, the true nature of public attitudes regarding local control is somewhat more complicated. Public opinion scholars are suspicious of claims that intergovernmental relations play a strong role in the formation of policy evaluations. People's attitudes on intergovernmental relations are neither strongly held nor sharply crystallized, and people often abandon their commitment to decentralization when centralized levels can better achieve desired policy outcomes (Thompson and Elling 1999; S. K. Schneider and Jacoby 2003). Certain factors fundamental to people's identity, such as race and ethnicity, ideology, and income, consistently have the greatest effects on evaluations of most policies. The general trend holds for attitudes about public education policies, where "respondents' views about which level of government should take the lead depend upon the aspect of 'public education' about which they are asked" (Cantril and Cantril 1999, 39). The public supports many state and federal regulations that make local leaders' lives difficult. In polls conducted annually from 2002 to 2007, between 55 and

TABLE 5.1. Reported Levels of Support for Which Level of Government Should Have the Greatest Influence over Public Schools

Poll and Year	Support for Each Level		
	Federal	State	Local
ABC 1990	20	29	50
NBC 1997	13	25	58
PDK/Gallup 2003	15	22	61
PDK/Gallup 2006	14	26	58
PDK/Gallup 2007	20	31	49

66 percent of respondents indicated that they believed that standardized testing should be continued at its current level or increased (Phi Delta Kappan and the Gallup Organization 2007).[2] No Child Left Behind (NCLB) greatly expanded the federal role in education and is reviled by Vermont's educational elites for its intrusion on local autonomy.[3] The public, however, generally approves of both NCLB's provisions and proposals to increase federal involvement even further. In a 2002 poll, 57 percent of the public believed that the greater federal role NCLB assumes is a good thing, and 68 percent favored requiring all states to use a national standardized test for the program's accountability provisions (Phi Delta Kappan and the Gallup Organization 2002). Why should attitudes on federalism trump such factors when people evaluate the particular issue of school finance reform?

Democracy or Separation: How and Why Localism Might Affect Policy Preferences

In trying to explore the relationship between local control and people's evaluations of school finance reform, part of the problem stems from the failure to specify exactly what "local control" means. The public's love for local control usually is simply asserted without much data or explanation to substantiate the claim (Wirt and Kirst 1997). As this book shows, local control is a multifaceted concept that different people may value for different reasons. One person might value local control of curriculum, while another may want to keep tax generation and collection local. When we say that both value "local control," we obscure meaningful differences between the two that may have critical relevance for policy evaluations. No scholar has empirically tested how variance in the aspect of local control respondents most support affects their evaluation of school finance reform. Beginning that analysis requires first identifying the features of local control to which people may be attracted.

Tocqueville and the Virtues of Small-Scale Democracy

The American political imagination has always held local government to be an essential part of democracy. Admirers have argued that local government allows individuals to manage their own affairs and participate in government, better responds to local circumstances and allows each area to craft policy suited to its unique needs, and increases public trust in government. As chapter 1 describes in greater detail, whether railing against "a bureaucratic elite in Washington" or praising local government as "the people's government . . . and more responsive to the individual person," elected officials often appeal to the unique democratic values local control can provide (Danielson 1976, 214). Even as he campaigned for the passage of NCLB, George W. Bush declared that he "believed strongly in the local control of schools. I trust local folks to chart the path to excellence" (Kincaid 2001, 33).

Many observers believe that the public's support for local control of schools stems from a desire to preserve these virtues and keep as much education governance as possible in the hands of everyday citizens. In explaining opposition to Maine's late-1990s school finance reform proposal, Governor John Rettie McKernan Jr. said, "We're the land of the town meeting and direct democracy. People in Brunswick don't want people in Topsham telling them how to run their schools" (Ferdinand 1998, A3). If this hypothesis is correct, people value keeping education politics local because doing so gives them a chance to be actively involved in the governance of their local schools and in many cases their children's education. Especially in an era of high-profile debates on the teaching of such subjects as evolution and sex education, parents might value local control as a way to ensure that the curriculum their children learn reflects their values.

Localism and Suburban Separation

Others argue that people embrace localism because it allows the more affluent to avoid paying for services designed to help the poor. American residential life is segregated by race and class. When policy decisions are made at the local level, more affluent citizens can use municipal boundaries to avoid paying for services for the less affluent, thus keeping taxes relatively low yet receiving a high level of services. The relationship between class and race means that whites often enjoy a high level of service without paying the taxes necessary to provide that same level of service for racial and ethnic minorities. Some observers argue that the affluent recognize this dynamic, and assert that the power of local control in finance debates stems from an opposition to redistributive spending: "To suburban dwellers, the appeal of returning federal power to states and localities is that it allows communities with relatively healthy tax bases and relatively few needy residents to keep taxes low and services high"

(Gainsborough 2001, 120). Localism thus becomes less about high-minded democratic ideals and more about exclusion and power. Scholars have shown that affluent whites' desire to remain separate from the poor and nonwhites affects evaluations of a host of educational policies designed to aid poor and minority children, including school choice and tracking (Wrinkle, Stewart, and Polinard 1999; Welner 2001; M. Schneider and Buckley 2002; Weiher and Tedin 2002).

Testing Localism: Regression Analysis

Polls

The best way to analyze the causes of opinion formation is through statistical analysis of polling data. The National Network of State Polls database[4] contains data sets from polls conducted in Alabama, Illinois, New Jersey, Tennessee, and Texas that asked questions about people's attitudes on both school finance reform and local control of education.[5] These five states are in different regions of the country and have very different political cultures. The polls analyze each state at different points in the school finance reform process. At the time the respective polls were conducted, the Illinois state government was not considering school finance reform; the issue's importance was rising in Texas and Tennessee; and Alabama and New Jersey were engaged in full-fledged policy wars. If commonalities exist between the views of citizens in these five situations, one can be reasonably confident that the findings apply to most other finance reform situations.

Methods and Dependent Variables

The dependent variable in each regression is support for equity-minded school finance reform. In the data sets from Texas, Tennessee, and Illinois, where the dependent variable is a simple "agree/disagree" variable, I estimated bivariate probit models. In the data sets from Alabama and New Jersey, in which the dependent variable was scaled as a four-category "strongly agree/mildly agree/mildly disagree/strongly disagree" variable, I estimated ordered probit models. These statistical tests show the independent effects of all of the variables on attitudes about school finance reform. In other words, these tests allow one to measure the effect of support for local control on a person's evaluations of school finance independent of other factors.

Controls

Commitment to local control is not the only thing that may drive people's resistance to school finance reform. Scholars of public attitudes may expect self-interest and symbolic politics to have a much larger effect on evaluation of finance reform than either of the local control hypotheses. Included in the models presented here are variables measuring factors that political science scholars have found shape people's general policy preferences. Studies have linked symbolic attitudes such as partisan identification, ideology, and racial prejudice to a host of relevant policies, including school funding (Swenson 2000; Wood and Theobald 2003), school desegregation (Sears et al. 1980; Citrin and Green 1990), and social welfare spending (Gilens 1999; Feldman and Huddy 2005). Because education and the welfare of children have always been considered "women's issues," women may be more likely than men to support school funding increases (Kahn 1994). Several factors related to calculation of self-interest may also affect people's attitudes on finance reform. Bowler and Donovan (1995) have found that people's resistance to state and local taxes varies with their income and property ownership.[6] Parents with school-age children are more likely to become active in anti-school-desegregation movements, which bear important similarities to school finance reform movements (Green and Cowden 1992). Older residents are more likely to favor reductions in school spending, especially when older whites perceive that their higher taxes will benefit minority children (Poterba 1997). Residents of poorer communities might favor finance reform because their districts would benefit.[7]

Measures of Local Control

Four of the data sets include variables suitable for measuring the hypothesis that people's evaluations of the democratic virtues of local education governance affect their evaluation of school finance reform. The second New Jersey poll asked respondents to rate the performance of their local districts. The Tennessee poll focused on trust, asking respondents how big a problem they thought corruption in local government was. The Alabama poll asked whether respondents supported the establishment of school-based management councils, a group of parents, teachers, and administrators at each school that assumes some of the powers traditionally exercised by state government. In Texas, surveyors asked whether respondents favored having the state set standards for local school construction. The four variables used to test this hypothesis tap into the public's trust in local government, desire to increase the opportunities for participation, and desire to strengthen local government against interference from the state. If the democratic virtues hypothesis is true, high levels of support for the local option in these questions should have a consistently depressing effect on people's support for finance reform. Such a result would suggest that local control affects people's views on finance reform because people value the flexibility, trustworthiness, and opportunities for participation local educational governance provides and fear that finance reform will endanger some or all of those features.

All six data sets contain measures adequate for testing the hypothesis that people's desire to separate their financial resources from the problems of less affluent districts affects views of school finance reform. The key unifying aspect of these variables is that they focus on the financial independence of local school boards. Most of these variables gauge how people feel about efforts to switch financial decision making from local school boards to state government. This strategy increases the potential for redistribution, thus reducing suburban districts' ability to separate their resources from the problems of urban schools. The Alabama poll asked whether respondents would increase state taxes to ensure school funding equity. Both the Tennessee and Illinois polls asked whether people supported shifting the funding of education by increasing state taxes and decreasing local taxes. The Texas poll measured whether people believed that the state should provide money for local school construction.[8] The first New Jersey poll measured whether respondents believed their districts would gain or lose state aid under finance reform, while the second New Jersey poll asked people to rate how their local school districts handled their funds. If this exclusion hypothesis is true, high levels of support for the local option in these variables should have a consistently depressing effect on people's support for finance reform. Such a result would suggest that local control affects people's views on finance reform because it allows them to keep their financial resources local.

Concerns about Regression Analysis

The complexity of the two hypotheses and the limitations of state polls make it difficult to find good measures of the hypotheses. The democratic virtues of localism include increased accountability, increased potential for participation, and greater policy intervention. The urge to keep financial resources may stem from a mixture of a host of different factors, including race and class and a belief in limited government. It would be difficult to construct a single question that captures all aspects of such hypotheses, let alone to find such a question in an existing survey. To compound the problem, poll questions vary from state to state, meaning that the local control variables measure slightly different phenomena depending on the poll.

That said, just because a question cannot be analyzed using ideal data does not make the question or its analysis any less important, and the data provide valuable information about how the public thinks about the Piper Link. Taken as a whole, the measures capture many of the different aspects and implications of the two local control hypotheses. The measures of the democratic virtues hypothesis describe people's feelings on a range of local government virtues, from the ability to inspire greater citizen trust in government performance (the second New Jersey and Tennessee polls) to the promotion of citizen participation (Alabama) to their freedom from state regulations and bureaucratic red tape (Texas). The measures of support for local financial control capture people's feelings regarding the financial performance of school boards and numerous strategies governments can employ to keep local districts financially independent. Although each of these measures captures a slightly different aspect of the two hypotheses, the direction of their effect is consistent across models. The consistency of the measures' effects should help alleviate concerns about their validity and provide confidence that the measures are united by the causal mechanisms the two hypotheses describe. Some readers may wonder whether it is possible to separate the two local control hypotheses as neatly as this study does. As table 5.2 shows, with one exception, the measures testing the two hypotheses on the surveys are not highly correlated, and removing one of the local control measures from each of the statistical model does not greatly change the other's ef-

TABLE 5.2. Correlations between Measures of Hypotheses 2a and 2b

Poll	Correlation between Measures
NNSP-AL-022	0.04
NNSP-NJ-093	0.56
NNSP-TN-004	0.03
NNSP-TX-013	0.04

fect size or statistical significance, suggesting that the variables test two distinct concepts.

An additional concern is that the measures of fit for the individual regressions are quite small. This finding is unfortunate but remains consistent with other studies of federalism and public opinion, almost all of which share a similar problem but have been accepted for their valuable insights into how the public thinks about federalism (Roeder 1994; Thompson and Elling 1999; Hetherington and Nugent 2001; S. K. Schneider and Jacoby 2003). The general consistency of the effects of the measures of the two hypotheses across the different regressions should allay most concerns about the model's fit and lend confidence to the interpretation offered here.

Supplemental Analysis

Despite these assurances, methodological concerns may continue to trouble some readers, so this chapter also presents results of an analysis of coverage from the *Birmingham News* and the *Houston Chronicle* of the finance reform movements in Alabama and Texas. The *Chronicle's* online search engine returned thirteen articles with the terms *local* and *school finance* or *school funding* from three years before to five years after the Texas poll was conducted. Using the same search terms and time frame, Lexis/Nexis returned twenty-four articles from the *News*. All articles were searched for instances in which either the reporter or an official quoted in the story attributed opposition to reform to reasons consistent with either local control hypothesis. A total of nine *Chronicle* and fifteen *News* articles contained language consistent with one of the two hypotheses. This examination is not a comprehensive content analysis. The results are included to provide additional evidence that the dynamics the statistical models demonstrate were present in the debates.

Results from Individual States

Alabama

On January 19, 1991, a group of parents filed the *Harper v. Hunt* lawsuit against the state of Alabama charging that its school funding system, with its high reliance on local taxes, did not allow less affluent districts to provide a quality education and therefore violated the state constitution.[9]

TABLE 5.3. Ordered Probit Estimates of Attitudes on School Finance Reform in Alabama, 1994

Independent Variables	Coefficient (S.E.)	Change in Variable from This to This	. . . Changes Probability That R Supported Reform by This Much[a]
Local Control Variables			
Support for school-based management councils	.2313 (.2522)	From "favor" to "oppose" (1,2)	−2.9%
Support for ensuring equity with centralized state taxes	.1603 (.1063)*	From "favor" to "oppose" (1,2)	−1.9%
Controls			
Education	.0340 (.0727)		
Age	.0635 (.0481)		
Rural resident?	.2525 (.1397)*	From "nonrural" to "rural" (0,1)	−3.2%
Income	−.0840 (.0408)**	From "less than 10K" to "more than 90k" (1,8)	+3.6%
School-age children	.0901 (.1423)		
Gender	−.1574 (.1359)		
Ideology	.0608 (.0692)		
Party	.0413 (.0975)		
Race	−.4446 (.1948)**	From "white" to "nonwhite" (0,1)	+3.0%
Model Summary Statistics			
Cut 1	−.3624 (.6458)		
Cut 2	1.9075 (.6532)		
Cut 3	2.5486 (.6643)		
N	338		
Log likelihood	−269.9095		
Pseudo R^2	0.0408		

Source: National Network of State Polls NSSP-AL-022, 1994.

Note: The dependent variable is a four category variable where 1 = strongly agree, 2 = mildly agree, 3 = mildly disagree, 4 = strongly disagree. Support for dependent variable (should state remedy inequities in school finance?) = 89.8 percent.

[a]Calculated by estimating how indicated value change in the independent variable would increase the likelihood of a person either strongly agreeing or mildly agreeing with the reform proposal.

*$z < .10$ **$z < .05$ ***$z < .01$

In 1993, Montgomery Circuit judge Gene Reese ruled the existing funding system unconstitutional and mandated that any new system fund different school districts more equally. Critics dubbed the response that Governor Fob James and the Alabama Legislature crafted "Fobin Hood," because it achieved greater equity by redistributing existing funds from relatively affluent districts to poorer districts.

Table 5.3 presents estimates of an ordered probit model of the 1994 Capstone Poll Omnibus Spring Survey, conducted by the University of Alabama as the state government debated its response to the *Harper* decision. The data set includes all of the independent variables described earlier except a measure of property ownership. Four variables are statistically significant predictors of Alabama residents' opinions on school finance reform. One is the measure of support for local financial control, which had a small but statistically significant effect on Alabamans' evaluation of school finance reform. People who approved of raising state income taxes to ensure equity were 1.9 percent more likely to support reform than those who opposed such a plan. The results are more mixed for the measure of support for the democratic virtues of local control. Moving from a position of support to opposition of school-based management councils results in 2.9 percent reduction in the chance that someone will support reform, but the effect is not statistically significant, severely compromising any confidence in it. The findings from Alabama support the hypothesis that localism played a factor in shaping Alabamans' opinions on school finance reform, but only through support for local financial control.

The coverage Alabama's school finance reform movement received from the *Birmingham News,* the state's largest paper, suggests that the statistical results accurately depict the roles of both types of localism in shaping public opinion. Factors associated with the democratic virtues of local government appear to have helped rally opposition early in the reform process. Some conservative groups feared that the curricular reforms the state hoped to pass as part of the finance reform package would force local school districts to teach values at odds with their beliefs. "There is one consistent school of thought in Alabama that assumes what you're going to do is devise objectives to ultimately measure students not against academic performance but against certain values like tolerance for homosexuals or rejection of God," said Auburn University history professor Wayne Flynt (Dean 1993, A1). The *Harper* plaintiffs did not allay such fears during the trial when they explicitly challenged local curriculum control and urged the court to use national standards to rate the system's ability to educate its students. After Governor James's response to *Harper* became public, however, concerns about local control of curriculum disappeared from the *News*'s coverage, suggesting that arguments consistent with this hypothesis did not resonate outside of a narrow segment of the population. Only four of the fifteen news articles included language that could be interpreted as invoking concerns about nonfinancial control.

By contrast, eleven of the fifteen articles described citizens opposing finance reform as a consequence of concerns about the challenge to local funding's supremacy. Under most proposed funding schemes, more affluent districts faced the possibility of funding millions of dollars below their previous levels while paying higher taxes (Dean 1995). Such concerns prompted residents of these districts to offer a vigorous defense of the virtues of local funding. "They want to take away my voluntary tax dollars to fund other schools. It's like welfare," said parent Pam Merrell (Dean 1995, A1). School board members from such districts worried that voters would not support the schools as generously as had previously been the case. "If and when we need another property tax increase, how would the voters vote knowing that the money might be taken and used somewhere else?" asked one board president (Pierce 1995, A1).

Another significant variable in the model table 5.3 describes is race. Nonwhites were 3.0 percent more likely than whites to support state attempts to remedy imbalanced funding. Rural residents were 3.2 percent less likely to support reform. These results may be linked. Plaintiffs explicitly linked their suit to Alabama's segregationist past, arguing that funding for public schools remained so low because the state maintained a system of all-white private schools designed to thwart integration during the 1950s and 1960s. Blacks would likely support reform presented in such terms, and the hostility of rural whites, who some observers have argued are among the most vehement opponents of racially targeted redistributive programs, could drive the effect of rural residency (Woodward 1966). The income variable is also significant. People making more than ninety thousand dollars a year were 3.6 percent more likely to support finance reform than those making less than ten thousand dollars a year. This effect shows that self-interest alone is a poor explanation for a person's evaluation of school finance. Perhaps the rich supported reform more because they were in a unique position to understand how Alabama's system of school funding left many of its students without the education needed to lead productive lives.

Texas

Texas has been the home to one of the longest-running school finance reform movements in the nation. In *Rodriguez v. San Antonio Independent School District*, the U.S. Supreme Court washed its hands of school finance reform and declared education funding a state issue.[10] In the late 1980s, thirteen poor Texas school districts filed *Edgewood v. Kirby*, and the state's supreme court unanimously found in favor of the plaintiffs in 1990.[11] Over the next three years, the same court rejected two different state plans designed to comply with the design, engendering widespread hostility. The court finally approved a third plan in 1994, but concerns about school finance have continued to dog the state. In 2005, more affluent districts won a decision in opposition to the *Edgewood* remedies that leaves the method of school funding in Texas in flux yet again. Some Texans blame *Edgewood* for its detrimental effects on local control, claiming that it limits local school boards' ability to raise funds and has forced consolidation of school districts (Pagel 1995).

Table 5.4 presents estimates from a bivariate probit model of the fall 1988 Texas Poll conducted by the University of Texas at Austin as the *Edgewood* suit was gaining greater notoriety. All independent variables described earlier except for measures of property ownership and whether a respondent had children are present. Three variables have a significant effect on support for equity between districts. The measure of local financial control—whether the state should provide money for local school construction—is once again significant. Those who approve of such measures are 2.7 percent more likely to support reform than those who oppose them. The measure of the democratic virtues of local control—whether people believe that the state should set standards for local school construction—does not influence opinions on reform at a statistically significant level. The contrast between the effects of these two variables is striking. The two questions have almost exactly the same wording, although one asks if the state should "set standards" while the other asks if the state should "provide funds." The former asks respondents to consider whether they would sacrifice control over an issue and does not have an effect on support for reform. The latter asks whether respondents would sacrifice their districts' financial independence and has a significant effect. Feelings about local control matter in the politics of school finance reform in Texas, but they matter strictly in a financial sense.

All nine of the articles from the search of the *Houston Chronicle*'s archives contained language describing opposition based on a loss of local financial control. Articles generally identified how much reform

TABLE 5.4. Probit Estimates of Attitudes on School Finance Reform in Texas, 1988

Independent Variables	Coefficient (S.E.)	Change in Variable from This to This	. . . Changes Probability That R Supported Reform by This Much
Local Control Variables			
Should state set standards for local school construction?	.0267 (.0907)		
Should state provide money for local school construction?	.0729 (.0368)**	from "yes" to "no" (1,2)	−2.7%
Controls			
Education	−.0338 (.0491)		
Age	.0550 (.0290)*	from "18–29" to ">70" (1,6)	−10.6%
Rural resident?	.0683 (.1032)		
Income	−.0210 (.0261)		
Gender	−.1441 (.0902)		
Ideology	.1655 (.0664)**	from "liberal" to "conservative" (1,7)	−12.8%
Party	−.0276 (.0244)		
Race	.0082 (.1160)		
Constant	−.5730 (.3857)		
Model Summary Statistics			
N	829		
Log likelihood	−542.3756		
Pseudo R^2	0.0214		

Source: National Network of State Polls NSSP-TX-013, 1988.
Note: The dependent variable is a two category variable where 0 = favor, 1 = oppose. Support for dependent variable (ensure equity between districts?) = 56.1 percent.
*z < .10   **z < .05   ***z < .01

would cost and whether state or local taxes should finance education as the two most contentious aspects of the finance reform debate. School finance opponents wanted to avoid an increase in state taxes or a redistribution of locally raised funds from rich to poor districts. A poll found that 69 percent of Republican state representatives did not want to increase state spending, even if the only alternative was to force local school districts to increase taxes. "They're going to have to increase local taxes, but local people are going to make that decision," state Republican chair Fred Meyer said. "That's consistent with Republican philosophy" (Robison 1990, C1). The superintendent from a wealthy district said that resistance to reform in his district was based almost solely on its perceived financial effect: "In any redistribution of state funds we would have lost a considerable amount" (Greene 1988, A1).

The table 5.4 model shows that local control's effect on people's attitudes pales in comparison to that of two other independent variables. The first is age. Texans over seventy were 10.6 percent less likely to support school finance reform than those aged between eighteen and twenty-nine. Older people appear to have calculated their self-interest and were not willing to pay higher taxes for educational programs of which they cannot take advantage, while younger residents may have wanted to ensure good schools for their children and thus approved of increasing educational spending. Second, ideology has a substantial and significant effect. A movement from strong liberalism to strong conservatism is associated with a 12.8 percent drop in support for reform. Conservatives resented the growth in government and additional spending that accompanied reform, while liberals may have valued the opportunity to improve poor people's education.

Tennessee

In 1988, seventy-seven rural Tennessee school districts filed a lawsuit claiming that the state's method of funding public schools was unconstitutional because of the inequities it allowed. In 1991, a superior court judge agreed with the plaintiffs, and the Tennessee Supreme Court affirmed this decision in 1993.[12] There is good reason to expect that feelings about localism affected people's attitudes on Tennessee's reform efforts. Residents have passionately resisted attempts to levy a state income tax and continue to favor local taxes such as the property tax (D. Firestone 2001). To this day, the state does not collect an income tax, even though former governor Ned McWherter explicitly linked the need for it with school finance reform in his initial response to the court ruling.

Table 5.5 presents estimates of a bivariate probit model of a survey conducted by the Social Science Research Institute at the University of Tennessee in the fall of 1990, when school finance reform was starting to become a notable issue in the state. The data include measures of all the independent variables described earlier except for whether respondents have school-age children. Table 5.5 shows that four of these variables are statistically significant predictors of people's views on school finance reform. People's position on replacing local property taxes with a state income tax was a significant predictor of opposition to reform. Moving from strong opposition to strong support for state taxation made people 7.9 percent more likely to support spending equity. This effect is more modest than that of the three other statistically significant variables but nonetheless indicates that stance on the proper taxing authority is an important cause of such attitudes. By contrast, belief in the corruption of local government was not a significant predictor of opposition. In Tennessee, trust in local government to do the right thing did not affect people's views on finance reform, but their desire to protect the property tax at the root of school finance inequities does have such an effect. Tennessee offers evidence in support of the local financial control hypothesis but not the democratic virtues hypothesis.

Three other variables influenced people's evaluations of finance reform in Tennessee. The more education people had received, the more likely they were to oppose reform. Someone who had completed some postgraduate work was 16 percent less likely to support reform than someone without a high school diploma. Such a result might seem counterintuitive, because those who know the value of education from personal experience might be expected to support extending it to everyone. However, education is a competitive good, and increasing the education some people receive decreases the relative utility of the education others already possess (Hochschild and Scovronick 2003). In Tennessee, the more educated appear to have wanted to protect their position of privilege, while the less educated wanted access to equal opportunity. Race and ideology were also statistically significant and have effects consistent with expectations. Finance reform in Tennessee promised to expand government and raise taxes, leading strong conservatives to be 15.7 percent less likely to support reform than were strong liberals. Nonwhites were 10.5 percent more likely to support reform than were whites, which is

TABLE 5.5. Probit Estimates of Attitudes on School Finance Reform in Tennessee, 1990

Independent Variables	Coefficient (S.E.)	Change in Variable from This to This	. . . Changes Probability That R Supported Reform by This Much
Local Control Variables			
How big a problem is corruption in local government?	−.0698 (.0744)		
Favor replacing local property tax with state income tax	−.0864 (.0430)**	from "strongly oppose" to "strongly support" (1,5)	−7.9%
Controls			
Education	.1240 (.0541)**	from "less than HS" to "postgraduate work" (1,5)	−16.0%
Age	.0308 (.0679)		
Rural resident?	−.1412 (.1696)		
Urban resident?	−.1007 (.1343)		
Income	−.0313 (.0518)		
Owner	−.0876 (.1462)		
Gender	−.1358 (.1185)		
Ideology	−.0810 (.0368)**	from "strong liberal" to "strong conservative" (1,7)	−15.7%
Party	−.0346 (.0320)		
Race	−.5035 (.2047)**	from "white" to "nonwhite" (0,1)	+10.5%
Constant	−.0211 (.5186)		

Model Summary Statistics

N	554
Log likelihood	−321.9674
Pseudo R^2	0.0433

Source: National Network of State Polls NSSP-TN-004, 1990.

Note: The dependent variable is a two category variable where 0 = favor ensuring all student receive the same level of funding, 1 = satisfied with existing school funding scheme. Support for dependent variable (ensure equity between districts?) = 62.9 percent.

*$z < .10$ **$z < .05$ ***$z < .01$

consistent with findings about redistributive policies from the public opinion literature and the reality that nonwhite populations benefit disproportionately from policies promoting equity.

New Jersey

Like Texas, New Jersey's school finance reform debate has been among the nation's most contentious and longest-running. *Robinson v. Cahill* (1973) was the first case in the nation where a state supreme court found that a system of school funding with a large local component violated a state constitution's educational provisions by creating spending inequities. Sixteen years later, in *Abbott v. Burke*, the court again ruled the system unconstitutional.[13] Governor Jim Florio's proposed remedy, the Quality Education Act of 1990 (QEA), touched off one of the most contentious policy debates in New Jersey history. Available evidence suggests that local control concerns played a large part in the state's finance reform history. Reed (2001) found that worries about local control drove New Jersey citizens' attitudes on the reform, and columnists in the state mourned how the QEA took decision-making authority out of the hands of local voters and placed it in the hands of the state bureaucracy (Ahearn 1992).

The Eagleton Institute at Rutgers University conducted the two polls used in the models described in this section, one each in July 1990 and September 1993. Using two polls from the same state at different times should demonstrate how public opinion on school finance changes over time and as debate becomes more heated. At the time the first poll was conducted, school finance reform was not as contentious as it would soon become. The New Jersey Supreme Court had just issued its ruling, and no one knew what kind of funding system the state would propose as a remedy. At the time of the second poll, resistance to the QEA and its tax increases had reached its highest level, the Democrats had lost control of the state legislature, and Florio was in the fight of his political life with Christie Todd Whitman, who ultimately succeeded him in large part as a result of his aggressive school finance reform proposal. Neither poll measured whether the respondent was a rural resident. The first poll did not contain variables suitable to test the democratic values hypothesis or a measure of property ownership. Otherwise, all of the key independent variables were present.

Table 5.6 presents estimates of an ordered probit model of the first New Jersey poll. The single most important predictor of people's opinion

TABLE 5.6. Ordered Probit Estimates of Attitudes on School Finance Reform in New Jersey, 1990

Independent Variables	Coefficient (S.E.)	Change in Variable from This to This	. . . Changes Probability That R Supported Reform by This Much[a]
Local Control Variables			
Believe own district will gain or lose state aid	.4576 (.0969)***	from "believe it will gain" to "believe it will lose" (1,2)	−18.0%
Controls			
Education	−.0918 (.0459)**	from "less than HS" to "college grad" (1,4)	+10.4%
Age	.0273 (.0311)		
Urban resident?	−.1394 (.1263)		
Income	.0341 (.0298)		
School-age children	.1721 (.0994)*	from "have kids" to "don't" (1,2)	−6.8%
Gender	.0252 (.0898)		
Ideology	.0265 (.0309)		
Party	.2150 (.0504)***	from "Democrat" to "Republican" (1,3)	−16.9%
Race	−.0836 (.1258)		
Model Summary Statistics			
Cut 1	.1256 (.4167)		
Cut 2	.8287 (.4170)		
Cut 3	1.4367 (.4190)		
N	625		
Log likelihood	−802.7078		
Pseudo R^2	0.0396		

Source: National Network of State Polls NSSP-NJ-079, 1990.

Note: The dependent variable is a four category variable where 1 = strongly approve, 2 = mildly approve, 3 = mildly disapprove, 4 = strongly disapprove. Support for dependent variable (approve of raising all districts' per pupil spending to minimum level?) = 53.3 percent.

[a]Calculated by estimating how indicated value change in the independent variable would increase the likelihood of a person either strongly agreeing or mildly agreeing with the reform proposal.

*z < .10   **z < .05   ***z < .01

TABLE 5.7. Ordered Probit Estimates of Attitudes on School Finance Reform in New Jersey, 1993

Independent Variables	Coefficient (S.E.)	Change in Variable from This to This	. . . Changes Probability That R Supported Reform by This Much[a]
Local Control Variables			
Rating of local school district	−.0176 (.0330)		
Rating of how local district handles money	−.0572 (.0272)**	from "excellent" to "poor" (1,4)	−3.2%
Controls			
Education	.1612 (.0449)***	from "less than HS" to "college grad" (1,4)	−11.3%
Age	.0892 (.0281)***	from "18–29" to ">69" (1,6)	−13.2%
Urban resident?	−.1087 (.1273)		
Income	.0356 (.0222)		
School-age children	−.0251 (.0909)		
Owner	.2922 (.1067)***	from "don't own" to "own" (1,2)	−6.1%
Gender	−.3511 (.0881)***	from "male" to "female" (1,2)	+4.9%
Ideology	.0441 (.0278)		
Party	.0533 (.0281)*	from "Democrat" to "Republican" (1,3)	−2.0%
Race	−.2180 (.1238)*	from "white" to "nonwhite" (0,1)	+3.3%
Model Summary Statistics			
Cut 1	.5884 (.3739)		
Cut 2	1.1743 (.3750)		
Cut 3	1.6007 (.3772)		
N	745		
Log likelihood	−819.16		
Pseudo R^2	0.0582		

Source: National Network of State Polls NSSP-NJ-094, 1990.

Note: The dependent variable is a four category variable where 1 = strongly agree, 2 = mildly agree, 3 = mildly disagree, 4 = strongly disagree. Support for dependent variable (agree with court ruling mandating equity?) = 74.4 percent.

[a]Calculated by estimating how indicated value change in the independent variable would increase the likelihood of a person either strongly agreeing or mildly agreeing with the reform proposal.

*z < .10   **z < .05   ***z < .01

on reform was the measure of local financial control. Respondents who believed that their home school districts would receive less funding from the state were 18 percent less likely to support raising all students' per-pupil spending to a minimum level than those who believed that their home districts would gain. The strength of this effect suggests that the desire to preserve local funding will be a particularly strong predictor of attitudes when people perceive a direct link between finance reform and its financial consequences for their districts. The education variable is statistically significant and exercises the same effect as in the Alabama poll but the opposite effect of the Tennessee poll. Increased education raises the likelihood that respondents will support finance reform, as college graduates are 10.4 percent more likely to support reform than people who lack high school diplomas. In addition, people who have school-age children are 6.8 percent less likely to support reform than those without children. Reform was also susceptible to partisan dynamics, as Democrats were 16.9 percent more likely to support it.

Table 5.7 presents the estimates of an ordered probit model of the second New Jersey poll. Attitudes about localism continued to matter in 1993, but not as much as in 1990. Those who believed that their local districts handled money well were 3.2 percent less likely to support reform than those who believed that their districts did a poor job. Because the wordings for the two questions are so different, comparing support for the local financial control hypothesis across the two New Jersey polls is difficult, but the variables' significance in both models suggests that the underlying effects of the hypothesized relationship are consistent and powerful. Conversely, as the reform debate in New Jersey progressed from 1990 to 1993, the size of local control's effect appears to have diminished substantially. In the table 5.7 model, people's more general ratings of their local school districts were not statistically significant predictors of opposition, so the democratic virtues hypothesis receives no support.

The table 5.7 model shows that the structure of the public's evaluation of school finance reform changed a great deal in the three years between polls. No longer is having school-aged children a significant predictor of opposition, and the effect of partisan identification diminishes greatly, perhaps because opposition to reform had spread across party lines. By 1993, Republicans were only 2 percent more likely to oppose reform than were Democrats. The role of education also changed dramatically. By 1993, college graduates were 11.3 percent more likely to oppose reform than those without high school diplomas, meaning that education had the opposite effect found in the 1990 poll. Age had a statistically significant and particularly prominent effect, with residents over sixty-nine 13.2 percent more likely to voice opposition than residents between the ages of eighteen and twenty-nine. Those who owned property were 6.1 percent more likely to oppose reform than those who did not. Two basic blocks of identity politics also become much more important. Women were 4.9 percent more likely to support reform than were men, and whites were 3.3 percent less likely to support finance reform than were nonwhites.

How can the differences between the two sets of results in New Jersey be explained? Methodological considerations about different samples and different question wordings for key variables undoubtedly played a role, but so too might changes in the dynamics of school finance reform debates as they unfold. These results suggest that people's perceptions of finance reform change over time and as competing considerations become apparent. School finance reform shifted from a novel and unknown program in 1990 toward one that evoked a more conventional structuring of beliefs in 1993; factors such as race and partisan identification, which public opinion scholars have long found to affect attitudes on redistribution, became important. In the case of New Jersey, conservatives' success in labeling school finance reform a program that dramatically raised taxes may well have helped define it as a redistributive program designed to help nonwhites. Similarly, the shift in the effect of education probably stems from the fact that people's understanding of the issue shifted from an abstract belief in the importance of education to a realization about the competition for scarce resources. Educated people may approve of a principle of equal educational opportunity, but when equal opportunity becomes a reality, they fall back on their desire to preserve their competitive advantage and oppose reform.

The most notable similarity between the two sets of results is that measures of local financial control remained a statistically significant determinant of people's opinions on school finance reform, even as the structure of the public opinion of finance reform in New Jersey changed and more accepted determinants of policy positions asserted their effects. Measures of the democratic virtues hypothesis were not significant. The New Jersey results provide more support for the local finance control hypothesis, with one caveat. In 1990, before the *Abbott* case became so well known and controversial, support for local control was a much more powerful determinant than in 1993, when its effect was real but not as large as other independent variables. As the issue became more contentious, attitudes about local control became relatively less important.

Illinois

Unlike the other four states this chapter considers, Illinois has never had a successful legal challenge to its school funding system. As a result, in the 2004–5 school year, local taxes generated 57.5 percent of all school funding in the state, making Illinois more reliant on local revenue sources than every state except Nevada (National Center for Education Statistics 2007). Thus, Illinois provides an opportunity to study how people think about finance reform before it becomes a contentious issue. The difference between local control's effect in low-intensity situations such as Illinois and states such as New Jersey and Tennessee, where the issue is more hotly contested, may help illustrate how local control's role changes as the issue gains greater attention and erupts into debate.

Table 5.8 presents the estimates of a bivariate probit model of the 1994 Illinois Policy Survey conducted by the Center for Governmental Studies at the University of Northern Illinois. The data do not contain measures of the democratic virtues of local control, whether people had children, or whether respondents lived in rural or urban areas. Only two variables are significant predictors of citizen opposition to increasing state funding to lessen inequality. Illinois residents over the age of seventy were 11.1 percent more likely to oppose lessening inequality than people between the ages of eighteen and twenty-nine. As in New Jersey and Texas, age demonstrates an apparent self-interest effect.

The single most important determinant of Illinois residents' evaluation of school finance reform was their opinion on shifting some of the burden of school funding to the state level. Those in favor of this proposal were 19.5 percent more likely to support reform than those who wanted to continue to fund schools primarily with local taxes, and the effect is statistically significant. Illinois offers the strongest support yet for local financial control's role in shaping attitudes about finance reform, but the large effect should be regarded with a healthy dose of caution. At the time the poll was conducted, Illinois lacked a strong finance reform movement, suggesting that feelings about local control may have their greatest predictive power in hypothetical situations, before people have thought much about how specific finance reform packages would apply to them. At such a point, the issue remains a matter of principle, and many people apparently value local education control enough that the principle can affect finance reform attitudes. Based on the results from New Jersey, the local financial control variable's effect might be expected to decrease in subsequent polls if a strong reform movement can gain court victories and pressure the state for new, more equitable funding formula.

The Results as a Whole

Table 5.9 summarizes the effects of all the independent variables across all six models. One of the most notable findings is that different factors influence people's evaluations of school finance in different situations in

TABLE 5.8. Probit Estimates of Attitudes on School Finance Reform in Illinois, 1994

Independent Variables	Coefficient (S.E.)	Change in Variable from This to This	. . . Changes Probability That R Supported Reform by This Much
Local Control Variable			
Increase state tax, reduce local tax	.8139 (.1164)***	from "yes" to "no" (1,2)	−19.5%
Controls			
Education	−.0045 (.0600)		
Age	.1074 (.0397)***	from "18–29" to ">70" (1,6)	−11.1%
Income	.0003 (.0025)		
Owner	.0744 (.1306)		
Gender	−.1901 (.1163)		
Ideology	.0444 (.0511)		
Party	.0852 (.0824)		
Race	.1019 (.1557)		
Constant	−2.4502 (.5327)		
Model Summary Statistics			
N	633		
Log likelihood	−317.85591		
Pseudo R^2	0.0920		

Source: National Network of State Polls NSSP-IL-012, 1994.

Note: The dependent variable is a two category variable where 0 = favor, 1 = oppose. Support for dependent variable (increase state funding to lessen inequity?) = 66.3 percent.

*z < .10   **z < .05   ***z < .01

different states. Almost all of the independent variables have a significant effect in at least one of the models, yet only one variable is significant in more than three models. Anyone seeking to understand the public opinion dynamics of specific school finance reform movements in specific states must understand the history of that particular debate and should be prepared to undertake qualitative analysis to complement any statistical work. That said, this chapter shows that some trends in public opinion about school finance cut across state lines. The structure of the public's evaluation of reform mirrors that of other redistributive policies. Race, age, ideology, party, and education were significant predictors of opposition in more than one poll. These results show that whites, older people, conservatives, Republicans, and the highly educated are more likely to oppose reform than their opposites.

TABLE 5.9. Summary of Independent Variables' Effects on Attitudes about School Finance Reform

Independent Variables	Alabama 1994	Illinois 1994	New Jersey 1990	New Jersey 1993	Tennessee 1990	Texas 1988
Hypothesis 2a						
Hypothesis 2b	N	N	N	N	N	N
Education			P	N	N	
Age		N		N		N
Rural residency	N					
Urban residency						
Income	P					
School-age children			N			
Owner				N		
Gender				P		
Ideology					N	N
Party			N	N		
Race	P			P	P	

Note: "P" indicates that an increase in the independent variable significantly increases the likelihood of a person supporting school finance reform. "N" indicates that an increase in the independent variable significantly decreases the likelihood of a person supporting school finance reform.

The variables with the most consistent effects were the measures of people's support for local financial control. The more people supported funding education through local taxes and believed their district would suffer from finance reform, the more likely they were to oppose reform. Considering that no other independent variable was significant in more than three models, the consistency of local control's effect is even more impressive. Regardless of the specific circumstances surrounding a state's reform debate, support for local control is the one factor that will consistently cause people to oppose reform. Although local financial support can be very important in the right set of circumstances, it is usually one of several factors that influence people's evaluations of reform. Except in Illinois and the first New Jersey poll, the effect of support for local control is modest compared to that of the other statistically significant factors in each regression. Support for local financial control matters but not dramatically more than the factors that scholars of public opinion have identified as determinants of people's attitudes on a wide range of social welfare policies. Local control's effect is also less pronounced in polls taken from high-intensity situations such as Alabama and New Jersey in 1993. Perhaps local control matters more in situations where the issue remains one of principle, as in Illinois, than when finance reform is an active issue that involves competition for scarce resources.

The results do not provide the same level of support for the democratic virtues hypothesis. None of the four variables testing this hypothesis was significant, and only in Alabama did it have anything close to a substantial effect on people's support. Chapters 3 and 4 suggest that keeping school funding local will not increase trust in government, citizen participation, or any of the other virtues democratic scholars have attributed to small-scale democratic bodies. This chapter shows that people either intuitively understand that finance centralization does not endanger these democratic goods or do not care enough about them to alter evaluations of finance reform. Local control's power to change people's attitudes comes not from their support for democracy or home rule but from their desire to keep their financial resources local and to avoid paying for solutions to other school districts' problems.

Discussion

Centralization of school finance may not compromise local autonomy, but people think it does, which accounts for its true power in school finance reform debates. The evidence this chapter presents confirms Reed's (2001) finding that the strength of one's commitment to local control is the most consistent predictor of such opposition, although he may have overstated its strength in relation to other factors. This chapter extends his separation and testing of two types of support for localism. The most consistent reason people oppose finance reform is their support for the financial separation that local control permits, but this opposition does not arise out of a desire to preserve the policy responsiveness, participation, and other democratic goods theorists attribute to local government. Passionate defenses of local control come not from a desire to protect control of curriculum and the like but from support for a school finance status quo that creates the spending inequities school finance reform seeks to remedy. This chapter has provided systematic support for the assertion of chapter 4's Vermont elites that public opposition to finance reform is based less on fears of compromised local autonomy and more on the financial consequences for the more affluent. As Texas District Court judge Scott McCown said, "Local control [is] a code word for the rich spending money the poor don't have" (Reed 2001, 78).

These results should also help us make sense of how the public values local control of public education more generally. People do not vote in school board elections or show up at meetings because they are not overly concerned with the policies school board sets. As long as school district lines continue to provide the ability to separate, the public is content. Commentators have noted that state and federal education reforms designed to aid minorities, beginning with *Brown v. Board of Education*, have succeeded only when they have not greatly disrupted affluent whites' way of life (Bell 1980). Federal and state school reforms such as desegregation and finance reform that aim to bring students and resources from across school district lines together will be among the most difficult to pass and implement, largely because such programs threaten the separation that is precisely what an influential segment of the public wants. Centralized levels of the American intergovernmental system can undertake reforms such as standardized testing and charter school legislation because they do not threaten what the public values in local control. Not by accident have charter schooling and curricular standards become some of the most widely adopted and least controversial education reforms. They allow government to do something to address the dire condition of public schools in the poorest areas but do not disturb the larger framework of separation.

The evidence this chapter presents offers a bleak forecast for equity-minded school finance reform movements. Ensuring equity in spending between rich and poor areas necessitates major changes in a system of local funding that is deeply entrenched and thus requires widespread public support, but the current system of school finance guarantees that a sizable, dedicated, politically powerful segment of the populace is getting exactly what it wants from the finance status quo and sees reform as an anathema. Advocates for finance reform have instinctively understood the dynamics of public opinion, largely forgoing lobbying elected branches of state government and focusing their energies on litigation. This strategy has had limited success. The research on courts and policy-making has shown that the judiciary cannot achieve the type of sweeping social change that ensuring equity would require without the support of the general public (Rosenberg 1991).[14] Substantial inequities remain even in states where courts have ruled in favor of the plaintiffs, especially in districts not included as plaintiffs in the lawsuits (Gittell 1998; Ritter and Lauver 2003).

The political challenges of trying to achieve funding equity have led reform movement leaders in most states to concentrate their efforts on getting adequate funding for poorer schools, to the point where a whole subfield in the study of education policy has developed to try to determine exactly how much money would be required to provide poor school districts with adequate curriculum, supplies, and so on. If one believes the poor need more money spent on their education than a system heavily reliant on local funding can generate, one should celebrate the successes school finance reforms have achieved. In Michigan, Proposal A provided a significant boost in funding for poor districts and narrowed the spending gap among districts, but it could only do so by ensuring that more affluent districts would receive funding increases and continue to enjoy a per-pupil spending advantage, even if that advantage shrank over time. Because their distinctiveness and competitive advantage were preserved, Michigan's affluent residents did not strongly oppose this proposal. This reaction contrasts sharply with that of the affluent in Vermont, where reformers achieved equity but stirred up a hornet's nest. As always, the perfect is the enemy of the good. As described in chapter 4, Vermont is exceptional in many ways. Elected officials in most states would fear the public backlash against funding equity far too much to ever achieve it. Michigan's school finance reform movement could not entirely eliminate spending gaps, and there is good reason to believe that spending gaps may contribute to a continued achievement gap between rich and poor. But Michigan did get more money to ensure that teachers would not have to pay for pencils for their students.

Liberals reading these results may bemoan another instance of mean, nasty suburbanites preserving a competitive advantage over the needy, but there are more charitable interpretations of opposition to school finance reform. Many residents of more affluent school districts have worked hard, sacrificed, and paid a premium to ensure that they could buy properties in high-quality school districts. Having done so much to ensure that their children have the best possible opportunity to succeed, they may resent funding proposals that take away that advantage and consequently reduce the resale values of their houses because they no longer provide access to a better-funded public education. It is possible to understand why finance reform upsets these people but nevertheless to disagree with their opinion. It can be argued that none of the adjustments or hardships the more affluent must bear when school spending is equalized can match those that poor parents face when spending is unequal. Other factors will ensure that what are considered good real estate locations remain so in the future, and removing the comparative advantage for rich children seems a small price to pay to ensure that every student has a fair chance of receiving a good education.

CHAPTER SIX

What Boiled the Frog

Unfunded Mandates and the Real Problem with Centralized-Level Funding

STEVE JEFFREY, THE EXECUTIVE DIRECTOR of the Vermont League of Cities and Towns, has probably spent as much time thinking about local control as anyone in the state. Local control, after all, is his business. He compares local control in Vermont to trying to boil a frog. If one turns up the heat on the stove too quickly, the frog will sense that something is amiss and jump out of the pot. To succeed, one must turn up the heat slowly, so that the frog will not notice the change until too late. Jeffrey's analogy helps make explicit a critical point with significant ramifications for the study of the Piper Link. The most convincing argument against blaming Act 60 for a loss of local control in Vermont is that local control was on life support well before Act 60. Finance reform opponents assume that strong local control currently exists in American education and that finance centralization can damage this control, an argument that is simply out of touch with the reality of contemporary education policy. Over the last half of the twentieth century, state and federal governments have become increasingly willing to regulate all aspects of public education, including curriculum, labor, construction, and a thousand other areas (Derthick 2001). As a result, local board members, administrators, and teachers across the nation have seen their ability to control their districts diminish.

These regulations have done far more to undermine local control than has centralized-level funding.

What upsets local officials most has been the insufficient funding centralized levels have provided to implement the mandates, regulations, and conditions attached to aid. State and federal governments are more than willing to regulate education policy without providing the money needed to implement the mandated changes, forcing local actors to dedicate scarce resources to these programs and limiting the time and money they can devote to their own independent policy activities. These regulations are not, strictly speaking, unfunded mandates. Some funding accompanies them, but it is not enough fully to cover the cost of the program's implementation. Local officials' real Piper Link concern is not that centralized-level funding comes with strings attached. It is that the strings lack enough funding.

The Rise of Regulation . . .

A large part of the history of U.S. intergovernmental relations has been the increasing power of federal and state governments relative to local government. As early as the late nineteenth century, James Bryce noted that local governments had lost some of their traditional autonomy to state and federal governments and that their power was at an all-time low (Zimmerman 1995). The early twentieth century saw the rise of the Progressives, who believed local politics, with its infamous machines such as Tammany Hall, to be the cause of government corruption and sought to vest the duties of local officials into a centralized, "scientific" bureaucracy. The New Deal ensured that the federal government would forever be the leader in poor relief. World War II and the Cold War caused the federal government to raise an incredible amount of revenue for defense spending. Another effect of the combined activities of the Roosevelt and Truman administrations was that the American public became accustomed to a huge federal government with the resources and inclination to become involved in an enormous array of policy areas. The civil rights movement established the federal government as the primary governmental protector of individual rights, and southern defenses of Jim Crow cast a lasting suspicion that any appeal to decentralization, local control, or states' rights was cover for more sinister motives. By the turn of the twenty-first century, the federal government was the biggest and most powerful governmental actor in almost every field where it chose to assume such a role, including the protection of rights, social welfare services, and economic, development, and transportation policy.

Given its expansion in other areas, state and federal involvement in public education was inevitable but lagged behind regulation of other policy areas. The norm of local educational control was firmly entrenched in American political culture, and parents cherished their ability to chart the course of their children's education. Through the 1960s, developments such as the perceived need to compete with the Soviet Union in science and math achievement and school desegregation spurred some centralized-level action, but school districts still had considerable latitude in most areas, including curriculum, student evaluation, and staffing (Macedo 2004).

The beginning of the contemporary era of state and federal education policy-making was the 1965 Elementary and Secondary Education Act (ESEA). The federal government offered huge new funding streams to local districts, provided they vigorously pursued school desegregation. The federal government used these carrots to compel southern school districts to accept desegregation. While desegregation was an unimpeachable goal, the federal government set an ominous precedent in the relationship between what it demanded and the funding it provided to implement the demands. Between 1965 and 1970, the federal government increased its annual spending on public K–12 schools by four billion dollars. This figure is impressive, but even if all of this increase went to schools in former Jim Crow states, it certainly did not cover all or even most of the cost of switching an entire region to a system of integrated schooling. Thus, the first great federal intervention into public education also saw the first instance of local officials having to spend a significant amount of their funding to implement a federal program.

Another aspect of the original ESEA was a significant increase in funding to state governments, which in exchange were charged with monitoring compliance with federal education laws. The number of employees at state education agencies doubled from 1965 to 1970, when it reached 22,000. By the 1992–93 school year, that number had risen further to 28,600 (Johnston and Sandham 1999). Today, the federal government provides more than 40 percent of the total operating budgets for most state departments of education, and it is not terribly surprising that employees hired with these funds tend to look favorably on most federal action and do whatever they can to promote compliance (Hill 2000).

Even through the 1970s, however, state and federal regulation was targeted primarily at specific programs and populations, such as special education, rather than at the entire public education system.[1] The 1983 release of the Reagan administration's landmark study, *A Nation at Risk*, changed this focus. The study began by warning that "the educational foundations of our society are presently being eroded by a rising tide of mediocrity that threatens our very future as a Nation and a people. What was unimaginable a generation ago has begun to occur—others are matching and surpassing our educational attainments" (U.S. Department of Education 1983, 1). With the release of *A Nation at Risk*, the days when local school systems were left alone and assumed to provide a world-class education were gone forever. For the first time, the federal government indicted the entire American public school system and its local foundations for their approach to education and indicated that the national government would be increasingly interested in the procedures local districts followed and the outcomes they produced.

A Nation at Risk recommended that all states adopt curricular standards and increased standardized testing. Buoyed by the federally financed expansion of their departments of education, the states met the report's challenge with relish. By 2003–4, forty-nine states had implemented curricular standards, and all fifty states required schools to administer standardized testing to measure student achievement. Forty-six states had provisions to hold at least some schools accountable for poor test results, and twenty-three did not let students advance to the next grade or graduate without passing state tests. Regulation was not limited to curriculum and evaluation. Forty-four states required teachers to pass tests to become certified. Forty-one states enacted bullying policies. Driven in part by school finance reformers' efforts, almost every state government dramatically increased its share of the public school finance burden. The list goes on (*Education Week* 2004). These numbers only begin to tell the story of state involvement in what was once an almost solely local policy sphere. A lobbyist for the American Association of School Administrators said, "In 1960, no state had more than one book of education laws, and now they are volumes long because states are regulating everything" (Johnston and Sandham 1999, 4).

The federal government's initial efforts at regulation after *A Nation at Risk* were less ambitious.[2] In 1994, Goals 2000 called on states to adopt stringent curricular standards but left compliance largely to the discretion of the states, with no penalties for failure to comply. With the 2001 passage of the No Child Left Behind Act (NCLB), the federal government took a more demanding stance. NCLB required states to adopt stringent standards and extensive testing and allowed parents to use federal funds for alternative schooling if their public schools failed to meet progress requirements on tests. The federal government threatened to withhold funding from any state or school that failed to comply. In so doing, it further curtailed schools' already limited discretion in curriculum design and evaluation and threatened local schools with losses of students and funding.[3]

In today's United States, state and federal governments have become involved in almost every aspect of K–12 public education, and almost every involved party has accepted and encouraged this centralization. The public may say it likes local control (although fewer people than ever go even that far), but as chapter 5 shows, it likes a very specific, limited, and financially based local control and is somewhat indifferent toward its other aspects. In 2007, for the first time, when asked which level of government should have the most control over the public schools, less than 50 percent of respondents chose local school boards (Phi Delta Kappan and the Gallup Organization 2007). Polls find consistently high levels of support for programs that increase state and federal regulation. Majorities approve of state high-stakes testing, minimum state curricular requirements, evaluating teachers by the standardized test scores of their students, increasing state mandatory attendance policies, using the federal government to narrow the achievement gap between white and minority students, and numerous other federal and state policies that intrude on local educational control (Phi Delta Kappan and the Gallup Organization 2004).[4] "How deep-seated could our commitment to 'local control' be if two-thirds to three-quarters of the American public are willing to jettison its most important manifestations?" (Finn 1992, 24).

Another reflection of the public's support for centralization is state and national politicians' success in using the rhetoric of education reform to get elected. In the 1980s, governors increasingly began to make education issues a central part of their campaign messages and used their authority to pass sweeping reforms (Mazzoni 1995). Patrick J. McGuinn (2006) summarizes recent presidential candidates' success in incorporating calls for an expanded federal role in education into their electoral appeals. To help establish his image as a "kinder, gentler" Republican, George H. W. Bush pledged to be an "education president" and called on the federal government to ensure student achievement through standards and testing. Bill Clinton trumpeted Arkansas's education reforms under his administration and painted Bush and his Republican colleagues as not fully committed to assuring universal student achievement. Bob Dole was the last presidential nominee for either major party to call for the dismantling of many federal education reforms and a return to stronger local educational control, but Clinton and the Democrats cast this stance as an abandonment of underachieving children. In 2000, perhaps tired of losing votes as a consequence of its commitment to local and state control, the Republican Party nominated George W. Bush, who made his success as an education reformer in Texas, which some dubbed the "Texas Miracle," a critical part of his platform. He and his presidential opponent, Democrat Al Gore, agreed that the federal government should adopt extensive programs to ensure improved learning for all students.

. . . and the Fall of Local Control

Scholars disagree about how much autonomy local governments can retain in the face of extensive regulation from centralized levels of an intergovernmental system. Some authors argue that regulation drastically changes the behavior of all local actors, including classroom teachers (Malen and Muncey 2000; Sipple, Killeen, and Monk 2004). Other observers argue that because centralized-level reforms often fail to establish conditions sufficient to guarantee their implementation, teachers and other local officials can interpret reforms to further their own goals (Fuhrman and Elmore 1990; Fairman and Firestone 2001; Percival, Neiman, and Fernandez 2005).[5] To call the dialogue between these two groups a debate is somewhat misleading. While they argue over the extent of centralized-level influence, even the latter group believes that regulation makes local school districts do things they otherwise would not. The majority of scholars and policymakers believe local control's best days are behind it. Said Professor Neil Theobald, "I don't think the public realizes the sea change that's occurred in who's responsible for schools. While we talk about local control, what we have is anything but local control." California governor Gray Davis went even further and labeled local control an "abject failure" (Johnston and Sandham 1999, 1).

The clearest illustration of diminished local control is the rapid decrease in the number of school districts throughout the twentieth century. More units of local governments ensure that each one will serve a smaller number of people, thereby giving rise to the benefits democratic theorists attribute to participatory democracy, including greater citizen participa-

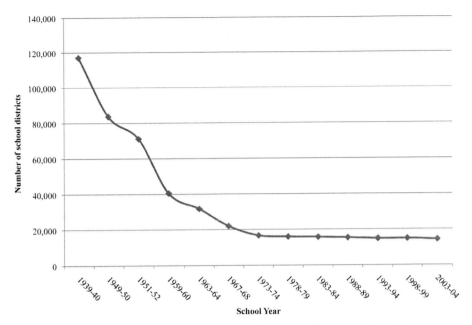

Fig. 6.1. Number of U.S. public school districts by selected years. (Data from National Center for Educational Statistics 2007, Table 83.)

tion and accessibility and the ability to enact different policies that reflect the country's diversity. While Vermont has remained committed to preserving school districts for many of its small towns, most states have not. Figure 6.1 shows that the number of public school districts in the United States decreased almost tenfold during the twentieth century between 1939–40 and 2003–4. During the school year beginning in 1939, the country had 117,108 school districts. Within twenty years, that number had dropped to 40,520, and by the 1978–79 school year, only 16,014 school districts existed, with a slow but steady trend toward consolidation continuing to this day. The great bulk of district consolidations occurred before the Supreme Court's 1973 *Rodriguez* ruling, which begat the modern movements to remedy school funding inequities in state courts. Thus, these movements and the 20–90 finance centralization involved in them do not appear to have been a significant cause of most of this consolidation.

The inevitable by-product of consolidation is a huge increase in the size of the average school district, as table 6.1 shows. As a result of limited data, one can only trace the average size of school district back to the

1990–91 school year, when 10.5 percent of school districts contained five thousand or more students and 51.3 percent of districts served fewer than one thousand students. By the 2003–4 school year, 13.3 percent of school districts served five thousand or more students, and 46.6 percent of districts served fewer than one thousand students. Contemporary school districts are large enough to require bureaucracies that can be as difficult to navigate as any state department of education, making it difficult for the average citizen to know where to inquire to address an issue.

Another impediment to meaningful local school board decision making is the complex and seemingly endless web of regulations. Any ambitious new school board member will quickly learn the difficulties of making meaningful reform at the local level, and most do not even try. Modern school boards rarely do more than ratify the policies their superintendents suggest (Iannaccone and Lutz 1970; Bolland and Redfield 1988). The only significant independent choice school boards make is often the hiring of the superintendent, but it is open to question how much effectiveness this decision has in transmitting all but the broadest policy preferences and in ensuring the superintendent's day-to-day accountability to the public.

Faced with a situation in which making a meaningful difference seems impossible, the public has responded accordingly. The low participation seen in Vermont is the norm for the rest of the country. Existing studies suggest that only 17 to 25 percent of those registered vote in local school board elections (Cameron, Underwood, and Fortune 1988; Hochschild 1997).[6] Local school politics also fail to inspire people to en-

TABLE 6.1. Size of school district, 1990–91 and 2003–4

	Size, 1990–91	Percentage of whole, 1990–91	Size, 2003–4	Percentage of whole, 2003–4
25,000 or more	190	1.2	256	1.8
10,000–24,999	489	3.2	594	4.1
5,000–9,999	937	6.1	1,058	7.4
2,500–4,999	1,940	12.6	2,031	14.1
1,000–2,499	3,542	23.1	3,421	23.8
600–999	1,799	11.7	1,728	12.0
300–599	2,275	14.8	1,981	13.8
1–299	3,816	24.8	2,994	20.8
Size not reported	370	2.4	320	2.2

Source: National Center for Education Statistics 2007, Table 84.

gage in other forms of political participation. From 1974 to 1987, the Roper Organization periodically polled the public about its attempts to engage the government. It found that between 16 and 20 percent of people reported "attending a public meeting on town or school affairs" (Hochschild and Scott 1998, 96). Low participation may allow special interests such as teachers' unions, evangelical Christian groups, or advocates of specific programs such as special education and bilingual education to mobilize members and exercise a disproportionate share of influence on the composition and policy of local boards (Moe and Koret Task Force on K–12 Education 2001). What citizen involvement exists in school activities is usually channeled to serve existing policies rather than bring new voices into government. Schools are happy to mobilize parent support into Parent-Teacher Associations (PTAs) and similar organizations, but scholars have not found PTAs to be important actors in the policy process.

> The American PTA is rarely anything more than a coffee and cookies organization based on vague goodwill and gullibility. It is chiefly useful to the administration for raising money for special projects and persuading parents who are interested enough to attend meetings that the local schools are in the front ranks of American education. (Koerner 1968, 167–68)

> Educators are very supportive of parental activity at home and of their volunteering as chaperones at school activities, but they often seem to prefer that parents accept a position of "distant assistants" and help teachers only when invited to do so. Professional educators and administrators express much lower levels of interest in community participation in other areas of public school life. (Doherty 1998, 233)

I do not intend to demean the importance of citizen participation in local school politics. At every public school in the country, many ordinary citizens, like the parents who built a fence around the playground at Vermont's Sherburne Elementary, toil anonymously and perform critical support roles. In light of the countless barriers state and federal governments place between citizens and direct democracy, this participation is all the more exceptional. The vast majority who do not participate can hardly be blamed for abandoning what has become a controlled and ceremonial process. State and federal regulations have increased, local control has diminished, and the public has adjusted its participation patterns to avoid taking part in an increasingly meaningless activity. Local school board politics are a far cry from the New England town meeting ideal of direct democracy. Small-scale, participatory "democratic local control of public education is a potent ideal; it also should be regarded as a myth" (McDermott 1999, 7).

Vermont Again

The Vermont interview subjects confirmed the sorry state of contemporary local educational control. As subject after subject pointed out, asking whether Act 60 had reduced local control presumed a relatively high level of pre–Act 60 local control, an idea they roundly rejected. As one board member said, "Local control is a thing of the past." They consistently mentioned that they controlled only a small portion of their operating budgets, with numerous respondents from both supervisory unions, including both of the administrators who supervise budget affairs, estimating that portion at about 10 percent. A former PS3 board member said, "Everybody hollers about not wanting to give up local control, but most of the budget is determined by the state grant." The interviewees reported that most of their efforts go toward reacting to the dictates of centralized levels, with little to no time or funding to innovate. Windsor Central superintendent Meg Gallagher indicated that most board policy is passed because the state requires every school board have a policy on a certain issue. As a RS1 board member put it,

> Independence is a dream. Local control is a wonderful thing, and you do have some. You have *responsibilities* that you might think are indicative of local control that are actually somebody telling you you are responsible for something. It's not necessarily something you'd want to do on your own if you had true local control.

The people with whom I spoke blamed their powerlessness on "unfunded mandates," the perennial bogeyman of local governments everywhere. Vermonters believe that the tendency of state and federal governments to regulate what goes on in public schools without paying for the associated costs has reached epidemic proportions. Says Ruth Anne Barker, "The issues would be alleviated significantly if the federal government would put the money into our states to support education and to support its mandates." Interviewees complained about mandates in a staggeringly wide array of policy areas. RS3 board member Rachel Benoit noted that the state forced her son's elementary school to have a library even though the town library was located in the building next door. One PS3 board member mentioned how the state required every school nurse to send the state a weekly report on how many children in the school had chicken pox, even if the illness was not present in the school. PS3 board member Connie Carroll talked about how a federal requirement that all classrooms have a minimum amount of square footage added a significant amount of money to a bond proposal that the citizens of her town ultimately rejected by one vote. A 2003 report identified twenty-nine different types of unfunded or underfunded mandates in such areas as curriculum, teacher certification, student health, standardized testing, and reporting to the state (Vermont School Board Association, Vermont Superintendents Association, and Vermont Principals Association 2003).

Out of all the mandates about which the interview respondents complained, two drew the most ire. The first was the vast web of federal requirements governing special education. These regulations mandate that schools spend an enormous share of their budgets on a small segment of the student population with limited beneficial externalities for the general student body. For example, Rutland Northeast director of finance Brenda Flemming estimated that 26 percent of the supervisory union's combined budget went to pay for special ed services that served approximately 13 percent of its students. Federal regulations require that the federal government pay 40 percent of the cost of special education. Although Washington sends only 10–15 percent of those funds, it still demands full compliance (Hochschild and Scovronick 2003). Local officials must divert scarce resources toward special education programs they did not pass and over which they have little control.

The clear winner of the Least Popular Mandate Award is NCLB. Vermont's local school elites regard NCLB's insistence on students achieving adequate yearly progress on standardized tests as unrealistic, and they loathe both its designation of schools that failed to achieve it as "needs improvement" and its threat to withhold funds from such schools.[7] They scoff at its criteria for what makes a highly qualified teacher, noting that NCLB classified both the National Teacher of the Year, who is from Vermont, and PS3's Teacher of the Year as unqualified. "We know who our well-qualified teachers are, and if they're not on the list that comes down, something's obviously wrong with it," said one PS3 board member. Finally, interviewees despised the fact that the Bush administration expected compliance with these regulations without significantly increasing its share of the school finance burden.

Interview subjects explicitly linked NCLB to a loss of local control. Reacting to NCLB's testing provisions, RS1 principal Marion Withum agreed that local taxpayers had a right to know how schools were performing, but such evaluation "is the job of the school board." Carroll claimed that NCLB was "an initiative crafted by this administration to try to bring everyone under the same umbrella, the same thought process," and Rutland Northeast superintendent William Mathis agreed:

> [NCLB] comes right into your school by a very narrow set of definitions of what the purpose of education is, meaning standardized test scores and gains on it. . . . [I]t doesn't mention anything about building a democratic society, a better society, people that vote, people that stay out of jail, people that contribute to their community—these are outcomes of education. This law doesn't care about that. When you've got a place like Vermont, where community is so precious, then for something to come in and on the basis of dumb test scores literally condemn your school and close it and change the organization, that's not only a threat to the communities here, it's a threat to democracy. It obliterates local control.

One Michigan observer lamented the same trend and told the story of a local boy who doctors predicted would never talk. By 2007, he had defied all expectations and was attending high school. The president of his district's school board said, "Rather than celebrating the accomplishments of students like him—and those of his therapists, aides and teachers—schools are feeling punished under the federal No Child Left Behind act when disabled students don't perform up to mandated standards" (Moore 2007, A1).

None of the interview respondents saw a link between the finance centralization of Act 60 and an increase in the number of state mandates. Some officials believed that Act 60 made existing mandates more bearable, because the state assumed a greater share of the cost of programs such as special education. Jeffrey characterized respondents' views on the link between the two when he remarked that the mandate situation had grown worse since 1998, but only because he believed the trends that had caused the mandate situation had only gotten more pronounced. He called mandates "a speeding bullet before Act 60 that hasn't slowed down."

Conclusion: What Does and Does Not Hurt Local Autonomy

The juxtaposition of local elites' attitudes on Act 60 and unfunded mandates helps us pinpoint exactly what kind of centralized action policymakers think is most harmful to local control. They welcome state funding because they generally feel that it increases their ability to do what needs doing. But local officials hate when central governments pass regulations without providing the funding to implement them. Such actions, officials believe, take up too much of their time, energy, and resources and inhibit their ability creatively to respond to local needs. Scholars of intergovernmental relations agree, having long recognized that un- and underfunded mandates are among the most damaging practices centralized levels can use in their interactions with local governments and change local government behavior far more than grants with no conditions attached (Zimmerman 1995; Kronebusch 2004). The tension that David R. Berman (2003) identifies between local officials' desire for both home rule and centralized-level funding is not irrational. Rather, it is an understandable reaction to the way state and federal governments sometimes treat their local governments and offers a simple remedy to revitalize locally controlled public education: worry less about some alleged link between finance centralization and state intrusiveness and more about NCLB and other programs that dictate policies available to local districts and siphon off scarce resources that local officials might otherwise spend on policies of their choosing. If anything, local officials wish that the Piper Link functioned more strongly in the 20–90 range, because the regulations they already endure would be accompanied by the funding necessary to implement them.

CHAPTER SEVEN

No Child Left Behind and the Power of 5 Percent

※ ※ ※

CHAPTER 6 SUGGESTS THAT "UNFUNDED" MANDATES such as special education and No Child Left Behind are far more harmful to local autonomy than finance centralization born out of state efforts to achieve a more equal funding distribution, but one critical question remains unanswered. If, as chapter 6 argues, local officials detest state and federal regulations that come without funding, why do local leaders comply? If mandates are "unfunded," local governments certainly risk nothing in noncompliance.

The answer to this question provides the final key to unlocking the Piper Link. This book has yet to examine whether finance centralization in the 0–20 range functions differently than finance centralization in the 20–90 range. The curved model of the Piper Link proposed in chapter 2 hypothesizes that local governments become dependent on even small amounts of funding from state and federal governments, thereby allowing centralized levels to achieve a large amount of control with relatively small funding contributions. In other words, the changes in centralized-level funding that truly compromise local autonomy are those where it moves from no contribution to even a small percentage of the total funding for a program. The best way to examine such shifts is to bring the third level of the U.S. intergovernmental system into the mix. The federal government contributes a very small share of the total U.S. K–12 public education funding, but it has still tried to exercise a tremendous amount of control over education policy and in the process state and local governments.

No Child Left Behind

In 2001, bipartisan majorities in both houses of Congress and President George W. Bush reauthorized the Elementary and Secondary Education Act (ESEA) in what became known as the No Child Left Behind Act (NCLB).[1] NCLB goes beyond all previous federal efforts to reform public education and signals that the federal government intends to play a part in every conceivable aspect of public education governance. NCLB demands that states annually test students in reading and mathematics in grades three through eight and in science once each in elementary, middle, and high school. States must also produce annual report cards with students' academic achievements and multiple other indicators of school district quality, with districts responsible for providing the same data on each school. States must ensure that all students reach proficiency on state tests by 2013–14 and that schools meet federal benchmarks for "adequate yearly progress" (AYP). Schools must meet AYP not just for their entire population but for each demographic subgroup, including traditionally underachieving populations. To give policymakers and the public a measure by which to judge the rigor of states' tests and student progress, a sample of each state's students must take the National Assessment of Educational Progress every other year. If a school receiving federal funds fails to meet AYP for multiple years in a row, it is deemed a "needs improvement" school and must face penalties of escalating severity, including offering students the ability to transfer to other schools in the district, providing supplemental educational services such as private tutoring, and ultimately being forced to "restructure" by changing the entire administration and teaching staff. Finally, states are expected to ensure that every teacher is "highly qualified," which NCLB defines as state certification and demonstrable proficiency in both pedagogy and subject area.[2]

Are States Complying?

Demands and Backlash

NCLB goes much further in demanding that state and local governments adopt certain programs and practices than any previous ESEA reauthorization. NCLB is rooted in both earlier federal efforts, such as 1994's Goals 2000, and state efforts over the past twenty-five years to establish accountability systems, but NCLB is the first time the federal government has mandated accountability systems, set ambitious timetables for reaching these goals, and placed stringent guidelines on the progress of regular education students that schools must fulfill to retain a portion of their federal funding. Earlier federal efforts suggested that state governments adopt certain accountability measures; NCLB demands that state governments do so.

NCLB has generated a firestorm of protest that meeting its goals and requirements lies beyond states' and localities' ability. In the years immediately after its passage, states struggled to meet the testing requirement, with only twenty states able to meet the English and math testing requirements by the 2003–4 target (*Education Week* 2004). States have also struggled to bring existing systems of curricular standards and testing in line with NCLB's demands, with the result that schools "must deal with two competing accountability systems, and conflicting rules and priorities have thoroughly frustrated and confused" them (Herrington 2004, A1). The demand that subgroups meet AYP goals means that states with high populations of racial and ethnic minorities have an even harder time meeting federal requirements (Tucker 2003; Shaul 2004). Local and state actors face significant challenges in collecting student achievement data for every subgroup in every school and providing the supplementary services NCLB requires for failing schools (Minnici 2007).[3] Critics argue that almost no district or state has developed sufficient capacity to accommodate student transfers out of "needs improvement" schools. Providing supplementary services and transfer options is a particular challenge for small rural school districts, many of whom have very few schools and face daunting costs in moving handfuls of students across geographically large districts. Observers have expressed skepticism that understaffed state departments of education can monitor the teaching force for compliance with the highly qualified teacher (HQT) standard, arguing that HQT makes staffing even more difficult for a nation that was already suffering from a teacher shortage. Rural and urban schools, which serve a disproportionate number of the hard-to-educate students NCLB seeks to help, have had the hardest time attracting qualified teachers, a task that the HQT requirement makes even more difficult (National Conference of State Legislatures 2005; Keller 2006). Utah state representative Patricia Jones claims the NCLB "has kind of forced us to be prostitutes for the federal government" (Davis 2005, 3). Even if NCLB's requirements were fully funded, they would place state governments and local school districts under significant strain.

What has infuriated state and local governments is that by almost all accounts, NCLB has not been fully funded. Instead, Republican senator Gary Schroeder of Idaho has called it "the largest unfunded mandate in the history of the United States" (National Education Association 2005, 1). In one survey, 93 percent of school superintendents and 88 percent of principals agreed that NCLB has resulted in "an enormous increase in responsibilities and mandates without . . . the resources necessary to fill them" (Public Agenda 2003). William Mathis conducted a metaanalysis of forty studies that have attempted to determine how much money it would cost individual states to ensure that all students passed the state tests that NCLB demands and increase state department of education size to a level sufficient to meet the new data reporting requirement:

> The new requirements for administering the new law require at least $11.3 billion in new funds. . . . Additional new costs to give all students standards-based opportunities are conservatively estimated at 27.5% or $137.8 billion in new money. Thus, implementation of the administrative and learning opportunities aspects of the law would require a new sum of $144.5 billion, or an increase of 29% in educational spending. (Mathis 2005, 93)

For the 2003–4 school year, the total federal Title I appropriation was $11.3 billion, and the administration's budget request of $12.3 billion fell below NCLB's authorized amount of $18 billion.[4] The $1.3 billion increase represents only 0.4 percent of the country's total educational spending, an amount which Mathis regards as monumentally insufficient to pay for the new costs. His conclusions reflect the overwhelming consensus that NCLB is significantly underfunded.[5] The only people who seem to believe that NCLB has been adequately funded are officials closely connected to the Bush administration, a group that includes the president, his staff, and the leaders of the U.S. Department of Education (DOE) that he selected. The DOE points to an alleged $6 billion in educational funding of which state and local governments have not taken advantage (U.S. Department of Education 2004). Mathis finds no empirical evidence to back up these claims, and if the studies he examines are even close to accurate, this funding would fall well short of what is required to fully pay for NCLB's components.

Resistance and Compliance

Given the tremendous strain NCLB has placed on state and local capacity, the federal government might be expected to have problems ensuring compliance, and some resistance has indeed developed. Numerous states have applied to the DOE for waivers from specific NCLB provisions, although the DOE has not always granted these requests. States and local school districts have made no secret of their desire to modify some of NCLB's most ambitious provisions and have pursued normal channels of lobbying to advance their views. Colorado, Maine, New Mexico, and Utah have passed laws that formally oppose various NCLB provisions, and Connecticut has filed a major lawsuit arguing that its existing system of student accountability better meets state needs than does the NCLB system. Local school districts from Michigan, Texas, and Vermont have joined the National Education Association (NEA) in filing *Pontiac v. Spellings*,[6] arguing that the federal government has failed to adequately fund NCLB and that local school districts nationwide face a twenty-seven billion dollar shortfall; six other states, the governor of Pennsylvania, and state and local officials from California have filed amicus briefs in support of the suit.[7] Illinois's Ottawa Township High School District 140 and a special education teacher from Kansas have filed independent lawsuits against the DOE.[8]

Yet the overwhelming state response to NCLB has been compliance. The Education Commission of the States (ECS), a nonprofit, nonpartisan research organization with representatives from forty-nine states and the District of Columbia on its board, has tracked whether each state has fully implemented, partially implemented, or not implemented thirty-eight separate NCLB provisions. Given ECS's reputation as an unbiased organization, these measures offer a very good sense of the general level of state compliance. Table 7.1 describes the findings for all fifty states. On average, states have fully implemented 31.1 of 38 provisions, or 81.6 percent. Every state has fully implemented at least 50 percent of the provisions, and only nine states have implemented fewer than 70 percent. If the analysis is expanded to include provisions that states have partially implemented, the level of compliance reaches 94.9 percent. Maine, Montana, Nebraska, North Dakota, Utah, and Wyoming are the only states to have fully or partially implemented less than 34 of the 38 provisions. Making this level of compliance even more significant is that ECS has updated its database "only periodically since Fall 2004," most likely because the organization found the level of compliance so high that it did not warrant further examination. The ECS ratings represent the general consensus of the public education community that states have implemented the vast majority of NCLB's provisions. The Center on Education Policy (CEP) has been at the forefront of measuring NCLB implementation and has issued multiple reports on different provisions: all of these reports have found that NCLB has already drastically changed American public education. Every state now measures whether students meet AYP, and "NCLB has spurred massive changes in and expansion of state testing programs" (2007b). The number of school restructurings in California doubled in one year to 8 percent of the state's schools, an increase the CEP attributes to schools' failure to make AYP for multiple years (2007a; see also Debray, McDermott, and Wohlstetter 2005).

Local school districts are also complying. Only 7 of the 14,383 U.S. school districts have opted out of NCLB, 83 percent claim to be on track to fully implement the HQT requirement, and 62 percent report increasing time spent on math and English and decreasing time spent on subjects for which NCLB does not require testing (McMurrer 2007a, 2007b). Only one Colorado school district has taken advantage of a state law allowing districts to choose not to comply by seeking voter approval of a mill levee to replace the lost funding. Phyllis McClure of the Title I Independent Review Panel has observed that NCLB "has really upset the status quo in state and local offices and has shaken the complacency of educators and parents about their schools' performance" (2004). Teachers perceive a high level of compliance in their individual schools, a phenomenon many educators deeply resent. The NEA has issued a 227-page report containing teachers' thoughts on NCLB, almost all of which are negative. Heather Mildon, a kindergarten teacher from Anchorage, Alaska, has a typical reaction:

> NCLB's adverse impact on my classroom also has been significant. It has changed the tone of kindergarten to resemble that of the first-grade classrooms of yesteryear. . . . This has meant less time to evaluate student needs and abilities, less time to formulate plans for improvement, and less time for one-on-one contact with students. Instead, teachers have been given a one-size-fits-all scripted text curriculum that does nothing to take into account students' varying abilities and experiences.

TABLE 7.1. Implementation of 38 NCLB Components by State[a]

State	NCLB Parts Fully Implemented	Percentage of 38 Possible Parts	NCLB Parts Fully or Partially Implemented	Percentage of 38 Possible Parts	Percentage Federal Funding	Percentage Title Funding[b]
Alabama	33	86.8	38	100	11.6	4.2
Alaska	36	94.7	38	100	17.7	3.0
Arizona	30	78.9	36	94.7	11.4	3.6
Arkansas	35	92.1	37	97.4	9.9	4.3
California	35	92.1	38	100	9.9	3.7
Colorado	37	97.4	38	100	6.5	2.2
Connecticut	34	89.5	38	100	5.2	1.7
Delaware	35	92.1	37	97.3	8.6	3.1
Florida	33	86.8	37	97.3	10.5	3.5
Georgia	35	92.1	38	100	8.1	3.2
Hawaii	24	63.2	37	97.4	8.2	2.4
Idaho	31	81.6	37	97.4	9.8	3.1
Illinois	35	92.1	38	100	8.5	3.0
Indiana	31	81.6	37	97.4	7.6	2.4
Iowa	32	84.2	37	97.4	7.4	1.8
Kansas	27	71.1	37	97.4	9.1	2.5
Kentucky	37	97.4	38	100	10.6	4.2
Louisiana	32	84.2	37	97.4	13.2	5.5
Maine	19	50	30	78.9	8.9	2.4
Maryland	36	94.7	38	100	6.7	2.1
Massachusetts	34	89.5	37	97.4	6.0	2.2
Michigan	30	78.9	38	100	7.8	2.6
Minnesota	25	65.8	34	89.5	5.9	1.4
Mississippi	31	81.6	37	97.4	15.4	5.6
Missouri	32	84.2	38	100	8.0	2.8
Montana	23	60.5	26	68.4	14.5	3.9
Nebraska	22	57.9	32	84.2	8.9	2.3
Nevada	34	89.5	37	97.4	7.0	2.6
NewHampshire	28	73.7	35	92.1	5.2	1.7
New Jersey	28	73.7	37	97.4	4.3	1.6
New Mexico	32	84.2	36	94.7	15.0	4.9
New York	35	92.1	38	100	7.0	3.6
North Carolina	35	92.1	37	97.4	9.6	3.4
North Dakota	24	63.2	31	81.6	15.3	4.2
Ohio	35	92.1	38	100	6.4	2.5
Oklahoma	35	92.1	36	94.7	12.7	3.9
Oregon	27	71.1	34	89.5	9.1	3.5
Pennsylvania	32	84.2	38	100	7.7	2.6
Rhode Island	29	76.3	38	100	6.5	2.9
South Carolina	31	81.6	36	94.7	9.8	3.3
South Dakota	35	92.1	38	100	15.7	4.1
Tennessee	35	92.1	37	97.4	10.0	3.7
Texas	31	81.6	36	94.7	9.9	3.8
Utah	24	63.2	31	81.6	9.3	2.1
Vermont	23	60.5	34	89.5	7.0	2.9

TABLE 7.1.—*continued*

State	NCLB Parts Fully Implemented	Percentage of 38 Possible Parts	NCLB Parts Fully or Partially Implemented	Percentage of 38 Possible Parts	Percentage Federal Funding	Percentage Title Funding[b]
Virginia	36	94.7	37	97.4	6.6	2.2
Washington	34	89.5	36	94.7	9.0	2.4
West Virginia	30	78.9	34	89.5	10.6	4.2
Wisconsin	30	78.9	37	97.4	6.1	2.0
Wyoming	23	60.5	30	78.9	8.8	3.6
50 state average	31.1	81.6	36.1	94.9	9.3	3.2

Source: Education Commission of the States 2006.

[a]The presented observations reflect the contents of the database through March 28, 2007. Since the fall of 2004, ECS has updated the database only on a periodic basis, as discussed in the text.

[b]These observations are taken from National Center for Educational Statistics 2007, Table 153.

Kindergarten students, once able to learn through play and experience, are now required to complete an endless string of worksheets with only one recess break in a full-day program. They are told there is no time for play, as there is too much curriculum to complete. Young children learn best through hands-on, real-life experiences that completely engage them. Since NCLB's inception, such practices have been swept aside like yesterday's news in favor of rote memorization of facts and figures that is supposed to ensure that our five- and six-year-olds score as proficient on end-of-the-year assessments. (National Education Association 2007, 7–8)[9]

Certain caveats must be borne in mind when discussing the level of state and local compliance with NCLB. NCLB provisions have not been implemented to the extent that ECS ratings suggest. State governments may have adopted the legal apparatus full implementation requires, but the size of state education bureaucracies has meant that monitoring every aspect of NCLB is difficult if not impossible. Perhaps as a result, states have used what flexibility NCLB gives to construct benchmarks for phenomena such as student progress and teacher subject mastery that are lower than some observers would like (Carey 2006).[10] Yet the fact that states lack the capacity fully to implement a huge federal program a scant five years after its implementation seems less relevant to the questions central to this book than the fact that states are following federal guidelines to the best of their abilities. Where implementation is at least somewhat of a choice and not an impossibility as a consequence of insufficient capacity, it is proceeding as quickly and thoroughly as possible. Nor do the data presented here imply that states and districts are completely passive in shaping the regulations they will follow. Through elected representatives and professional organizations, states are agitating for favorable changes to the most burdensome provisions in the 2007 reauthorization, have pursued waivers regarding particular provisions, and have introduced state legislative bills challenging NCLB. These efforts do not change the high level of implementation of NCLB as it currently exists. When the federal government has denied waiver requests, state and local governments, with very few exceptions, have complied.

Why Compliance?

NCLB is a burdensome federal law that has outraged numerous state officials, teachers, and other educational professionals, but it is clearly and dramatically changing how states, districts, and individual classrooms treat public education. Very few states and districts have opted out, and the vast majority of its provisions are being implemented. As the resistance that has developed suggests, this high level of compliance is not a given, because the federal government has not technically required that all states must adopt NCLB. So why has NCLB been so faithfully implemented? There are three possible answers to this question, and they help to complete our picture of the Piper Link and the relationship between money and control in education policy.

Possibility 1: They Are Not Coerced

The first possibility is that the high level of implementation for NCLB's provisions does not mean that the federal government has coerced state governments, school districts, and individual schools into accepting something they oppose. State and local governments may feel neutral toward certain parts of NCLB and have no strong reason to oppose them. Some provisions extend the philosophy of existing state-level reforms. The federal government's traditionally secondary role in education means that it would not have been able to accomplish its education policy goals on its own. Instead, it had to utilize the accountability systems states had already developed. State officials may chafe at the scope and stringency of NCLB's requirements but support its philosophy and basic approach, so to regard federal-state relations surrounding NCLB as strictly adversarial is a mistake (McDonnell 2005; Manna 2006).

Decentralized-level actors may even welcome some provisions that enable certain actions. This hypothesis mirrors the suggestion of former Vermont principal Peter Mello (chapter 4) that centralized-level action may enable decentralized-level actors to do things they support but cannot do without prompting and/or the political cover the centralized level can provide. Decentralized-level officials can then claim that they are simply doing what the federal government requires. For example, state and local decision makers may want all of their teachers to meet NCLB's HQT provisions, but this requirement would force all teachers to be certified and receive further education to demonstrate mastery of pedagogy and subject matter. Under most collective bargaining agreements, school districts are required to pay certified teachers more than uncertified teachers, and additional coursework may trigger mandatory salary raises. Taxes in the district would go up, and school board members might find themselves booted out of office and vilified, particularly in poor areas where tax increases hit the hardest. With the federal government demanding such qualifications, however, state and local governments can blame any tax increases on Washington while still implementing a regulation they feel will help children.

The furor surrounding NCLB suggests that this logic has extremely limited utility in explaining compliance, particularly at the local level. Some local actors support NCLB, but their support is public, and they are in a definite minority. The vast majority of local actors' statements show deep, vehement resentment of NCLB. One survey found that 66 percent of districts believe the HQT requirement has little or no effect on student learning and that 75 percent believe it has little to no effect on teacher quality, yet a sizable majority of local districts are still implementing it (McMurrer 2007b). At the state level, officials could be talking out of both sides of their mouths. To appease teachers, suburban residents, and other key constituencies, officials may publicly renounce NCLB but secretly support the law's goals and means of promoting universal achievement. Opposition from most state officials is so passionate that this idea seems implausible. If Senator Schroeder and others secretly supported NCLB, they might choose to criticize it with less incendiary language. One cannot rule out the possibility that a few local and state officials support

NCLB's goals and are happy to implement them, but to attribute more than a small amount of the high level of compliance to state and local indifference or support for its provisions would be a mistake.

Possibility 2: Nonfinancial Mechanisms

Political scientists have identified several nonfinancial mechanisms by which the federal government seeks to influence state and local policy. From the 1970s onward, the federal government has sought to influence state and local policy less through funding mechanisms such as grants-in-aid and more through un- and underfunded regulations, even though this strategy can put significant strain on decentralized-level officials. John Kincaid (1990) and others have labeled this approach "coercive federalism," and it has proven effective in compelling decentralized levels to follow regulations because such officials face a daunting array of factors that promote compliance with the regulations even when little or no money accompanies them.

The first nonfinancial mechanism that may promote state and local compliance with federal regulations is the overlapping nature of interest groups at the state and federal levels. Regulations enacted at the federal level have gained acceptance from either Congress or bureaucracies such as the DOE, suggesting that powerful interest groups, many of which have lobbying presences in state capitols, want to see these regulations implemented. Any state or local government that wants to buck a federal regulation must contend with the mobilization of such groups. These political dynamics have functioned within states to facilitate NCLB implementation. Both major political parties share their governing philosophy across intergovernmental lines, so the bipartisan consensus behind NCLB at the federal level extends at least somewhat to state officials, most of whom embrace the idea of accountability through standards and testing. The history of the standards movement in individual states also means that interest groups that support this approach are already active in many states and are ready to mobilize in favor of NCLB.

Perhaps NCLB's most important allies are organizations that represent poor and minority students. At the local level, some of NCLB's strongest supporters have been urban principals and superintendents who believe that NCLB's insistence on subgroup progress will force the nation to acknowledge the monumental challenge of educating poor and minority students and eventually force centralized levels to commit the effort and resources necessary to bring these students up to proficiency. The Education Trust, an organization dedicated to universal student achievement and to narrowing the achievement gap, authored a letter to the U.S. Congress signed by approximately one hundred black and Hispanic superintendents in support of NCLB's efforts to provide "information about the achievement of low-income and minority students in every school. Where large problems are plainly evident, schools, districts, and states must take steps to improve" (2003, 1). Numerous minority interest groups have pressured state governments fully to implement NCLB. In Connecticut, the National Association for the Advancement of Colored People has sided with the federal government and argued that the state's lawsuit against NCLB is rooted in fears that extensive testing will show that the state is failing to educate African American children. In Utah, Robert Gallegos, president of the Raza Political Action Committee, wrote that his organization "did not support Utah's wanting to disregard the law's accountability system in favor of Utah's own system, which is one of the weakest in the country" (Davis and Archer 2005, 4). Blacks and Hispanics generally support NCLB more than whites do, which may bring further pressure to bear on state governments (Phi Delta Kappan and the Gallup Organization 2006).

NCLB's allies have allowed it partially to overcome the powerful interests that usually dominate education politics at the state level. In the past, because of teacher union resources and the presumption that no one better understands what kids need than those who teach them, education professionals have enjoyed a preeminent role in determining which state education policy proposals get adopted. Were this the case with NCLB, the NEA's steadfast opposition would surely have doomed the provisions of which it disapproves. The support for NCLB's basic approach among both parties means that groups that oppose it, including the NEA, may find state government support for strong challenges to the law fleeting and tepid at best. Minority groups' support brings political pressure on states to implement NCLB, helps legitimize the law's approach to school improvement, and means that the community of mainstream educators can no longer claim exclusive ownership of the moral high ground. When NCLB receives support from so many of the groups that public education has underserved, unions have a much harder time arguing that NCLB is not a sincere attempt at achieving universal student proficiency.

A second factor that has hindered decentralized levels' ability to slow NCLB implementation is the diminishing importance of constitutional safeguards against regulation in federal court decisions. While the Tenth Amendment of the Constitution reserves all powers not explicitly delegated to the federal government for the states, decisions of the past thirty years have almost always allowed the federal government complete freedom from any limits on its ability to regulate. This greater leeway stems from the increased federal use of conditional grants mandating that decentralized levels adopt certain policies in exchange for federal funding. Judges have ruled that states can reject the money if the conditions are too burdensome, making conditional grants a voluntary program for which the federal government can impose almost any terms. That most states could not reject federal grants and maintain comparable levels of service has not deterred judges from allowing conditions to stand (McDermott and Jensen 2005).

The Constitution does not enumerate public education as one of the federal government's areas of concern, which courts could interpret to mean that the governance of public education is reserved for the states. Yet most decisions of the past twenty-five years have allowed federal regulation of public education to grow. Any judicial barriers against federal action in public education have long since eroded, and today's legal system works in favor of the federal government in most disputes with state and local governments.[11] This trend has held in the two major lawsuits against NCLB. In 2005, a Michigan federal district court rejected the NEA coalition's claim that NCLB violated its own statutory language prohibiting any provision of NCLB from becoming an unfunded mandate and dismissed *Pontiac v. Spellings*.[12] In 2006, a federal court in Connecticut dismissed three of the four claims in the state's lawsuit against the DOE, claiming that the court lacks jurisdiction to hear the claims. Federal judges have also dismissed both local suits against the federal government. The lack of judicial support for the few NCLB cases that have been filed should deter future cases, meaning that states and districts wishing to challenge NCLB or slow implementation largely cannot use this avenue to air their grievances.

While internal state political dynamics and legal support for NCLB have helped speed NCLB implementation, they cannot fully explain the rapid compliance. Opponents of NCLB still have a wide variety of viable partners that can bring the resources and moral authority necessary to challenge it. For the former, NCLB opponents can look to the NEA, which has been willing to bankroll challenges and tireless in its lobbying efforts to modify NCLB. For the latter, the majority of the ground-level educators oppose NCLB, providing powerful testimony to the extreme stress NCLB has placed on schools. Likewise, the inhospitable climate for legal challenges to NCLB has not stopped all legal and legislative challenges from arising, showing that they are at least possible. Those charged with implementing NCLB have not cited pressure from interest groups or an inhospitable legal climate as the reasons for high compliance. Almost without exception, these people identify fear of loss of federal funding as the critical mechanism driving implementation.

Possibility 3: The Effect of Money

In the 2004–5 school year, the federal government contributed $54 billion to public education. If states or school districts fail to comply with NCLB, the DOE has threatened to withhold Title I funding, block grants to states for school improvement, and school assistance for federally affected areas. In 2004–5, these three categories of aid accounted for approximately $20.5 billion of federal education spending. Of these three categories, Title I, which distributes funding to schools and districts that serve low-income students, is the largest at $13.6 billion (National Center for Education Statistics 2007, table 361). Title I funding follows students in poverty rather than going directly to the most impoverished schools, which means that even schools with relatively small impoverished populations can receive Title I funding. In the 2003–4 year, 50 percent of the nation's schools received Title I funding (U.S. Department of Education 2006). The last two columns of table 7.1 show the percentage of each state's school spending that comes from federal funding and Title I. On average, each state receives 9.3 percent of its funds from the federal government, with a high of 17.7 in Alaska and a low of 4.3 in New Jersey. Title I funding makes up a much smaller percentage of the total K–12 public education burden. On average, states receive 3.2 percent of their K–12 public education funding from Title I, with a high of 5.6 percent in Louisiana and a low of 1.4 percent in Minnesota.

In the past, Title I funding came with few strings attached, allowing districts to fund technical assistance, in-service training, coordinating services, and almost any other program that they could argue benefited disadvantaged students. Districts often used Title I funding to craft programs designed to help the entire student body, not just impoverished populations. "An associate superintendent once told me that the reason she liked Title I so much was that she didn't have to do anything to get it"

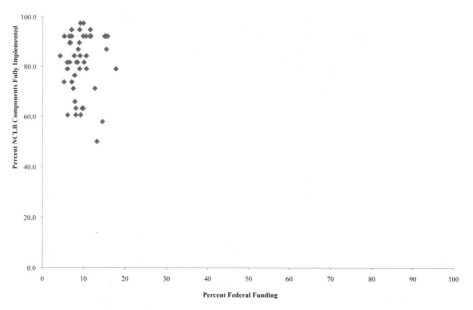

Fig. 7.1. Percentage federal funding and percentage NCLB components fully implemented by state

(McClure 2004). NCLB has eliminated much of this freedom. The night after President Bush signed it into law, secretary of education Roderick Paige met with thirty state education chiefs, intimated that he would not grant waivers regarding any of the measure's provisions, and threatened to withhold federal funds for noncompliance. "States that fail to comply with the law risk losing those record federal investments in their states and in their children," said DOE spokesman Dan Langan. "We would hope that states wouldn't jeopardize their funding" (Prah 2003). This position put states and school districts, which had come to depend on Title I funding to make their budgets work, in a position where ignoring NCLB would force them to cut back services.

Figures 7.1 and 7.2 plot each state in terms of the percentage of its total education funding received from the federal government (figure 7.1) and from Title I (figure 7.2) and the percentage of NCLB components with which it has fully complied according to ECS. Figure 7.1 shows that states are complying with NCLB at an extremely high level despite receiving federal funding that makes up a very small part of the total

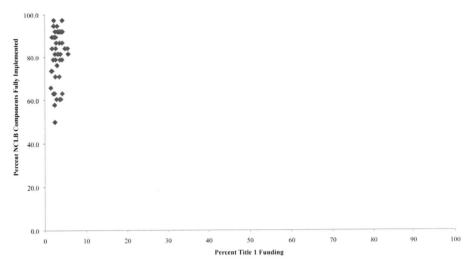

Fig. 7.2.   Percentage Title I of total funding and percentage NCLB components fully implemented by state

school funding. Figure 7.2 shows that state compliance is high even though Title I funding, which represents the bulk of the money NCLB noncompliance endangers, is such a small part of the total. Whichever measure of jeopardized funding one prefers, the federal government clearly has accomplished its goals very effectively while contributing a disproportionately small share of the funding. These data imply that the relatively small funding share the federal government provides has had a strong causal effect in compelling state NCLB compliance and deterring resistance.

In explaining their compliance with the unpopular law, officials have cited the fear of funding loss far more than any other reason. In most cases, the threat has forced states to avoid strong formal challenges against NCLB, as in Utah and Connecticut. Instead, states have either passed far less confrontational resolutions asking the federal government to reconsider some provisions or abandoned legislative and legal challenges altogether. Mathis estimates that twenty-five states have considered opting out of NCLB but declined to do so because of concerns about loss of federal funding. Fearing the loss of more than half a billion dollars, Arizona refused to allow school districts to opt out. State senator Barbara Leff is no supporter of NCLB but looks at the issue pragmatically:

I don't think it's a question of whether No Child Left Behind is a good thing. The question is whether we jeopardize federal dollars by [refusing to comply]. If you want to send a message, we do a postcard. If we do a bill and we jeopardize all of our federal money, that's not doing a service to anyone. (Biscobing 2007)

The threat of lost funding has forced even the states most willing to challenge NCLB to limit the scope of their efforts. Utah's law stating that it would follow its own student accountability system wherever it conflicted with NCLB is much milder in its language and goals than the bill originally introduced, which called for a full boycott of NCLB. State representative Margaret Dayton, who introduced the original bill and is widely credited as one of the driving forces behind Utah's resistance, endorsed the weaker bill: "I still think opting out is worthy of a serious discussion. But we also have to deal with the reality of the lack of support when it comes to losing $106 million—even though that's such a small percentage of our education budget" (Lynn 2005, A1). In 2003–4, Utah's total funding for K–12 public education topped $3 billion, meaning that Utah scaled back its challenge as a result of the perception that it might forfeit 3.5 percent of its total school funding. In 2005, Connecticut education commissioner Betty J. Sternberg claimed that she would defy NCLB's accountability provisions, an important step in the state's eventual decision to sue the federal government, but she ultimately decided that completely opting out of NCLB was not feasible because of the $109 million in annual federal subsidies the state could lose (Dobbs 2005, A10). In 2003–4, Connecticut spent $7.4 billion on K–12 public education. One of the reasons that Connecticut, Colorado, Maine, and Utah may have been willing to push their challenges as far as they have is because Title I funding makes up 1.7, 2.2, 2.1, and 2.2 percent of their respective total education funds, significantly less than the national average of 3.2 percent.[13] While these states are not willing to do very much that would jeopardize Title I funding, they are generally willing to do more than states that rely more heavily on Title I.[14]

At the local level, the story is the same. School districts refrain from challenging the law because of the threat of lost federal funding, even though the funding at risk makes up a very small percentage of their total budget. A study by the state of Minnesota found that despite overwhelming sentiment that NCLB was "costly, unrealistic, and punitive," fewer than 20 percent of the state's superintendents favored opting out of

NCLB for fear of losing the state's $216 million in federal funding, most of which eventually found its way to the local level (Minnesota 2004). California's Santa Cruz City School District rejected a proposal to opt out of certain NCLB requirements as a result of fears that doing so would endanger its $1.2 million annual Title I grant even though the district's total budget for the 2006–7 school year was about $60 million (King 2006). The fear of the loss of funding runs strongest in less affluent school districts, which serve the largest populations of Title I students and therefore stand to lose a higher percentage of their total funding. Because federal funding financed full-day kindergarten at twenty area elementary schools, educators in the Reno area strongly opposed Nevada's efforts to withdraw from NCLB. Principal Patricia Casarez said, "If we were to opt out of federal money, it would probably be a big mistake. This is how at-risk schools survive. If you pull away the federal money, that's just unthinkable" (Hagar 2005, A1).

Only eight school districts have opted out of NCLB. Table 7.2 describes each of these districts, their total 2005–6 educational budgets, their total federal funding, their total Title I funding, the percentage of their total budgets that come from federal and Title I funding, and their median incomes. All of these districts depend on federal and Title I funding far less than the average school district, with Title I funding making up 1.1 percent or less of the total budget. For districts that rely so little on federal funding, the increased testing and reporting requirements may exceed the funding jeopardized or at least approach a break-even point, allowing districts to regard opting out as a feasible strategy. Such is not the case in Santa Cruz or the vast majority of the nation's school districts, where although NCLB adds new costs to the school system, the total Title I and other federal appropriations at risk through noncompliance outweigh these new costs. Seven of the eight districts have median household incomes well above the national average. Such affluence may make these districts more confident in their ability to absorb and offset losses of federal funding. As discussed in chapter 4, affluent districts can raise large amounts of school funding with relatively low tax rates. Board members in the seven wealthy districts opting out of NCLB may have believed that district voters would accept slight increases in their low tax rates to retain control of the areas in which NCLB sets policy. Of course, raising taxes as a consequence of refusing to accept funding from other sources is a very tough sell for elected representatives, regardless of how low tax rates are or how small a percentage of the total budget is involved. This rationale explains why very few affluent districts have opted out of NCLB and why officials in the rebellious districts are not sure how long they will continue their challenges. The vice chair of the Arlington, Virginia, school board admits that the threat of lost federal funding may make the district's challenge temporary: the DOE has "got the hammer, and they've got the big stick. I suppose they can force these districts to bend to their will" (Glod 2007, B1).

Legal action offers another potential avenue for states and localities to challenge NCLB, but to date only four lawsuits have been filed against the federal government. Because lawsuits take significant money, it is not surprising that no districts have filed independent lawsuits against an opponent with far superior resources and a determination to get its way. Without a strong sponsor such as the NEA to offset the resource imbalance, a legal challenge must seem almost impossible. In addition, any state pursuing a lawsuit will also have to answer voters' questions about why money that could be spent on children is being spent on a lawsuit.

In summary, federal funding is the key reason why states and school districts comply with NCLB. Decentralized levels are implementing

TABLE 7.2. Characteristics of School Districts Opting out of NCLB

School District	Total Educational Revenue ($)	Total Federal Revenue ($)	Percentage Federally Funded	Total Title I ($)	Percentage Title I of Total Revenue	Median Household Income
Arlington (VA)	325,607,000	13,882,000	4.2	2,704,360	0.8	63,001
Cheshire (CN)	56,844,000	828,000	1.5	79,600	0.1	80,466
Consolidated High School District 230 (IL)	106,737,000	1,835,000	1.7	145,297	0.1	63,183
Fairfax (VA)	1,893,101,000	72,613,000	3.4	9,000,000	0.0	81,050
Kit Carson (CO)	2,075,000	44,000	2.1	22,638	1.1	29,000
Marlborough (CN)	8,422,000	117,000	1.4	8,000	0.0	80,265
Somers (CN)	18,140,000	312,000	1.7	43,000	0.2	65,273
Township High School District 211 (IL)	179,048,000	2,703,000	1.5	296,856	0.2	63,627
National K–12 (in thousands)	440,157,299	37,515,909	8.5	13,566,485	3.0	41,994

Source: For columns 2 and 3, National Center for Education Statistics, *Common Core of Data.* Data accurate for the 2004–5 school year. For column 5, state Department of Education Web sites. Data accurate for the 2004–5 school year. For column 6, U.S. Census Bureau, School District Demographic System, Table P53. Data reflects median household income for 1999.

NCLB at very high rates and citing fears of loss of funding as their reason for doing so, even though the share of the total school finance burden that noncompliance endangers is very low. While decentralized-level actors may implement some provisions because they approve of or are neutral toward them and nonfinancial mechanisms are pushing them toward compliance, fear of a loss of a small portion of the total education funding appears to be the strongest weapon in the federal compliance arsenal.

Implications for the Piper Link

There is good reason to believe that money's role in ensuring NCLB compliance represents a general trend in which a small amount of the total funding burden is enough to ensure decentralized-level compliance with centralized-level education regulation. The consensus within the education community is that special education is a remarkably costly program that the federal government does not adequately fund but that local school districts feel they have no choice but to implement (Hochschild and Scovronick 2003). Despite the disproportionate share of the budget these regulations consume, and even though the federal government contributes significantly less than its statutes require, these elites implement these regulations to the best of their ability. Such regulations are not *un*funded. The centralized levels do not provide adequate money to implement these measures but provide enough that decentralized levels will suffer should they opt not to implement the mandate. Decentralized levels build centralized-level funding into their budgets and thus feel unable to turn down the money.

School desegregation may be the most notable example of the role a small amount of funding can play in ensuring compliance with ambitious regulations. As chapter 6 describes in greater detail, the original ESEA of 1965 offered significant new federal funding to school districts, and its authors designed it so that school districts in the South would receive a disproportionate amount. The catch was that any district accepting these funds needed to enact aggressive desegregation plans. Strictly in terms of integrating schools, the federal government achieved its goals quickly and impressively. In 1968, 77.8 percent of black students in the South attended schools where the total population was made up of 90–100 percent minority students. By 1972, that figure had dropped to 24.7 percent (Hochschild 1984). The federal courts' and bureaucracy's support for desegregation certainly played a role in this achievement, but most studies attribute a major role to southern school districts' desire to partake in the new funding (Orfield 1969; Clotfelter 2004). In absolute terms, the funding increases were significant. In 1965, the federal government contributed $1.9 billion to K–12 education. By 1970, that amount had more than tripled to $5.8 billion. Yet in relative terms, the size of the federal share increased only from 4.4 percent for the 1963–64 school year to 8.4 percent in 1970–71 (National Center for Education Statistics 2007, tables 162, 360). It seems safe to assume that the size of the federal contribution needed to ensure compliance with school desegregation falls in that range. If ever a small amount of funding would not force compliance with centralized-level regulation, desegregation would be the issue. It is hard to imagine another contemporary U.S. domestic issue that would arouse nearly the level of passionate resistance generated by school desegregation, which challenged the entire southern way of life. If less than 10 percent of the total funding share is enough to play a major role in ensuring compliance with desegregation, a smaller share should be sufficient to ensure compliance with even the most ambitious and controversial contemporary centralized-level regulations.

Federal power over state governments and local school districts with NCLB and the effectiveness of other underfunded regulations in compelling decentralized-level compliance show that centralized levels can gain tremendous control over public education with very small amounts of money. Particularly at the local level, officials face tight budget constraints. Affluent interests' ability to move with little effort if tax rates become too high places significant constraints on the amount of revenue local governments can generate (Peterson 1981). To a lesser extent, the same dynamic holds true for state governments, which may drive out businesses by levying high taxes. If decentralized levels seek to offer anything more than skeletal services, they must accept any centralized-level funding offered, regardless of the strings attached. Public opinion dynamics also push decentralized-level officials toward accepting grants despite the attached conditions. Refusing funds means answering to a public likely to be angry that real dollars that could help children were rejected in favor of an abstraction called autonomy. Finally, many of these officials have dedicated a significant amount of their lives to helping children through autonomy and may not want to turn down the money. However cumbersome centralized-level conditions can be, they are usually well-intentioned. As resentful as decentralized-level officials might be, they might believe they have a duty to implement potentially useful programs.

Because compliance, control, and most of the other key concepts relevant to the Piper Link are very difficult to measure, it is not possible to specify exactly what percentage of the total finance burden a centralized level must contribute to get exactly, say, 81 percent control; we can speak only of "greater," "less," and "almost complete" control. Many different aspects of decentralized-level autonomy exist, and it is reasonable to hypothesize that the federal government's small contribution gives it more control over the areas that NCLB regulates (for example, curriculum, evaluation, and teacher certification) than over, say, local and state school tax rates. Because of these challenges, it is not possible to determine the exact level of funding needed to gain the level of control the federal government has exercised with NCLB, but it is almost certainly less than the 8.5 percent the federal government contributed to total education spending in the 2002–3 school year, since NCLB noncompliance did not jeopardize all or even most of that funding.

The amount of control gained with relatively small contributions explains the findings of chapters 3 and 4 that show increases of state finance share from 20 to 90 percent yield no appreciable gains in state control and why the Vermont elites felt that state control was equally extensive before and after finance reform. States that contribute the highest relative share of school funding have no more leverage to mandate that their districts adopt education reform than do states with the smallest relative share, because even a share of 20 percent of the total funding is much more than a state government would need to expect faithful implementation of almost any regulation. Schools in Vermont were just as dependent on the 29 percent of the total education funding the state provided prior to Act 60 as they were on the 75 percent of the total the state provided after the act's implementation. Because centralized levels gain so much control while contributing such a relatively small part of the total financing of a project, they cannot gain much more with additional increases.

To return to the two visual representations of the Piper Link presented in chapter 3, the evidence this book presents overwhelmingly suggests that the curved model better captures the true causal effect of centralized-level finance share on centralized-level control of other aspects of a policy and decentralized-level autonomy. Figures 7.1 and 7.2, showing compliance with NCLB as a function of the federal contribution to each state's finance share, suggest almost exactly the same steep gain in control in the first small contributions to the funding burden above zero that figure 7.3 hypothesizes. With so much control gained with such small contribu-

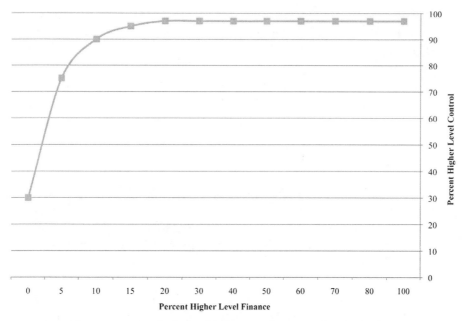

Fig. 7.3.   A curved relationship between finance and control redux

tions, greater contributions will inevitably yield gains in control of rapidly decreasing size.

Thus, no control is at stake in school finance reform battles because the critical threshold is much lower than 20 percent, which is the contribution state governments make even in states with the most decentralized finance systems. Once this threshold is passed, the centralized level simply cannot gain much more control by assuming a greater share of the school finance burden. States can move within the 20–90 range to further equity goals without affecting local control in the least, and if reestablishing local control is the goal, states would be far better served by reducing or fully funding regulation. State governments have contributed more than 15 percent of the total U.S. K–12 public education funding since the DOE began keeping records in the 1919–20 school year (National Center for Education Statistics 2007, table 162). No one believes state funding will ever again drop to such low levels, let alone dip to the point where states would lose the ability to compel compliance with regulations. No change in the state share of school funding will ever compromise what is left of local educational control.

CHAPTER EIGHT

Brave New World

Local Control and the Future of American Education

THIS BOOK'S CENTRAL QUESTION has been whether funding from state and federal governments disrupts local educational control in the United States. The evidence presented suggests that the Piper Link functions but does not follow a simple "money equals control" formula. Relatively small contributions to the total funding burden give state and federal governments a tremendous amount of leverage and allow them to compel local government obedience to most regulations. As the centralized level's share of the total funding burden increases, it provides diminishing returns in terms of the control because centralized levels gain so much control with contributions of less than 10 percent of the total funding. The best simple expression of the Piper Link is that a little money equals a lot of control, and a lot of money does not increase the amount of control much if at all. To conclude, this book will consider what the evidence in total suggests about school finance reform, No Child Left Behind (NCLB), and the future of intergovernmental relations.

School Finance Reform: A Green Light

State governments' most common reform strategy to achieve a more equitable distribution of resources has been to increase their share of the school finance burden, allowing for an easier redistribution of funds across district lines. All of the evidence in this book suggests that states may pursue this strategy free of concerns that this approach will compromise local autonomy. Current state contributions to the total spent on public education range roughly from 20 to 90 percent, and the possibility that a state contribution will sink lower than 20 percent is minute. This book finds that because a 20 percent contribution is much more than enough for state governments to expect compliance with almost any regulation, no difference exists between the amount of control a state can exert at any point in the 20–90 spectrum. The only appreciable loss of local control this work finds is the loss of more affluent districts' ability to spend above the rest of the state's districts, but Michigan's school finance reform under Governor John Engler shows that even that problem can be ameliorated or eliminated. Moreover, finance reform will have no effect on local educational governing institutions' ability to deliver the results participatory democrats might desire, from increased accountability and citizen participation to policy more tailored to meet local conditions.

While finance reform does not harm local control, the public thinks it will, which accounts for finance reform's power in rallying opposition. How much this opposition truly stems from a love of "local control" and how much of it stems from some local control's less democratic side effects is very debatable. As chapter 5 shows, the public both supports regulations such as standardized testing that centralize important educational decisions and is indifferent to how finance reform will affect local school governments' ability to deliver on their democratic potential. These results suggest that people care less about local control and more about preserving a system that allows the more affluent to fund their children's education at a high level without paying the taxes necessary to ensure that all children have similar resources available for their education.

Stated in this way, affinity for local control seems less a matter of principle and more a rationalization of power politics, but it is possible to make a strong ethical defense based on this rationale. Samuel Adams did not throw tea into Boston Harbor because he thought England did not distribute its taxes equitably, and Patrick Henry did not say, "Give me equity or give me death!" The right of U.S. citizens to economic liberty—to reap the rewards of their individual efforts without the government taking an unfair share—is one of the country's most lasting and cherished ideals. Of course, so is equality. As countless policy debates since the country's founding have shown, these ideals are sometimes hard to reconcile, and school finance reform evidences these tensions. Reformers on all sides need to be honest that these ideals are at stake in reform debates. Reform opponents should build their case using arguments about personal liberty and avoid resorting to scare tactics that make parents worry about losing all influence on their local schools and their children's education. Doing so will allow the public to make decisions about the distribution of billions of dollars with an understanding of the real stakes at hand.

NCLB and Underfunded Regulations: The Real Problem

Instead of school finance reform, those who are concerned about the Piper Link's real and pernicious effects on local education governance should focus on the effects of underfunded state and federal regulations. The results presented in chapters 6 and 7 show that the real link between centralization of finance and local autonomy is created when centralized levels of government increase their funding share from 0 to some small percentage of the total burden. Local governments are constrained in their ability to raise funds, and local officials are likely to face significant public outrage for rejecting any funding available for their district's children. Thus, state and federal governments can contribute a very small share of a program's funding and expect local officials to try fully to comply with any regulation.

Consciously or not, state and federal officials have exploited this dynamic since the middle of the twentieth century, regulating education without providing funding sufficient to cover the cost of implementation. This practice forces local governments to divert funds toward implementing regulations and therefore greatly hampers localities' ability to undertake independent policy proposals. Of course, the regulations themselves also greatly curtail local autonomy. Federal special education regulations and school desegregation orders dictate that districts treat certain students a certain way. State curricular standards and standardized testing, especially in the NCLB era, demand that certain concepts be emphasized in the classroom. State teacher certification requirements determine whom schools can hire for classroom instruction. And so on. All of these programs dictate specific requirements that curtail local actors' options. All do more far more to curtail local autonomy than does funding from centralized levels of government that comes with no conditions attached.

The Piper Link Outside of Education

Further research is needed to answer definitively the question of whether the findings presented here apply to policies outside of education, but the existing literature on federalism and state and local politics suggests that the dynamics of the Piper Link function similarly across a wide spectrum of issues for local governments' relationship with the state and federal levels and the states' relationship with the federal government. Because they face significant constraints on their ability to raise revenue, state and especially local governments rely on higher-level funding to provide the level of service constituents expect. Localities may not be able to replace even relatively small funding losses, and turning down money that pays for tangible programs in favor of an ideal such as autonomy figures to anger the public. Thus, higher levels may be able to use relatively small funding contributions to compel lower-level compliance. When stated in its most basic form, the version of the Piper Link this book promotes sounds like it should hold for nearly all intergovernmental situations.

At first glance, significant developments in intergovernmental relations in the latter half of the 2000s appear to exhibit this relationship between money and control. Chapter 1 describes how several Republican governors threatened to refuse funding from the 2009 federal stimulus package, which came with a laundry list of conditions on how it could be spent that the reticent governors feared would expand their costs beyond the monies that the stimulus provided. One of the main areas of contention was the condition that states expand unemployment eligibility requirements. Governors feared that after the stimulus money was spent, their states would be left with much larger unemployment rolls that the federal government would not continue to help fund. To get any of the stimulus's roughly $100 billion earmarked for education, state and local governments had to agree to "assurances" that demanded increases in the difficulty of standardized tests and commitment to ensuring that effective teachers were distributed evenly across school districts of different socioeconomic strata. A spokeswoman for the House education committee said, "This couldn't just be free money. We had to get something in return" (Dillon 2009, A12). Some went so far as to label the stimulus as a Democratic "tool for rewriting the social contract with the poor, the uninsured, and the unemployed, in ways they have long yearned to do" (Pear 2009, A1).

States and localities eventually accepted and even competed vigorously for this money.[1] Given the huge amounts at stake, this acceptance should have been expected. What is notable is how little money the governors who railed against the stimulus refused. Governor Bobby Jindal of Louisiana warned that after federal funding for expanded unemployment benefits ran out, "our businesses would then be stuck paying the bill. We must be careful and thoughtful as we examine all the strings attached to the funding in this package" (Burns 2009). Jindal ultimately accepted all but $98 million of the $3.8 billion offered to Louisiana, meaning that he rejected roughly 2.6 percent of the total (Moller 2009). Alaska governor Sarah Palin indicated that she would reject $288 million of the $930.7 million allocated to her state, saying that "we are not requesting funds intended to just grow government. In essence we say no to operating funds for more positions in government. To me it's a bribe" (Cockerham 2009, A1). Faced with significant opposition, especially from an education community angered by her proposed rejection of $172 million for schools, Palin changed her mind three days later and ended up rejecting only $28 million, or 3 percent of the total. Even that fraction of the total caused the Alaska Legislature to consider using a provision in the stimulus legislation to override her rejection (Holland, Hopkins, and Komarnitsky 2009). Texas governor Rick Perry made passing references to the possibility of secession over the stimulus but eventually accepted all but $555 million (3.3 percent) of the $17 billion available to his state (Hoppe and Garrett 2009).

These percentages closely resemble the percentage of total education funding the states and school districts that threatened to opt out of NCLB endangered (chapter 7). In retrospect, that even six governors threatened to refuse stimulus funding is surprising, given the predictable and almost universal criticism they faced in their states and the deficits facing states as a result of the recession in the late 2000s. At the end of the day, the governors could do little more than reject a small percentage of their stimulus dollars to save face. Many regarded their resistance as political posturing among Republicans seeking to position themselves for their party's 2012 presidential nomination, but all of them arguably deserve credit for at least trying to inject federalism concerns into a debate of such immediacy.[2] Ultimately, however, the dynamics of the Piper Link seem to have forced them into actions in conflict with their initial reactions. The pattern of the responses shows that the dynamics of the curved Piper Link this book posits seem to play out in other policy areas, although proving this contention requires far more extensive study.

Should the Piper Link Work?

Policymakers should take a long look at how much they follow the dynamics of the Piper Link and try to avoid doing so in the future. To truly Machiavellian higher-level officials, the Piper Link may seem an invitation to try to have the best of both worlds. Officials can mandate that lower levels undertake certain actions but provide little money to do so. The lower levels will protect even small funding streams through diligent compliance, and higher-level officials can avoid passing unpopular taxes designed to fund these programs while still claiming credit for legislative "successes."

This calculus ignores the long-term ramifications of such crass thinking. Setting unrealistic requirements for those charged with implementing programs is a way to guarantee their failure. Even if higher-level politicians are not punished at the ballot box for exploiting the Piper Link, they still have to sleep at night. The United States faces serious problems that require government actions undertaken in good faith and with the potential to make a real difference. Because high local and state taxes can drive tax bases to other localities, decentralized levels must cap their tax rates and probably cannot raise enough funding on their own to comply with ambitious federal regulations at the levels needed to ensure this success (Peterson 1995). The need to balance budgets annually makes the fund-raising constraints on state and local governments even more cumbersome.

Nowhere is the ethical imperative for higher levels adequately to fund programs more pressing or apparent than in public education. Whereas other developed nations provide a system of social welfare services that includes relatively generous health care, unemployment, and basic income programs, the United States relies on schools to provide poor children with the tools to become upwardly mobile in what is supposed to be a meritocratic society. In a very real way, the U.S. claim to being a just society rests on its public education system (Hochschild and Scovronick 2003). Setting aside, if only for a moment, practical concerns about individual programs, no one can disagree with NCLB's fundamental goal of providing poor children with the essentials necessary to achieve a decent life. If federal policymakers truly think that NCLB is the best strategy to help all students achieve, they have a responsibility to raise the funds necessary to ensure its success. By all accounts outside of the Bush administration, the federal government is not doing so. State and local governments have shown that they will implement to the full extent of their ability to avoid losing the small amount of money at risk, but their legal compliance has masked the tremendous strain NCLB has placed on lower levels. Local schools and school boards have been unable to provide NCLB's mandated services at the required levels. Whether the Obama administration and Congress continue to support NCLB or embark on another course, the logic is the same. If the federal government is to continue its expanded role in public education and demand that state and local governments set ambitious goals, it must provide the resources necessary to achieve them.

Can Local Control Be Revitalized?

The findings in this book also point toward strategies that could revive localities as strong intergovernmental partners capable of autonomous decisions. Perhaps the most obvious recommendation is that at least in one policy area, local governments need more money with fewer strings attached. Local school officials face a host of federal and state regulations with only the flimsiest pretense of being fully funded but are not in a position to turn down any funding stream. Declining even small amounts of federal or state funding could very well lead schools to have to sacrifice educational necessities such as textbooks and writing materials, a disturbing possibility given that many poor schools already struggle to provide such items. Because local officials are unable to adopt a more confrontational stance, the onus is on state and federal governments to undertake reasonable estimates of the cost of their regulations and provide that level of funding. Centralized-level politicians need to resist the temptation to pass legislation without enacting the unpopular tax hikes needed to fund it. Doing so will result in policies more likely to succeed and local governments that have a fighting chance of funding other programs of their own design.

Policymakers at all levels should remember that state regulation and local autonomy need not be a zero-sum game. In Vermont, the state government held regional meetings to solicit ordinary citizens' input into the process of designing curricular standards. In turn, local leaders expressed relief when the state provided challenging but attainable standards to guide instruction. Local officials also felt that the Act 60's action planning process helped reengage citizens in school affairs and gave them a structure that allowed them to make real, important decisions.

Similarly, the Kentucky Education Reform Act of 1991 created school councils of parents, teachers, and administrators that assumed control for a host of decisions previously made at more centralized levels.

To give such bodies as these even more influence, state and federal agencies could use as a model a structure the Environmental Protection Agency (EPA) has employed when considering regulations that disproportionately affect particular localities. Proposed environmental regulations often cause hardships to local manufacturing and therefore hurt the local economy. The balance between a cleaner environment and a thriving local economy is inherently controversial and will affect no one as much as local citizens. When trying to decide such cases, the EPA sometimes invites the public to meetings where both environmental activists and local businesses can present evidence supporting their positions. After the presentation, the EPA solicits the public's recommendations and usually implements programs in keeping with those suggestions (Webler and Tuler 2006). No obvious reason exists why this model could not be applied to education or even expanded so that government agencies educate the public on, for example, the scientific evidence on the theory of evolution but leave the decision about what to teach to local people.

State and federal officials can and should identify these and other ways in which citizens can become more involved in the design and implementation of education policy, even though none of these three proposals fulfills the most ambitious goals of strong local control proponents. Kentucky, Vermont, and the EPA use their small groups as advisory or implementation bodies rather than autonomous decision makers with broad discretionary powers, but something is better than nothing. State and federal regulation has diminished participation in local school politics and left those still participating resentful and neutered; state and federal governments bear some responsibility for reviving participation. By involving local actors more closely in the design of their programs, state and federal governments can take large steps toward both revitalizing ordinary citizen participation and governance and ensuring that regulations make reasonable demands of local actors. Those interested in achieving school finance reform equity should also note that Act 60's accommodations of local control may have helped Vermont's finance reform survive the powerful forces opposing it. Empowering local actors may change opponents to supporters or, more realistically, sap opponents of their certainty that school finance reform packages have no positives, making rallying the kind of venomous opposition seen in states such as New Jersey more difficult.

Should Local Control Be Saved?

Adequately funded regulations and greater citizen involvement in their design can help, but if the United States is serious about reviving the power of local government to rival its place in the American political imagination, regulation must not merely be approached differently. Strong local autonomy demands that local governments make decisions about important issues. Even if fully funded, programs such as NCLB and special education greatly curtail the choices available to local school boards, administrators, and teachers. To have truly powerful local control, local actors need to decide what curriculum to teach, how students with learning disabilities should be treated, and so on. Freed from state and federal regulations, schools may fulfill the dreams democratic theorists attribute to small-scale democracy—adopting innovative practices, adopting curriculum that meets local needs, and having enough meaningful decisions to make people again participate in school governance.

But should the United States want to revive strong local control? Before special education legislation, students with all but the most extreme learning disabilities remained undiagnosed and often did not receive the instruction necessary for an adequate education. Before curricular standards, local superintendents had far less guidance in choosing what to teach. Before state standardized testing, parents' only evidence about the performance of their children's school came from teachers, who had an obvious interest in making schools look good, and the local school board, which, as chapter 6 describes, was usually in a very disadvantageous position to question claims made by teachers and their powerful unions. This book has treated the strength of local autonomy as an empirical relationship worthy of social science study, but on questions of this magnitude, data can take the argument only so far. The question of how much power local government should have is inherently normative.

A national expansion of local autonomy in education governance is significantly more problematic than wanting to bring back the Rockwellian vision of the little red schoolhouse. As chapter 5 shows, local control can trigger opposition to education reforms designed to ameliorate the effects of racial, ethnic, and class divides. The lure of the traditional local school district, though its powers have waned, has proven able to frustrate ambitious reform proposals from both the Left (desegregation and finance reform) and the Right (school choice). A stronger norm of local control might make programs designed to help those children but in conflict with the traditional system even harder to enact.

Local control may also allow illiberal attitudes to gain an undue influence over public education in large parts of the country. Where citizens have complete control, they can engage in classic participatory democracy, ensure that all relevant viewpoints have a chance to be heard, and still choose a science curriculum that teaches that a mad scientist named Yakub genetically engineered white people, as orthodox Nation of Islam doctrine states. Parts of the South may still want to offer decidedly skewed lessons on the "War of Northern Aggression." These examples are extreme, but the threat of local control leading to curriculum chosen for reasons other than its accuracy is very real. Despite the overwhelming consensus among scientists that evolution alone explains the origins of life, 64 percent of respondents to one survey favored teaching biblical creationism alongside evolution (Keeter and Horowitz 2009). Absent the restraining hand of the federal judiciary, much of the country might have already opted to teach the Bible as the scientific equivalent of Darwin. Adults have a right to decide their own affairs, but children have a right to an education that prepares them to achieve their goals. Experts in science, social science, history, pedagogy, and a hundred other scholarly fields may be the most qualified to design curriculum that best readies American students for the challenges of the twenty-first century. This type of expertise figures to flow from some of the world's most elite institutions, including central government bureaucracies and universities. This is undoubtedly a form of centralization. It may also be best for children.

Another potential drawback of strong local control is that it may contribute to the balkanization of the country. Hypothetical parents who lose a battle to include creationism in their school district's science curriculum may indeed vote with their feet and move to a district that has adopted a curriculum more to their liking. Even when concerns about the teaching of incorrect information are set aside, one may wonder how healthy it is to accept a system in which different children learn different things based on where they live. Many observers believe that U.S. public education must provide a common core of knowledge that enables citizens to live together and be part of a vibrant democracy that respects the rights of those whose outlooks on life fundamentally differ (Hochschild and Scovronick 2003). If local governments can choose curriculum without restriction, the common education that every public school student receives may be drastically curtailed at the expense of future generations' ability to unite and participate in a democracy. People already are participating less every year in all aspects of civic life (Putnam 2000). If Americans are increasingly "bowling alone," sacrificing or failing to strengthen the lessons of diversity, social cohesion, and common purpose that centralized school governance facilitates seems dangerous.

Proponents of local control strongly rebut these charges. The belief that elites alone must determine a public education curriculum shows a lack of faith in the everyday citizen that is unbefitting a democracy. Compared to one hundred years ago, overt racial, ethnic, and gender biases have fallen dramatically, and the South need not suffer forever for its Jim Crow crimes before it can be trusted to construct a balanced history curriculum. No parent desires that his or her child receive an education that severely hampers his or her ability to become a happy, productive citizen, so with guidance similar to what the EPA gives, why cannot ordinary citizens weigh evidence and make hard choices about what is to be taught? Through such a process, elites will have their opportunity to present their case for a core of knowledge that all democratic citizens must learn, and it is hard to imagine most parts of the United States rejecting the civics skills that are sure to be part of such a curriculum. The millions of children who attend parochial schools routinely outperform their public school counterparts on civics tests (Peterson and Campbell 2001). In addition, if Americans are bowling alone more often, what the country needs is not a civics education dictated by the state or federal government but the more meaningful opportunities for group interaction that returning more power to local government will provide.

As with all big normative questions, no correct answer exists. People's deepest political beliefs will determine the extent to which they want to revitalize local government or ensure other outcomes more easily achieved through state and federal governments. This book offers the lesson that the United States can make that choice. Powerful forces are pushing the country toward entrusting more and more responsibilities to centralized levels of government, but all evidence suggests that the country can take steps to revitalize local government power. The country is free to centralize funding and decentralize policy-making, or vice versa. In short, the United States still has the ability to get the local control and the federalism of its choosing.

Notes

✳ ✳ ✳

Chapter One

1. I use the terms *local control* and *local autonomy* interchangeably.

2. Nationally, in 2002, rich districts spent $868 more per student than did poor districts (Winter 2004). In Illinois, Missouri, and New York, rich districts spend up to 20 percent more per student (Rothstein 2000).

3. These figures do not include states that undertook school finance reform and centralization without judicial prodding. Updates on school finance litigation are available at the National Center on Education Finance's Web site, http://www.ncsl.org/programs/educ/NCEF.htm (accessed July 1, 2008).

4. For a description of the dynamics and extent of public resistance to school finance reform in New Jersey, see Goertz 1998; Scovronick and Corcoran 1998; Reed 2001, chapter 7.

5. Scholars have identified a host of other reasons why finance reform movements fail, including but not limited to the alignment of special interests around the status quo, the size of current discrepancies in tax rates between poor and rich areas, questions about the relationships between funding and student performance, courts' limited power to make policy, concerns about the effect of reform on housing prices, and misperceptions about the need for and results of reform.

6. President Obama's stimulus money may temporarily increase the federal share of education spending, but that funding stream is designed to provide one-time grants to help schools get through the current recession.

7. Chapter 2 discusses the few empirical studies of the Piper Link.

8. For example, Pfiffner 1983 claims that "state aid . . . often diminishes home rule and increases the centralization of control at centralized levels of government" (37; see also Montgomery 2002; Verstegen 2002). Others argue that financial centralization does not disrupt but rather reinforces existing patterns and practices of local school boards (Garms 1978, 152; Clark and Ferguson 1983, 225–27).

9. Frank Bryan's epic work on modern New England town meetings, *Real Democracy* (2004), has a Rockwell painting of a town meeting on its cover.

10. One can argue that the increased centralization of general government responsibility at the federal level has made localism more important in determining people's attitudes about school finance. Iannaccone and Lutz (1970) believe that the public becomes more attached to local control of education as more and more decision-making authority in other policy areas becomes increasingly centralized.

11. The precise origins of this saying are unknown. Independent Doctors of New York 2004 attributes it to James Monroe, but no other source confirms the attribution.

Chapter Two

1. Wirt 1985 summarizes the older literature on the topic. A normative longing that the Piper Link should be true often seems to color claims that it actually is. For example, a United Kingdom task force on intergovernmental relations recommended that the country assign responsibilities for funding and other aspects of a policy to the same level of government as a way to enhance democratic accountability (D. King 1997). The same longing is present in school finance debates. The New Hampshire Supreme Court ruled that "the state may not take the position that the minimum standards form an essential component of the delivery of a constitutionally adequate education and yet allow for the financial constraints of a school or school district to excuse compliance with those standards" (quoted in Viadero 2002).

2. Of course, we all care deeply about whether students graduate and go on to rewarding careers, but one would need to undertake a Herculean amount of advanced statistical analysis to examine whether local control is essential to promoting these goals.

3. State regulations may come in the form of conditions attached to grants, which in theory allow local government to choose to refuse both the grant and the conditions attached. In practice, however, local governments can ill afford to refuse any funding and therefore may feel compelled to accept even those grants with unwanted stipulations. As Grodzins 1966, Derthick 2001, and a host of others point out, such grants have traditionally been among the most successful ways state and national governments have influenced the policies of local governments. The role of conditional grants is discussed in detail in chapter 6.

4. I have borrowed the positive and negative phrasing from Berlin 1969. Berlin's concepts of positive and negative liberty inspired and informed my thinking on the topic of local autonomy, but I mean to imply no other connection to Berlin's work, let alone make any argument that one can or should extend his theories to local government specifically or to collective bodies generally.

5. Throughout the text, I note when the topic at hand is the relationship between state funding and local autonomy and when it is the relationship between all centralized-level funding and all decentralized-level autonomy.

6. See chapter 7.

7. Extending the decentralized bound of possible state contribution to the

funding burden to 20 percent allows the study to account for the fact that some states, including Vermont, have recently contributed less than 30 percent of the total finance burden. According to the U.S. Department of Education's *Digest of Education Statistics,* since at least the 1999–2000 school year, no state has contributed less than 20 percent of the total finance burden, and only New Hampshire contributed less than 20 percent in the previous fifteen school years.

8. A third feature of the model is that 100 percent centralized-level funding does not lead to 100 percent state control. Scholars have found that even in areas of heavy state regulation, local actors remain "street-level bureaucrats" with some leeway in how they implement or subvert state programs (Malen 2003).

Because this book does not purport to specify the exact mathematical relationship between finance and control, the assumption of a linear relationship in figure 2.2 and a simple curved model in figure 2.3 only facilitates a better understanding of the two hypotheses.

Chapter Three

1. All state regulations discussed in this section are explained more fully later in the chapter.

2. Other scholars have employed this measure to measure union strength across the states; see, for example, Steelman, Powell, and Carini 2000. I estimated similar models substituting the percentage of Hispanic and African American children and total school spending for the appropriate concepts. The results presented here are robust for these alternate specifications.

3. I estimated each of these models with finance share observations ranging from two to ten years prior to the observations used for the dependent variable. The results presented here are robust regardless of what observations for the finance share variable are used, which is not unexpected given that state finance share varies only slightly from year to year in almost every case.

4. A final set of independent variables are controls for the levels of the dependent variables in previous years. This study seeks to analyze finance share's effect on changes in the dependent variable, which requires the use of a control variable to account for prior levels of the dependent variable. Each model contains a control measuring the dependent variable at a point a few years before the observations employed in the dependent variable. Due to data limitations, the year of the observations for each of the controls varies.

5. As later chapters discuss, NCLB made states rework their existing standards extensively, so standardized testing and high-stakes testing policies after 2002 are not satisfactory measures of state regulation. Therefore, the data set uses observations prior to NCLB implementation for the two dependent variables measuring these concepts.

6. For example, a plan put forth by Lieutenant Governor Mark Schweiker to reform Philadelphia schools divided schools by their scores on the National Assessment of Educational Progress. Schools that performed well were allowed to continue their operations with little state interference, but those that performed poorly faced state regulation of their curriculum and instruction and possible

takeover by community groups or private interests (Snyder and Mezzacappa 2001; see also Malen 2003). State takeovers of school districts are discussed later in the chapter.

7. Because the dependent variable is ordered and categorical, ordered logit estimation is appropriate.

8. This book treats as real effects those that meet the conventional definition of statistical significance of p or $z \leq .05$.

9. A fascinating study might examine whether Bush's advocacy of NCLB has weakened the relationship between party and standardized testing, but that analysis is beyond the scope of this chapter.

10. Because the dependent variable is binary, logistical regression is appropriate.

11. Although this effect falls outside of conventional definitions of statistical significance, one can be reasonably sure its effect is real ($z = .147$).

12. Not all public school teachers are certified—in fact, one of the most cited reasons behind the decay of urban schools is the number of uncertified teachers such districts are forced to employ. Nonetheless, state certification is almost always valued, and nearly all districts that can afford to be somewhat selective about who they employ choose to hire certified teachers.

13. NCLB has made these three tests required for all teachers. As with the testing variables, to avoid the influence of NCLB's highly qualified teacher requirement on state teaching regulations, the observations for the dependent variable are taken from years prior to NCLB's implementation.

14. The union share variable approaches statistical significance but moves in the opposite direction of what is expected, with centralized union share associated with fewer, not more, requirements. This effect almost certainly results from multicollinearity problems with the Bush vote variable. These two variables have a correlation coefficient of $-.4290$. When the Bush vote variable is removed, the union share effect vanishes. When the union share variable is removed, the Bush vote effect remains robust and even strengthens. I thus conclude that the Bush vote effect is real, but the union vote not.

15. $z = .092$.

16. One of the factors that might increase the likelihood that school safety legislation will be adopted is previous instances of violent crimes in school. Preliminary models employed a dummy variable recording whether a state had endured at least one murder in school in any school year between 1992–93 and 2000–2001. This variable's effect did not approach statistical significance, probably because forty-one states had seen murders in schools during that time period. For the sake of presenting consistent results for the all the estimations described in this chapter, I do not present the model estimations containing the school violence variable.

17. These two variables show how policymakers sometimes follow perception rather than reality. Most infamous instances of school violence have occurred in predominantly white schools. While some studies have suggested that more school violence takes place in poorer areas, affluent areas (including Columbine) have also endured it (Center for the Study and Prevention of Violence 1998).

18. The union share variable is included in Models 3 and 4 because its effect

approaches significance in Model 1 more closely than any excluded independent variable. Nevertheless, its effect is not close enough to significance in any of the models to provide any evidence of a real effect on the dependent variable.

19. When modeling a dependent variable that records a limited number of events, Poisson maximum likelihood estimation is an appropriate technique.

20. $z = .101$.

21. $z = .174$.

Chapter Four

1. *Amanda Brigham et al. v. State of Vermont*, 692 A. 2d 384, 166 Vt. 246, 117 Ed Law Rep. 667 (1997), No. 96-502, February 5, 1997. The key constitutional provisions were Articles 7, 9, and 68 of the Vermont State Constitution. Article 7 of the Vermont State Constitution states that "government is, or ought to be, instituted for the common benefit, protection, and security of the people, nation, or community, and not for the particular emolument or advantage of any single person, family, or set of persons, who are a part only of that community." Article 9 claims that every citizen of Vermont "is bound to contribute the member's proportion towards the expense of . . . their common good." Article 68 says that "a competent number of schools ought to be maintained in each town" (Vermont 1786).

The Brigham case was not the first attempt to make the state take on a greater role in school finance. The state legislature passed a law in 1969 mandating that the state share of public school funding be no less than 40 percent of total spending. Inevitably, however, during hard economic times, the state found its law easy enough to ignore and curtailed its contribution to education (Rebell and Metzler 2002). Several of the people interviewed for this project believe that Act 60 would never have been necessary if the state had appropriately funded the existing formula.

2. Act 60 did not go into effect until the 1998–99 school year. Its funding scheme was then phased in over a three-year period.

3. For any cosmopolitan academic looking to emulate Thoreau and return to the soil, Bryan provides quite a role model. "Burly and hairy, Bryan is built more like a logger than a college professor. When he speaks, the expletives drop like dead leaves in November." His first question to a journalist interviewing him was, "Where did you get the shoulders? You didn't get them sitting behind a computer" (Jensen 2001). Bryan's professional Web site cites the article containing these quotations.

4. For example, in 2002–3, the Whiting Village School had twenty-three students in grades K–6. Information on enrollment totals is available at http://www.state.vt.us/educ/new/pdfdoc/data/enroll_03.pdf (accessed December 23, 2003). I discuss the economic incentives for and against consolidation later in the chapter. Because Vermont's mountains make transportation difficult, the cost/benefit analysis for consolidation may be slightly more favorable than in most other states.

5. As in most other states, municipal and school governments are separate entities; however, each town operates its own school district.

6. In Killington, resistance to Act 60 was so intense that the town voted to se-

cede from Vermont and join New Hampshire in 2004. This vote was largely symbolic, and no one believes that either state government can or will allow Killington to switch states.

7. Socioeconomic indicators for Vermont's towns are available at http://maps.vcgi.org/indicators/.

8. I am indebted to McCracken 1988 and Leech et al. 2002 for their instruction in preparing and conducting elite interviews.

9. Iannaccone and Lutz 1970 find that this dynamic characterizes the relationship between local school boards and their superintendents.

10. In 2002, a fire destroyed the Windsor Central Supervisory Union building and the official copies of the three schools' school board minutes. My access to minutes from RS2 and RS3 was thus limited. I owe a huge debt of gratitude to Tom Bourne for allowing me access to his private stack of old school board minutes, which dated as far back as December 1997. I owe a similar debt to the staff of RS2 for helping me locate the old minutes for that institution.

11. McDermott's system has six separate classifications. "School operations" refers to motions dealing with transportation, construction, and the like. "Curriculum and instruction" includes textbook selection, approval of field trips, and the like. "Community relations" includes decisions to let community groups use school facilities. "Board operations" includes the approval of minutes and agendas and electing board officers. "Labor" includes negotiations and personnel decisions. "Budget" includes anything pertaining to the setting of the annual budget and individual appropriations decisions.

12. Some readers may find simple count data to be inelegant, but these data are not meant as primary evidence. Rather, information about school elections and school board meetings is secondary evidence to support the interviewees' claims.

13. These figures also show that tax relief did not last in part because of a new financial formula implemented under Act 68, the successor to Act 60 (discussed later in the chapter).

14. Because total town educational spending includes money that Killington and Woodstock contributed to the sharing pool, it is not an ideal measure of how schools fared financially under Act 60. Unfortunately, exact per-pupil spending totals for these six schools were not available. Each supervisory unit's budget coordinator assured me that per-pupil spending decreased in the three Windsor Central schools and increased in the three Rutland Northeast schools.

15. Conversely, the paucity of curriculum-related motions across all years may discourage advocates of local control and speaks to the centralization of educational decision making discussed in later chapters.

16. As the last part of this sentence implies, school board minutes varied in their detail depending on who was taking the notes. For that reason, one should not attempt to compare any of the measures of what goes on at school board meetings across the six schools.

17. The framework also requires students to show proficiency in communication skills, reasoning and problem solving, personal development skills, and civic and social skills. A copy of the standards is available at http://www.state.vt.us/educ/new/pdfdoc/pubs/framework.pdf (accessed December 14, 2003).

18. Also as part of the Green Mountain Challenge, the state legislature passed Act 230 of 1990, which drastically increased state regulation of special education (Roach and Caruso 1997; Furney et al. 2003).

19. Vermont is not the only state that took preemptive steps against possible Piper Link effects. The Massachusetts Education Reform Act of 1993, which increased funding for less affluent districts, also contained provisions that that decentralized decision-making power within school districts (Anthony and Rossman 1994; Dee and Levine 2004).

20. The respondents feel very differently about NCLB testing. Some interview subjects expressed concern that the rise of standardized testing was narrowing the scope of curriculum and putting schools under a great deal of unfair pressure. As Sherburne principal Marion Withum put it, the community has a right to know how schools are performing, "but that's the job of the school board and the community." Such sentiments express fears about a loss of local control but were always offered as criticisms of NCLB's testing provisions rather than of Act 60. None of the subjects thought that Act 60's standards or testing components compromised local control.

21. Outside of Vermont, Ehrenberg et al. 2004 find that increases in state aid do not make people less likely to support school budgets.

22. The minutes from RS2 and PS3 did not contain reliable records of the number of attendees at each meeting.

23. Unlike the other three towns discussed in this paper, Killington does not hold elections by Australian ballot, where people vote for candidates, budget proposals, and so forth in booths. All of Killington's decisions are made on the floor at town meeting.

24. Leicester proposed a series of four construction measures to its voters during the 2002–3 school year, and voter turnout for those measures (281, 500, 315, and 332 respectively) was among the highest for any election since 1991. This high turnout also offers evidence against the hypothesis that Act 60 depressed citizen interest in school affairs.

25. Vermont was selected precisely because it is exceptional. The results presented in chapter 3 buck the conventional wisdom that money must influence control, so I selected a case where the Piper Link had the best chance to show its effects. Vermont's rhetorical commitment to local control is unsurpassed, meaning that enough local control may have remained for finance centralization to harm it and people may have perceived its effects.

26. The author is indebted to Courant and Loeb 1997 and Cullen and Loeb 2004 for their presentation of the history of Michigan's reform efforts.

27. Chapter 5 says more about how affluent districts reacted to Proposal A.

28. See Lubienki 2001; Moe and Koret 2001.

29. No existing studies have examined charter schools' effect on local control as this book defines it. The evidence that exists on charter schools' effects on surrounding traditional public schools is limited and is mixed (Horn and Miron 1999; Bettinger 2005).

30. It is possible to acknowledge that the movement to lessen property taxes was the key motivating force behind Proposal A's passage and still accept that Engler's support for school choice played a role or at least that finance centralization itself did not cause charter legislation.

31. A survey from the Education Policy Center at Michigan State University raises the question of whether consolidation is really as unpopular as academics and some Vermont elites believe. In the poll, 47 percent of residents and 46 percent of parents supported consolidation of school districts. About half of those who initially indicated opposition changed their answer when asked if they would change their answer if they knew that consolidation would cut costs and/or provide more specialized offerings for students (Ray and Plank 2003).

Chapter Five

1. The authors of the study find that ratings of the federal government jumped above those of state and local governments in response to the events of September 11, 2001. For the previous fifteen years, however, the federal government was the least popular, and subsequent polls showed that the change was temporary. In recent polls, state and local governments have again garnered their typically high levels of support.

2. Evidence suggests that support for specific standards and testing proposals is even greater. For example, in Washington, 80 percent of those polled supported setting even stronger centralized standards than the ones currently in use and using testing to measure achievement of these standards (Jacobson 2001).

3. See chapter 6.

4. Hosted by the Odum Institute at the University of North Carolina (http://www.irss.unc.edu/data_archive/home.asp [accessed January 15, 2001]). Given the differences in the wordings of questions serving as measures of the dependent and local control variables from poll to poll, the data sets could not be pooled.

5. I used two polls from New Jersey conducted approximately two years apart and discuss my reasons for doing so later in the chapter. Throughout the remainder of this chapter, I refer to NJ-NSSP-079 as the first New Jersey poll and NJ-NSSP-094 as the second New Jersey poll.

6. Political science scholars are generally skeptical of claims that financial self-interest influences people's policy evaluations when the monetary stakes are large and visible and the connection between the proposal and centralized tax rates is clear. School finance reform may meet these criteria—it promises to redistribute huge amounts of money, it is always one of the most contentious issues in state capitols, and opponents of reform often stress how it might lead to centralized taxes (Scovronick and Corcoran 1998).

7. Not all of the polls contained all of the independent variables.

8. Those who value local control might fear that increased state funding would lead to state regulation and thus oppose state grants for school construction.

9. Opinion of the Justices, 624 So. 2nd 107 (Ala. 1993). *Coalition for Equity et al. v. Hunt*, CIV. A. Nos. CV-90-883-R, *Harper v. Hunt* CV-91-0117.

10. See chapter 1 for discussion on *Rodriguez* (411 U.S. 1 [1973]).

11. *Edgewood Independent School District et al. v. William Kirby et al.*, No. C-8353, Supreme Court of Texas, October 2, 1989.

12. *Tennessee Small School Systems v. McWerter* 851 S.W. 2d 139 (Tenn. 1993).

13. *Robinson v. Cahill*, 69 N.J. 449 (1976) 355 A.2d 129, The Supreme Court of New Jersey (argued November 24, 1975, decided January 30, 1976); *Abbott v. Burke*, 119 N.J. 287 (1990) 575 A.2d 359, The Supreme Court of New Jersey (argued September 25, 1989, decided June 5, 1990).

14. Nor, however, are courts powerless. When additional spending on poorer districts has taken place, it is largely a result of judicial intervention (and, to be sure, the persistence of the plaintiffs), so entirely discounting this strategy would be foolish. Several studies have found that favorable court rulings can substantially reduce inequalities in school funding (Murray, Evans, and Schwab 1998; Grider and Verstegen 2000; Reed 2001).

Chapter Six

1. As described later in this chapter, even though federal programs such as special education target a limited population, they may still have a huge impact on local autonomy.

2. The federal government's initial unwillingness strongly to regulate education stems from a variety of factors, including Republicans' traditional respect for local and state control of education, Democrats' indebtedness to teachers' unions, and the lack of constitutional provision for its involvement. See chapter 7; McGuinn 2006.

3. Chapter 7 discusses NCLB at length.

4. A 2002 survey found that 66 percent of the population believes that standardized testing should be continued at its current level or increased, and 63 percent favors using such tests to hold schools accountable to national and state learning standards (Phi Delta Kappan and the Gallup Organization 2002). In 2007, 55 percent of respondents believed that there was either "not enough emphasis" or "just the right amount of emphasis" on standardized testing (Phi Delta Kappan and the Gallup Organization 2007); in 2003, 66 percent of the public fell into these categories (Phi Delta Kappan and the Gallup Organization 2003). The drop may indicate that support for standardized testing is eroding as NCLB makes the strategy more conspicuous or that the public joined Vermont interview respondents in preferring state standards and testing, which may be more suited for local circumstances. Nevertheless, a majority of the public still either approves of the current testing system or wants it expanded.

5. In this group, political science scholars will recognize echoes of the concept of street-level bureaucrats (Lipsky 1971).

6. Turnout in the 1998 congressional election was 36 percent of registered voters (U.S. Federal Elections Commission 1998). McDermott also found that voting in local school elections was 20–60 percent lower than voting in national elections (1999).

7. The difference in attitudes on NCLB and Act 60 testing is notable. Respondents thought Act 60's testing provisions helped them diagnose problems rather than punishing them for failure to achieve unrealistic expectations.

Chapter Seven

1. By law, the ESEA must be reauthorized every five years.

2. A full summary of NCLB is available at Education Commission of the States 2002.

3. Part of the reason for the strong language state actors have employed against NCLB may stem from their fear that the failure of a large number of schools in their state to meet the act's ambitious new performance standards will result in a loss of votes or jobs.

4. William Mathis is also the superintendent of the Rutland Northeast Supervisory Union in Vermont (chapters 4, 6). Title I funding is defined and discussed in greater detail later in the chapter.

5. A host of other studies described shortfalls in NCLB funding, including Joyce 2002; Greenblatt 2004.

6. *School District of the City of Pontiac vs. Margaret Spellings*, filed November 23, 2005, in United States District Court, Eastern District of Michigan, Southern Division, Civil Action 05-CV-71535-DT.

7. The overwhelming majority of professional educators and the organizations that represent them have little positive to say about NCLB. A total of 121 organizations have signed an National Education Association statement calling for changes to its measurement of student progress, requirements for assessment and supplementary services, and funding. Teachers are extremely frustrated with what they regard as impossible expectations for student progress, unreasonable demands for midcareer teachers to meet the HQT standard, and the narrowing of curriculum. "It's just teaching to the test," claims Betty Olson of the Oakland Education Association. "That is what teachers are being forced to do. Students are being put through test prep after test prep while they lose art, while they lose science, while they lose music" (Melendez 2007).

Among elected representatives, a bipartisan consensus in favor of NCLB's basic accountability strategy remains, but nearly everyone believes that NCLB must be fundamentally changed. In March 2007, fifty Republican members of the House and Senate introduced legislation allowing states to opt out of NCLB's testing requirements. A separate letter from ten Democratic senators calls NCLB's testing requirements "unsustainable" and recommends fundamental changes.

8. *Board of Education of Ottawa Township High School District 140 v. Spellings*, United States Court of Appeals, Seventh Circuit, No. 07-2008 (argued January 15–February 11, 2008); *Kegerreis v. United States of America*, No. Civ. A. 03-2232-KHV (D. Kan. October 9, 2003).

9. Combined with the data described earlier, the general acceptance of such statements strongly suggests that local actors are not using their position as street-level bureaucrats to frustrate implementation. Against the wishes of local actors, the situation really does seem to be changing. Malen, the leading authority on the consequences of state and federal regulation of local autonomy, ultimately argues that the available evidence overwhelmingly supports the argument that state and federal laws severely curtail local autonomy and local actors have only minimal ability to derail a policy by dragging their feet on implementation or implementing in a way that furthers their own goals (2003).

10. The most infamous example comes from Mississippi. On the state-designed test used to judge AYP, 89 percent were judged proficient or advanced. On the NAEP, 18 percent passed (Lips and Feinberg 2008).

11. Those who wish to pursue legal challenges to NCLB also cannot expect to find much sympathy from state judges. Article VI of the Constitution establishes federal law as binding to judges of every state. Given that federal law is designed by the same bodies that pass regulation, all courts can be expected to look favorably on federal regulation.

12. On January 7, 2008, the U.S. Court of Appeals for the Sixth Circuit reversed the district court's decision and agreed that the lawsuit had merit enough to warrant a trial. While this decision is a triumph for the NEA coalition, it does not indicate that the courts will eventually decide in the coalition's favor and rule that the federal government must either pay for NCLB or abandon it.

13. Dayton either has more accurate data than are publicly available or has miscalculated the amount of funding jeopardized.

14. New Mexico relies on Title I for 4.9 percent of its total K–12 funding but still passed a law opting out of some NCLB provisions, representing a deviation from this trend.

Chapter Eight

1. When announcing plans to spend $341 million of its $492 million highway allotment from the stimulus, the State of Washington did not include any projects within Seattle city limits, angering local officials (Wingfield and Eaton 2009). New York's two senators offered to take any funding that other states refused (Bendavid 2009).

2. South Carolina governor Mark Sanford resisted taking stimulus funding as vocally as any governor in the nation. How South Carolina's stimulus debate would have played out in the absence of the adultery scandal that crippled his governorship would have been interesting.

References

�֍ ✖ ✖

Access. 2005a. *"Equity" and "adequacy" school finance decisions.* Available at http://www.schoolfunding.info/litigation/equityandadequacytable11-22-04.pdf. Accessed May 3, 2005.

Access. 2005b. *Litigation homepage.* Available at http://www.schoolfunding .info/litigation/litigation.php3. Accessed May 1, 2005.

Act60.org. 1997. *Local control.* Available at http://www.act60.org/goals.htm#local. Accessed April 1, 2004.

Addonizio, Michael F. 2005. *Putting off problems: Michigan school finance update 2005.* Detroit: Wayne State University.

Ahearn, James. 1992. It's New Jersey vs. democracy in Ridgefield Park. *Bergen County Record,* May 13.

Anthony, Patricia G., and Gretchen B. Rossman. 1994. *The Massachusetts Education Reform Act: What is it and will it work?* Lanham, MD: Educational Resources Information Center.

Anton, Thomas Julius. 1989. *American federalism and public policy: How the system works.* New York: Random House.

Arsen, David, and David N. Plank. 2003. *Michigan school finance under Proposal A: State control, local consequences.* East Lansing: Michigan State University.

Arsen, David, David N. Plank, and Gary Sykes. 1999. *School choice policies in Michigan: The rules matter.* Available at http://edtech.connect.msu.edu/choice/conference/default.asp. Accessed June 13, 2009.

Associated Press. 1998. Act 60 lives, but attitudes have evolved. November 15.

Baicker, Katherine, and Nora Gordon. 2004. The effect of mandated state education spending on total local resources. In *TAPES Conference on Fiscal Federalism.* Munich: CESIFO.

Baker, Bruce D. 2001. Balancing equity for students and taxpayers: Evaluating school finance reform in Vermont. *Journal of Education Finance* 26:239–48.

Barrilleaux, Charles. 1997. A test of the independent influences of electoral competition and party strength in a model of state policy-making. *American Journal of Political Science* 41:1462–66.

Bell, David A. 1980. *Brown v. Board of Education* and the interest convergence dilemma. *Harvard Law Review* 93:518–33.

Bendavid, Naftali. 2009. Lawmakers say N.Y. will gladly take funds GOP governors reject. *Wall Street Journal*, February 23.

Berlin, Isaiah. 1969. Two concepts of liberty. In *Four essays on liberty*. London: Oxford University Press.

Berman, David R. 2003. *Local government and the states: Autonomy, politics, and policy*. Armonk, NY: Sharpe.

Bettinger, Eric P. 2005. The effect of charter schools on charter students and public schools. *Economics of Education Review* 24:133–47.

Biscobing, David. 2007. *Senate votes down bill to allow opt-out from "No Child" act*. Cronkite News Service, February 19. Available at https://cronkite.blog.asu.edu/2007/02/19/bc-cns-no-child440/?triedWebauth=1. Accessed April 25, 2007.

Blendon, Robert J., John M. Benson, Richard Morin, Drew E. Altman, Mollyann Brodie, Mario Brossard, and Matt James. 1997. Changing attitudes in America. In *Why people don't trust government*, edited by E. J. S. Nye, P. D. Zelikow, and D. C. King. Cambridge: Harvard University Press.

Bolland, John M., and Kent D. Redfield. 1988. The limits to [U.S.] citizen participation in local education: A cognitive interpretation. *Journal of Politics* 50:1033–46.

Bowler, Shaun, and Todd Donovan. 1995. Popular responsiveness to taxation. *Political Research Quarterly* 48:79–99.

Bowman, Ann O'M. 2002. American federalism on the horizon. *Publius: The Journal of Federalism* 32:3–22.

Briffault, Richard. 1992. The role of local control in school finance reform. *Connecticut Law Review* 34:773–811.

Bryan, Frank M. 2004. *Real democracy: The New England town meeting and how it works*. Chicago: University of Chicago Press.

Bryce, James. 1910. *The American commonwealth*. New ed. New York: Macmillan.

Burns, Alexander. 2009. *Jindal to refuse some stimulus money*. Yahoo! News, February 20. Available at http://news.yahoo.com/s/politico/20090220/pl_politico/19092. Accessed May 11, 2009.

Burstein, Paul. 2003. The impact of public opinion on public policy: A review and an agenda. *Political Research Quarterly* 56:29–40.

Cameron, Beatrice H., Kenneth E. Underwood, and Jim C. Fortune. 1988. Politics and power: How you're selected and elected to lead this nation's schools. *American School Board Journal* 175:17–19.

Cantril, Albert Hadley, and Susan Davis Cantril. 1999. *Reading mixed signals: Ambivalence in American public opinion about government*. Washington, DC: Woodrow Wilson Center Press/Johns Hopkins University Press.

Carey, Kevin. 2006. Hot air: How states inflate their educational progress under NCLB. In *The evidence suggests otherwise*. Washington, DC: Education Sector.

Carnoy, Martin, and Susanna Loeb. 2002. Does external accountability affect student outcomes? A cross-state analysis. *Educational Evaluation and Policy Analysis* 24:305–31.

Center for Rural Studies, University of Vermont. 2002. *The 2002 Vermonter poll.* Available at http://crs.uvm.edu/vtrpoll/2002. Accessed April 9, 2004.

Center for the Study and Prevention of Violence. 1998. *CSPV school violence fact sheet.* Boulder, CO: Institute of Behavioral Science, University of Colorado.

Center on Education Policy. 2007a. *Beyond the mountains: An early look at restructuring results in California.* Washington, DC: Center on Education Policy.

Center on Education Policy. 2007b. *No Child Left Behind at five: A review of changes to state accountability plans.* Washington, DC: Center on Education Policy.

Cho, Chung-Lae, and Deil S. Wright. 2001. Managing carrots and sticks: Changes in state administrators' perception of cooperative and coercive federalism during the 1990s. *Publius: The Journal of Federalism* 31:57–80.

Chubb, John E. 2001. The system. In *A primer on America's schools,* edited by T. M. Moe and Koret Task Force on K–12 Education. Stanford, CA: Hoover Institution Press, Stanford University.

Citrin, Jack, and Donald Phillip Green. 1990. The self-interest motive in American public opinion. In *Research in Micropolitics,* edited by S. Long. Greenwich, CT: Jai.

Clark, Terry N., and Lorna C. Ferguson. 1983. *City money: Political processes, fiscal strain, and retrenchment.* New York: Columbia University Press.

Clarke, John H. 2001. Teaching each and all: Harnessing dynamic tension in school reform. *NASSP Bulletin* 85:75–80.

Clotfelter, Charles T. 2004. *After Brown: The rise and retreat of school desegregation.* Princeton: Princeton University Press.

Cockerham, Sean. 2009. Palin rejects over 30% of stimulus money. *Anchorage Daily News,* March 19.

Cole, Richard L., John Kincaid, and Andrew Parkin. 2002. Public opinion on federalism in the United States and Canada in 2002: The aftermath of terror. *Publius: The Journal of Federalism* 32:123–48.

Conlan, Timothy. 1993. Federal, state, or local? Trends in the public's judgment. *Public Perspective* 4:3–5.

Connors, Richard J., and William J. Dunham. 1993. *The government of New Jersey: An introduction.* Rev. ed. Lanham, MD: University Press of America.

Courant, Paul N., Edward M. Gramlich, and Susanna Loeb. 1995. Michigan's recent school finance reforms: A preliminary report. *American Economic Review* 85:372–77.

Courant, Paul N., and Susanna Loeb. 1997. Centralization of school finance in Michigan. *Journal of Policy Analysis and Management* 16:114–36.

Crain's Detroit Business. 1994. Can reform make grade: School overhaul may not be ideal. *Crain's Detroit Business,* February 28.

Cullen, Julie Berry, and Susanna Loeb. 2004. School finance reform in Michigan: Evaluating Proposal A. In *Helping children left behind: State aid and the pursuit of educational equity,* edited by J. Yinger. Cambridge: MIT Press.

Danielson, Michael N. 1976. *The politics of exclusion.* New York: Columbia University Press.

Darling, Martha. 1998. Necessary but not sufficient: Moving from school finance reform to education reform in Washington state. In *Strategies for school equity: Creating productive schools in a just society*, edited by M. Gittell. New Haven: Yale University Press.

Davis, Michelle R. 2005. Utah is unlikely fly in Bush's school ointment. *Education Week*, February 9.

Davis, Michelle R., and Jeff Archer. 2005. Complaint targets Utah NCLB law. *Education Week*, May 10.

Dean, Charles J. 1993. Panel on school standards meets, faces opposition. *Birmingham News*, September 30.

Dean, Charles J. 1995. Local school leaders oppose James' plan. *Birmingham News*, May 14.

Debray, Elizabeth H., Kathryn A. McDermott, and Priscilla Wohlstetter. 2005. Introduction to special issue on Federalism reconsidered: The case of the No Child Left Behind Act. *Peabody Journal of Education* 80:1–18.

Dee, Thomas S., and Jeffrey Levine. 2004. The fate of new funding: Evidence from Massachusetts education finance reforms. *Educational Evaluation and Policy Analysis* 26:199–215.

Derthick, Martha. 2001. *Keeping the compound republic: Essays on American federalism*. Washington, DC: Brookings Institution.

Dillon, Sam. 2004. Voters to decide on charter schools. *New York Times*, October 25.

Dillon, Sam. 2007. Battle grows over renewing landmark education law. *New York Times*, April 7.

Dillon, Sam. 2009. Education standards likely to see toughening. *New York Times*, April 15.

Dinan, John. 1997. State government influence in the national policy process: Lessons from the 104th Congress. *Publius: The Journal of Federalism* 27, no. 2: 129–42.

Dobbs, Michael. 2005. Conn. stands in defiance on enforcing "No Child." *Washington Post*, May 8.

Doherty, Kathryn M. 1998. Changing urban education: Defining the issues. In *Changing Urban Education*, edited by C. N. Stone. Lawrence: University Press of Kansas.

Education Commission of the States. 1998. State takeovers and reconstitutions. Denver, CO: ECS.

Education Commission of the States. 2002. No state left behind: The challenges and opportunities of ESEA. Denver, CO: ECS.

Education Commission of the States. 2006. *NCLB Database*. Available at http://nclb2.ecs.org/NCLBSURVEY/nclb.aspx?Target=SS. Accessed March 30, 2006.

Education Trust. 2003. *Don't turn back the clock*. Washington, DC: Education Trust.

Education Week. 2004. Quality counts 2004: Count me in: Special education in an era of standards.

Ehrenberg, Ronald G., Randy A. Ehrenberg, Christopher L. Smith, and Liang Zhang. 2004. Why do school district budget referenda fail? *Educational Evaluation and Policy Analysis* 26:111–25.

Fairman, Janet, and William A. Firestone. 2001. The district role in state assessment policy: An exploratory study. In *From the capitol to the classroom: Standards-based reform in the states,* edited by S. Fuhrman. Chicago: National Society for the Study of Education.

Feldman, Stanley, and Leonie Huddy. 2005. Racial resentment and white opposition to race-conscious programs: Principles or prejudice? *American Journal of Political Science* 49:168–83.

Ferdinand, Paul. 1998. Education funding issue colors New England fall. *Washington Post,* October 18.

Feuerstein, Abe, and Jonathan A. Dietrich. 2003. State standards in the local context: A survey of school board members and superintendents. *Educational Policy* 17:237–56.

Finn, Chester E. 1992. Reinventing local control. In *School boards: Changing local control,* edited by P. F. First and H. J. Walberg. Berkeley, CA: McCutchan.

Firestone, David. 2001. Tennessee's fiscal stature dives after futile push for income tax. *New York Times,* August 23.

Firestone, William A., David Mayrowetz, and Janet Fairman. 1998. Performance-based assessment and instructional change: The effects of testing in Maine and Maryland. *Educational Evaluation and Policy Analysis* 20:95–113.

Fisher, Ronald C., and Robert W. Wassmer. 1995. Centralizing educational responsibility in Michigan and other states: New constraints on states. *National Tax Journal* 48:417–28.

Fuhrman, Susan H., and Richard F. Elmore. 1990. Understanding local control in the wake of state education reform. *Educational Evaluation and Policy Analysis* 12:82–96.

Furney, Katharine S., Susan Brody Hasazi, Kelly Clark-Keefe, and Johnette Hartnell. 2003. A longitudinal analysis of shifting policy landscapes in special and general education reform. *Exceptional Children* 70:81–94.

Gainsborough, Juliet F. 2001. *Fenced off: The suburbanization of American politics.* Washington, DC: Georgetown University Press.

Garms, Walter I. 1978. *School finance: The economics and politics of public education.* Englewood Cliffs, NJ: Prentice Hall.

Gehring, John. 2004. Bailout deal reached for Baltimore schools. *Education Week,* February 25.

Gilens, Martin. 1999. *Why Americans hate welfare: Race, media, and the politics of antipoverty policy.* Chicago: University of Chicago Press.

Gittell, Marilyn. 1998. Foreword to *Strategies for school equity: Creating productive schools in a just society,* edited by M. Gittell. New Haven: Yale University Press.

Glod, Maria. 2007. Fairfax schools could lose millions for defying "No Child." *Washington Post,* February 23.

Goertz, Margaret E. 1998. Steady work: The courts and school finance reform in New Jersey. In *Strategies for school equity: Creating productive schools in a just society,* edited by M. Gittell. New Haven: Yale University Press.

Goodman, David. 1999. America's newest. *Mother Jones,* September–October 1999, 68–75.

Government Finance Review. 1999. Americans place most trust in local governments. *Government Finance Review* 15:5.

Gray, Virginia, David Lowery, Matthew Fellowes, and Andrea McAtee. 2004. Public opinion, public policy, and organized interests in the American states. *Political Research Quarterly* 57:411–20.

Green, Donald Phillip, and Jonathan A. Cowden. 1992. Who protests: Self-interest and white opposition to busing. *Journal of Politics* 54:471–96.

Greenblatt, Alan. 2004. The left behind syndrome. *Governing Magazine,* September.

Greene, Andrea D. 1988. Lawmakers, teachers greet funding ruling/Most area school officials voice relief. *Houston Chronicle,* December 15.

Grider, Andrew, and Deborah A. Verstegen. 2000. Legislation, litigation, and rural and small schools: A survey of the states. *Journal of Education Finance* 26:103–19.

Grodzins, Morton. 1966. *The American system: A new view of government in the United States.* Chicago: Rand McNally.

Gruenewald, David A. 2003. The best of both worlds: A critical pedagogy of place. *Educational Researcher* 32:3–11.

Hagar, Ray. 2005. Legislators threaten to defy education law. *Reno Gazette-Journal,* May 27.

Hero, Rodney, and Caroline J. Tolbert. 1996. A racial/ethnic diversity interpretation of politics and policy in the states of the U.S. *American Journal of Political Science* 40:851–71.

Herrington, Stephanie. 2004. No Child Left Behind leaves school districts behind. *Santa Cruz Sentinel,* June 13.

Hetherington, Marc J., and John D. Nugent. 2001. Explaining support for devolution: The role of political trust. In *What is it about government that Americans dislike?* edited by J. R. Hibbing and E. Theiss-Morse. Cambridge: Cambridge University Press.

Hill, Paul T. 2000. The federal role in education. *Brookings Papers on Education Policy* 2000:11–40.

Hochschild, Jennifer L. 1984. *The new American dilemma: Liberal democracy and school desegregation.* New Haven: Yale University Press.

Hochschild, Jennifer L. 1997. *Public involvement in decisions about public education.* Washington, DC: National Academy of Sciences Committee on Educational Finance.

Hochschild, Jennifer L., and Bridget Scott. 1998. Governance and reform of public education in the United States. *Public Opinion Quarterly* 62:79–120.

Hochschild, Jennifer, and Nathan B. Scovronick. 2003. *The American dream and the public schools.* New York: Addison Wesley, Longman.

Holland, Megan, Kyle Hopkins, and S. J. Komarnitsky. 2009. School officials turn to legislature to save stimulus funds. *Anchorage Daily News,* March 20.

Hoppe, Christy, and Robert T. Garrett. 2009. Texas gov. Rick Perry rejects stimulus money for jobless claims. *Dallas Morning News,* March 13.

Horn, Jerry, and Gary Miron. 1999. Evaluation of the Michigan Public School Academy Initiative. Kalamazoo: Western Michigan University.

Hovey, Harold A. 1989. Analytic approaches to state-local relations. In *A decade of devolution: Perspectives on state-local relations,* edited by E. B. Liner and J. A. Brizius. Washington, DC: Urban Institute Press.

Hoxby, Caroline M. 1997. Local property tax-based funding of public schools. *Heartland Policy Study* 82:1–23.

Hunter, Kennith G., Gregory G. Brunk, and Laura A. Wilson. 2002. Organizing for public policy effect: Aggregate affiliated interests in the American states. *Public Organization Review* 2:117–39.

Iannaccone, Laurence, and Frank W. Lutz. 1970. *Politics, power, and policy: The governing of local school districts.* Columbus, OH: Merrill.

Independent Doctors of New York. 2004. *Your freedom of choice in healthcare.* Available at http://www.idny.org/idny/static/origins.html. Accessed December 20, 2004.

Jacobson, Linda. 2001. Washington state groups build support for standards, tests. *Education Week*, April 18.

Jacoby, William G., and Saundra K. Schneider. 2001. Variability in state policy priorities: An empirical analysis. *Journal of Politics* 63:544–68.

Jensen, Dennis. 2001. Frankly speaking: An interview with UVM professor Frank Bryan. *Vermont Magazine*, November–December, 43–46.

Jimerson, Lorna. 2002. *Still "a reasonably equal share": Update on educational equity in Vermont: Year 2001–2002.* Burlington, VT: Rural School and Community Trust.

Johnston, Robert C., and Jessica L. Sandham. 1999. States increasingly flexing their policy muscle. *Education Week*, April 14.

Joyce, Mark V. 2002. "Analysis of cost impact of ESEA—No Child Left Behind Act—on New Hampshire." In *NHSSA Memorandum of 26 November 2002.* Peacock, NH.

Kahn, Kim Fridkin. 1994. Does gender make a difference? An experimental examination of sex stereotypes and press patterns in statewide campaigns. *American Journal of Political Science* 38:162–95.

Keeter, Scott, and Juliana Horowitz. 2009. *On Darwin's 200th birthday, Americans still divided about evolution.* Pew Research Center, February 5. Available at http://pewresearch.org/pubs/1107/polling-evolution-creationism. Accessed July 25, 2009.

Keller, Bess. 2006. No state meeting teacher provisions of "No Child" law. *Education Week*, May 24.

Kilborn, Peter T. 1999. Vermont spending plan seems to help schools. *New York Times*, January 31.

Kincaid, John. 1990. From cooperative to coercive federalism. *Annals of the American Academy of Political and Social Science* 509:139–52.

Kincaid, John. 1998. The devolution tortoise and the centralization hare. *New England Economic Review* 1998:13–40.

Kincaid, John. 2001. The state of U.S. federalism. *Publius: The Journal of Federalism* 31:1–69.

King, David. 1997. Intergovernmental fiscal relations: Concepts and models. In *Intergovernmental fiscal relations*, edited by R. C. Fisher. Boston: Kluwer Academic.

King, Matt. 2006. Santa Cruz schools consider leaving No Child Left Behind behind. *Santa Cruz Sentinel*, August 31.

Koerner, James D. 1968. *Who controls American education? A guide for laymen.* Boston: Beacon.

Kosar, Kevin. 2001. The demise of antistatism in federal education policy. Paper presented at the annual meeting of the Northeastern Political Science Association, Philadelphia.

Kronebusch, Karl. 2004. Matching rates and mandates: Federalism and children's Medicaid enrollment. *Policy Studies Journal* 32:317–39.

LaHaye, Beverly. 1997. The left and the right in education: A battle between federal and local control. *Contemporary Education* 68:239–42.

Lane, Robin. 2002. Understanding Act 60 and education finance: An objective look at the content, context, and implications of Vermont's current education finance legislation. Unpublished paper, Department of Education, Vermont College.

Leech, Beth L., John D. Aberbach, Bert A. Rockman, Jeffrey M. Berry, Kenneth Goldstein, Polina M. Kozyreva, Sharon Werning Rivera, Eduard G. Sarovskii, and Laura R. Woliver. 2002. Interview methods in political science. *PS: Political Science and Politics* 35:663–88.

Lips, Dan, and Evan Feinberg. 2008. *No Child Left Behind and the race to the bottom.* Available at http://www.heritage.org/research/education/ednotes77.cfm. Accessed July 5, 2009.

Lipsky, Michael. 1971. Toward a theory of street-level bureaucracy. *Urban Affairs Quarterly* 6:391–409.

Lubienski, Chris. 2001. Redefining "public" education: Charter schools, common schools, and the rhetoric of reform. *Teachers College Record* 103:634–66.

Lynn, Ronnie. 2005. Bill would buck federal rules on public schools. *Salt Lake Tribune,* February 1.

Macedo, Stephen. 2003. School reform and equal opportunity in America's geography of inequality. *Perspectives on Politics* 1:743–45.

Madden, Mike, and Gabriel Winant. 2009. *GOP governors take the (stimulus) money and run.* Salon.com, February 20. Available at http://www.salon.com/news/feature/2009/02/20/gop_governors/. Accessed May 15, 2009.

Malen, Betty. 2000. Recent litigation and its impact. In *Balancing local control and state responsibility for K–12 education,* edited by N. D. Theobald and B. Malen. Larchmont, NY: Eye on Education.

Malen, Betty. 2003. Tightening the grip? The impact of state activism on local school systems. *Educational Policy* 17:195–216.

Malen, Betty, and Donna Muncey. 2000. Creating "a new set of givens?" The impact of state activism on school autonomy. In *Balancing local control and state responsibility for K–12 education,* edited by N. D. Theobald and B. Malen. Larchmont, NY: Eye on Education.

Manna, Paul. 2006. *School's in: Federalism and the national education agenda.* Washington, DC: Georgetown University Press.

Mansfield, Harvey C. 1967. Functions of state and local governments. In *The 50 states and their local governments,* edited by J. W. Fesler, K. A. Bosworth, and American Assembly. New York: Knopf.

Mathis, William J. 2000. *Civil society and school reform: Vermont's Act 60.* Available at http://www.ids.ac.uk/ids/civsoc/final/usa/USA17.doc. Accessed April 21, 2003.

Mathis, William J. 2005. The cost of implementing the federal No Child Left Behind: Different assumptions, different answers. *Peabody Journal of Education* 80:90–119.

Mazzoni, Tim L. 1995. State policymaking and school reform: Influences and influentials. In *The study of education politics,* edited by J. D. Scribner and D. H. Layton. New York: Routledge.

McClaughry, John. 1997. *Local control R.I.P.* Available at http://www.act60.org/ethan.htm. Accessed March 31, 2003.

McClure, Phyllis. 2004. Grassroots resistance to NCLB. *Education Gadfly.* Available at http://www.edexcellence.net/gadfly/index.cfm?issue=140#a1723. Accessed August 30, 2010.

McCracken, Grant David. 1988. The long interview. In *Qualitative research methods,* vol. 13. Newbury Park, CA: Sage.

McDermott, Kathryn A. 1999. *Controlling public education: Localism versus equity.* Lawrence: University Press of Kansas.

McDermott, Kathryn A., and Laura S. Jensen. 2005. Dubious sovereignty: Federal conditions of aid and the No Child Left Behind Act. *Peabody Journal of Education* 80:39–56.

McDonnell, Lorraine M. 2005. No Child Left Behind and the federal role in education: Evolution or revolution? *Peabody Journal of Education* 80:19–38.

McGuinn, Patrick J. 2006. *No Child Left Behind and the transformation of federal education policy, 1965–2005.* Lawrence: University Press of Kansas.

McMurrer, Jennifer. 2007a. Choices, changes, and challenges: Curriculum and instruction in the NCLB era. Washington, DC: Center on Education Policy.

McMurrer, Jennifer. 2007b. Implementing the No Child Left Behind teacher requirements. Washington, DC: Center on Education Policy.

Melendez, Lyanne. 2007. *Local teachers campaign against No Child Left Behind.* May 9. Available at http://abclocal.go.com/kgo/story?section=education&id=5290030. Accessed May 10, 2007.

Memphis Commercial Appeal. 1995. Back state millage, school heads urge. *Memphis Commercial Appeal,* May 11.

Michigan Department of Education. 2009. Number of schools in Michigan 2009 (cited June 16). Available from http://www.michigan.gov/mde/0,1607,7-140-6530_6605-36877—,00.html.

Minnesota. 2004. *No Child Left Behind.* Minneapolis: Office of the Legislative Auditor.

Minnici, Angela. 2007. Educational architects: Do state education agencies have the tools necessary to implement NCLB? Washington, DC: Center on Education Policy.

Mintrom, Michael, and Sandra Vergari. 1998. Policy networks and innovation diffusion: The case of state education reforms. *Journal of Politics* 60:126–48.

Moe, Terry M., and Koret Task Force on K–12 Education. 2001. *A primer on America's schools.* Stanford, CA: Hoover Institution Press, Stanford University.

Moller, Jan. 2009. Jindal's stimulus opposition taken to national audience. *New Orleans Times-Picayune,* February 23.

Mondale, Sarah, and Sarah B. Patton. 2001. *School: The story of American public education.* Boston: Beacon.

Moore, Lynn. 2007. Schools sound off on no-child law. *Muskegon Chronicle,* February 22.

Morgan, David R., and Laura A. Wilson. 1990. Diversity in the American states: Updating the Sullivan index. *Publius: The Journal of Federalism* 20:71–81.

Morris, Jerome E. 2004. Can anything good come from Nazareth? Race, class, and African American schooling and community in the urban South and Midwest. *American Educational Research Journal* 41:69–112.

Murray, Sheila E., William N. Evans, and Robert M. Schwab. 1998. Education finance reform and the distribution of educational resources. *American Economic Review* 88:789–812.

National Center for Education Statistics. 1999. *Digest of education statistics 1999.* Washington, DC: U.S. Department of Education.

National Center for Education Statistics. 2001. *Digest of education statistics 2001.* Washington, DC: U.S. Department of Education.

National Center for Education Statistics. 2005. *1999–2000 Schools and Staffing Survey (SASS) and 2000–01 Teacher Follow-Up Survey (TFS) CD-ROM: Public-use data with electronic codebook.* Washington, DC: U.S. Department of Education.

National Center for Education Statistics. 2006. Common core of data 2006 (cited June 12). Available from http://nces.ed.gov/ccd/.

National Center for Education Statistics. 2007. *Digest of education statistics.* Available at http://nces.ed.gov/programs/digest/d05_tf.asp. Accessed February 8, 2007.

National Conference of State Legislatures. 2005. *NCSL task force on No Child Left Behind: Executive summary.* Washington, DC: NCSL.

National Education Association. 2004. *Joint organizational statement on "No Child Left Behind."* Washington, DC: NEA.

National Education Association. 2005. *Growing chorus of voices calls for adequate funding of "No Child Left Behind."* Washington, DC: NEA.

National Education Association. 2007. *NCLB/ESEA it's time for a change: Voices from America's classrooms.* Washington, DC: NEA.

Nelson, John. 2004. Re: Act 60 study, e-mail communication to author, May 11.

Oliver, J. Eric. 2001. *Democracy in suburbia.* Princeton: Princeton University Press.

Orfield, Gary. 1969. *The reconstruction of southern education; The schools and the 1964 Civil rights act.* New York: Wiley-Interscience.

Pagel, Jean. 1995. Small, oil-rich districts face deep cuts; some west Texas districts merge after sharing their wealth with poorer areas. *Austin American-Statesman,* August 17.

Pear, Robert. 2009. Relief seen for jobless and states in health care plan. *New York Times,* January 28.

Percival, Garrick, Max Neiman, and Kenneth E. Fernandez. 2005. Initiatives, mandates, and the persistence of local politics: Substance abuse and the three strikes in California. Paper presented at the annual meeting of the Midwest Political Science Association, Chicago.

Peterson, Paul E. 1981. *City limits.* Chicago: University of Chicago Press.

Peterson, Paul E. 1995. *The price of federalism.* Washington, DC: Brookings.

Peterson, Paul E., and David E. Campbell. 2001. *Charters, vouchers, and public education.* Washington, DC: Brookings Institution Press.

Pfiffner, James P. 1983. Inflexible budgets, fiscal stress, and the tax revolt. In *The municipal money chase: The politics of local government finance,* edited by A. M. Sbragia. Boulder: Westview Press.

Phi Delta Kappan and the Gallup Organization. 2002. *The 34th annual Phi Delta Kappa/Gallup poll of the public's attitudes toward the public schools.* Bloomington, IN: Phi Delta Kappa and Gallup.

Phi Delta Kappan and the Gallup Organization. 2003. *The 35th annual Phi Delta Kappa/Gallup poll of the public's attitudes toward the public schools.* Bloomington, IN: Phi Delta Kappa and Gallup.

Phi Delta Kappan and the Gallup Organization. 2004. *The 36th annual Phi Delta Kappa/Gallup poll of the public's attitudes toward the public schools.* Bloomington, IN: Phi Delta Kappa and Gallup.

Phi Delta Kappan and the Gallup Organization. 2006. *The 38th annual Phi Delta Kappa/Gallup poll of the public's attitudes toward the public schools.* Bloomington, IN: Phi Delta Kappa and Gallup.

Phi Delta Kappan and the Gallup Organization. 2007. *The 39th annual Phi Delta Kappa/Gallup poll of the public's attitudes toward the public schools.* Bloomington, IN: Phi Delta Kappa and Gallup.

Pierce, Phil. 1995. Hoover schools fear funding plan system "coming up short," Yeager says. *Birmingham News,* May 3.

Plank, David N., and Gary Sykes. 1999. How choice changes the education system: A Michigan case study. *International Review of Education/Internationale Zeitschrift für Erziehungswissenschaft/Revue Internationale de l'Education* 45:385–416.

Posner, Paul. 1997. Unfunded Mandates Reform Act: 1996 and beyond. *Publius: The Journal of Federalism* 27:53–71.

Poterba, James. 1997. Demographic structure and the political economy of public education. *Journal of Policy Analysis and Management* 16:48–66.

Prah, Pamela. 2003. *Lawmakers balk at cost of fed education law.* Available at http://www.stateline.org/live/ViewPage.action?siteNodeId=136&languageId=1&contentId=15212. Accessed May 2, 2007.

President's Commission on School Finance and Urban Institute. 1972. *Public school finance: Present disparities and fiscal alternatives.* Washington, DC: President's Commission on School Finance.

Public Agenda. 2003. Rolling up their sleeves: Superintendents and principals talk about what's needed to fix public schools. Washington, DC: Public Agenda.

Putnam, Robert D. 2000. *Bowling alone: The collapse and revival of American community.* New York: Simon and Schuster.

Ray, Lisa, and David Plank. 2003. *Consolidation of Michigan's schools: Results from the 2002 State of the State survey.* East Lansing: Michigan State University.

Rebell, Michael A., and Jeffrey Metzler. 2002. Rapid response, radical reform: The story of school finance litigation in Vermont. *Journal of Law and Education* 31:167–89.

Reed, Douglas S. 2001. *On equal terms: The constitutional politics of educational opportunity.* Princeton: Princeton University Press.

Ritter, Gary W., and Sherri C. Lauver. 2003. School finance reform in New Jersey: A piecemeal response to a systematic problem. *Journal of Education Finance* 28:575–98.

Roach, Virginia, and Michael G. Caruso. 1997. Policy and practice: Observations and recommendations to promote inclusive practices. *Education and Treatment of Children* 20:105–21.

Robison, Clay. 1990. Smoke blown on school finance. *Houston Chronicle*, April 8.

Roderick, Melissa, Brian A. Jacob, and Anthony S. Bryk. 2002. The impact of high-stakes testing in Chicago on student achievement in promotional grade gains. *Educational Evaluation and Policy Analysis* 24:333–57.

Roeder, Phillip W. 1994. *Public opinion and policy leadership in the American states.* Tuscaloosa: University of Alabama Press for the Institute for Social Science Research.

Rosenberg, Gerald N. 1991. *The hollow hope: Can courts bring about social change?* Chicago: University of Chicago Press.

Rothstein, Richard. 2000. Equalizing education resources on behalf of disadvantaged children. In *A notion at risk: Preserving public education as an engine for social mobility,* edited by R. D. Kahlenberg: Century Foundation Press.

Sack, Joetta L. 1998. In Vermont's funding shakeup, a bitter pill for the "gold towns." *Education Week*, October 28.

Sandberg, Louise. 1997. *Big brother's version of local control.* Available at http:// www.act60.org/sandberg.htm. Accessed March 12, 2004.

Schneider, Mark, and Jack Buckley. 2002. What do parents want from schools? Evidence from the Internet. *Educational Evaluation and Policy Analysis* 24:133–44.

Schneider, Saundra K., and William G. Jacoby. 2003. Public attitudes toward the policy responsibilities of the national and state governments: Evidence from South Carolina. *State Politics and Policy* 3:246–69.

Schwartz, John. 2009. Obama seems to be open to a broader role for states. *New York Times*, January 30.

Scovronick, Nate, and Tom Corcoran. 1998. More than equal: New Jersey's Quality Education Act. In *Strategies for school equity: Creating productive schools in a just society,* edited by M. Gittell. New Haven: Yale University Press.

Sears, David O., Richard R. Lau, Tom R. Tyler, and Harris M. Allen. 1980. Self-interest vs. symbolic politics in policy attitudes and presidential voting. *American Political Science Review* 74:670–84.

Shannon, Thomas A. 1994. The changing local community school board. *Phi Delta Kappan* 75:387–90.

Shaul, Marnie S. 2004. No Child Left Behind Act: Improvements needed in Education's process for tracking states' implementation of key provisions. Washington, DC: U.S. Government Accountability Office.

Shelly, Bryan. 2008. Rebels and their causes: State resistance to No Child Left Behind. *Publius: The Journal of Federalism* 38:444–68.

Sipple, John W., Kieran Killeen, and David H. Monk. 2004. Adoption and adaptation: School district responses to state imposed learning and graduation requirements. *Educational Evaluation and Policy Analysis* 26:143–68.

Snyder, Susan, and Dale Mezzacappa. 2001. For Gov. Schweicker's plan, a categorization challenge. *Philadelphia Inquirer*, November 4.

Spectrum. 1997. What Americans think: The state of disunion. *Spectrum: The Journal of State Government* 70:11.

Steelman, Lala Carr, Brian Powell, and Robert M. Carini. 2000. Do teacher unions hinder educational performance? Lessons learned from state SAT and ACT scores. *Harvard Educational Review* 70:437–77.

Stone, Clarence N., Jeffrey R. Henig, Bryan D. Jones, and Carol Pierannunzi. 2001. *Building civic capacity: The politics of reforming urban schools.* Lawrence: University Press of Kansas.

Swanson, Christopher B., and David Lee Stevenson. 2002. Standards-based reform in practice: Evidence on state policy and classroom instruction from the NAEP state assessments. *Educational Evaluation and Policy Analysis* 24:1–28.

Swenson, Karen. 2000. School finance reform litigation: Why are some state supreme courts activists and others restrained? *Albany Law Review* 63:1147–82.

Thompson, Lyke, and Richard Elling. 1999. Let them eat marblecake: The preferences of Michigan citizens for devolution and intergovernmental service provision. *Publius: The Journal of Federalism* 29:139–53.

Tiebout, Charles M. 1956. A pure theory of local expenditures. *Journal of Political Economy* 64:416–24.

Tocqueville, Alexis de. 1969. *Democracy in America.* Edited by J. P. Mayer. Garden City, NY: Doubleday.

Tucker, Marc. 2003. The issue of state capacity. Paper presented at conference on Implementing the No Child Left Behind Act, Washington, DC.

U.S. Census Bureau. 2000. *U.S. Census 2000.* Available at http://www.census .gov/main/www/cen2000.html. Accessed May 25, 2005.

U.S. Census Bureau. 2007. *State and local government finances by level of government and by state, 2004–05.* Available at http://www.census.gov/govs/esti mate/0600ussl_1.htm. Accessed October 13, 2007.

U.S. Census Bureau. 2010. *School district demographic system.* Available at http://nces.ed.gov/surveys/sdds/index.aspx. Accessed October 23, 2010.

U.S. Department of Education. 1983. *A nation at risk.* Washington, DC: Department of Education.

U.S. Department of Education. 2004. *Two years of accomplishment with No Child Left Behind.* Washington, DC: U.S. Department of Education.

U.S. Department of Education. 2006. *Improving basic program operated by local education agencies (Title I, Part A).* Available at http://www.gao.gov/mobile/con tent?path=htext/d10807.html. Accessed July 12, 2007.

U.S. Federal Elections Commission. 1998. Voter registration and turnout—1998. Available at http://www.fec.gov/pages/98demog/98demog.html. Accessed October 23, 2010.

Vermont. 1786. *Constitution of the state of Vermont.* Available at http://www.leg .state.vt.us/statutes/const2.htm. Accessed June 22, 2004.

Vermont. Department of Education. 1992. Vermont's core curriculum. Montpelier: Vermont Department of Education.

Vermont. Department of Education. 1993. *A Green Mountain challenge: Very high skills for every student—no exceptions, no excuses.* Montpelier: Vermont Department of Education. 31 pages.

Vermont Department of Education. 1996. *Vermont's framework of standards and learning opportunities.* Montpelier: Vermont Department of Education.

Vermont. Department of Education. 1999. *Vermont school quality standards.* Burlington: Vermont Department of Education.

Vermont School Board Association, Vermont Superintendents Association, and

Vermont Principals Association. 2003. *Report on education mandates and the removal of burdensome requirements.* Montpelier: Vermont School Boards Association, Vermont Superintendents Association, and Vermont Principals Association.

Verstegen, Deborah A. 2002. Financing the new adequacy: Toward new models of state education finance systems that support standards based reform. *Journal of Education Finance* 27:749–81.

Viadero, Debra. 2002. N. H. court: Accountability a constitutional duty. *Education Week,* May 1.

Webler, Thomas, and Seth Tuler. 2006. Four perspectives on public participation process in environmental assessment and decision making: Combined results from 10 states. *Policy Studies Journal* 34:699–721.

Weiher, Gregory R., and Kent L. Tedin. 2002. Does choice lead to racially distinctive schools? Charter schools and household preferences. *Journal of Policy Analysis and Management* 21:79–92.

Welner, Kevin Grant. 2001. *Legal rights, local wrongs: When community control collides with educational equity.* Albany: State University of New York Press.

West, Phil. 2009. Mississippi's governor shuns stimulus, stuns lawmaker. *Memphis Commercial Appeal,* February 3.

Williamson, Richard S. 1989. *Reagan's federalism: His efforts to decentralize government.* Lanham, MD, and Philadelphia: University Press of America and Center for the Study of Federalism.

Wingfield, Nick, and Leslie Eaton. 2009. States, cities in tug-of-war over stimulus funds. *Wall Street Journal,* February 28.

Winter, Greg. 2004. Wider gap found between wealthy and poor schools. *New York Times,* October 6.

Wirt, Frederick M. 1982. Does control follow the dollar? School policy, state-local linkages, and political culture. In *Political culture, public policy, and the American states,* edited by J. Kincaid. Philadelphia: Institute for the Study of Human Issues.

Wirt, Frederick M. 1985. The dependent city? External influences upon local control. *Journal of Politics* 47:83–112.

Wirt, Frederick M., and Michael W. Kirst. 1997. *The political dynamics of American education.* Berkeley, CA: McCutchan.

Wood, B. Dan, and Nick A. Theobald. 2003. Political responsiveness and equity in public education finance reform. *Journal of Politics* 65:718–38.

Woodward, C. Vann. 1966. *The strange career of Jim Crow.* 2nd rev. ed. New York: Oxford University Press.

Wrinkle, Robert D., Joseph Stewart, and J. L. Polinard. 1999. Public school quality, private schools, and race. *American Journal of Political Science* 43:1248–53.

Zimmer, Ron, and John T. Jones. 2005. Unintended consequence of centralized public school funding in Michigan education. *Southern Economic Journal* 71:534–44.

Zimmerman, Joseph Francis. 1995. *State-local relations: A partnership approach.* 2nd ed. Westport, CT: Praeger.

Index

✻ ✻ ✻